The Kidnap Business

The Kidnap Business

Mark Bles and Robert Low

A STAR BOOK
published by
the Paperback Division of
WH Allen & Co Plc

A Star Book
Published in 1988
by the Paperback Division of
WH Allen & Co Plc
44 Hill Street
London W1X 8LB

First published in Great Britain by Pelham Books Ltd, 1987

Printed and bound in Great Britain by
Anchor Brendon Ltd, Tiptree, Essex

ISBN 0 352 32163 6

Contents

Acknowledgements

We are particularly grateful to the four victims whose stories make up Part I of this book. Three of them asked us to use different names, for the sake of relatives, though they understandably want their accounts recorded for the benefit of others and in the hope that something may be done to prevent kidnaps recurring. We believe they each want their experiences — the most dramatic of their lives — recorded, lest, with the passage of time, they fade in significance and memory. This must not happen. Russell Stendal has written his own fascinating account of his months with the F.A.R.C. (*Fuerzas Armadas Revolutionarias de Colombia*) in the jungle in his book, *Rescue the Captors*, published by the appropriately named Ransom Press, in Minnesota, U.S.A. All the victims, and their families, spent hours talking to us about their cases. In the text, 'I' refers to Mark Bles throughout and the opinions expressed are his.

We spent more hours talking to many others in the researches for this book and are most grateful for the time given us by everyone, particularly the police in various countries to whom we hope this book will be of some use. We are especially grateful to Raymond Kendal, Acting Secretary-General of Interpol, at the Headquarters of the Organisation Internationale de Police Criminelle (O.I.P.C.), Paris, during this period.

We are indebted to the following officers, departments and

libraries: Dr Guiseppe Fera, Dr Patuto and the Direzzione Centrale de Polizia Criminale, Criminalpol, E.U.R., Rome; Dr Prof. Proc. Antonino Lazzoni, Head of the Crimes of Violence Group, O.I.P.C., Paris; Commissaris van Rijkspolitie T. J. Platenkamp and Director Jan van Straten at the Centrale Recherche Informatiedienst in The Hague; Commander Kees Sietstma, Police Headquarters, Amsterdam; Abstellungspräsident Gerhard Folger, Director Jurgen Storbeck, Superintendent Schmitt-Nothen and Arno Falk of the Pressestelle, in the Bundeskriminalamt, Wiesbaden; many senior officers of London's Metropolitan Police; also Special Agents and Heads of Departments in the Federal Bureau of Investigation Headquarters, Washington, and the Academy Library, Quantico, Virginia, were extraordinarily helpful but we are not permitted to detail their names; staff of the United States Embassy, Bogotá; the Press Association Library; the Reuters Library; and the El País Library, Madrid.

We are most grateful also to the following for their invaluable assistance and for putting up with our persistent inquiries: Nancy Abel, Susan Allott, the late Viscount Bearsted, Peter Brodie, Jeffrey Care, Iñaki Echevarria, Juan Felix Eriz, Roy Furness, Leslie Gardner, James Glerum, Jane Grose, Dr Ugo Leone, Tessi Miles, Adolfo Roldáu, Chad, Pat and Russell Stendal, Janet Stobart, and Dr Geoffrey Williams.

Above all, thanks are due to our wives, Rebecca, and Angela Levin, for their outstanding support and patience.

ONE

An Introduction: The Road to Rome

Outside, the traffic poured towards the Rome suburbs. Inside, the office was unremarkable. The walls were sparsely decorated, largely with testimonials from other offices of the giant multinational corporation for which the occupant worked as managing director of its Rome branch. There were framed letters from Frankfurt and Brussels: 'I greatly appreciated your hospitality on my first visit to Rome. I look forward to helping you meet your record sales targets for the coming year.' There was just one out-of-place photograph up there alongside them. It looked like any other office party. The managing director and his wife appeared to be receiving some sort of presentation from the staff, who were all raising their glasses to the happy couple. As we rose to leave after our conversation, he caught sight of us looking at the photograph. He explained: 'That was the party the staff threw to celebrate my release by the kidnappers.'

It was difficult to associate this prosperous pillar of the Rome monied classes with the haggard, bearded tramp whose photograph had appeared in the newspapers a few years previously. Then, he had been released from captivity after four months in the hands of one of the kidnap gangs which flourished in Rome and the rest of Italy during the 1970s and early 1980s.

I had never met him before, but I felt I knew him well. I had been instrumental in securing his release, for when he was a captive I had been a member of a trade with very few practitioners: I was a kidnap negotiator.

During his long disappearance I had worked with his family, advising them on the best way of getting him back alive. I had studied the kidnap gang's messages—some in writing, but most of them brief and one-sided telephone calls. I had analysed the character of the gang and of their victims, both the captive and his family. I had studied other kidnaps to see if they contained any similarities to this case. I had researched the hostage's financial circumstances. Using this and much other material I had worked out a negotiating strategy. On its success a man's life depended. In the end it was successful, after a fashion. The gang had started out demanding an astronomical 10 billion lire (10 *miliardi*, as the Italians say). The hostage's wife ended up paying a lot less—800 million lire (£400,000), to be precise.

She also got her husband back, unlike some families who paid ransoms and never saw their loved ones again. He is grateful to be alive and reunited with his family, but the bitterness at what the kidnappers did to him after a lifetime of honest work still remains. The ransom took up a lifetime's savings—and probably more besides. 'What right do these people have to do such things?' he asked angrily.

For most of our conversation he appeared calm and composed. It was only towards the end that the signs of strain began to show and he gave increasing indications that the experience of reliving his captivity was not a pleasant one. He begged us not to use his name or in any way reveal his identity. Was it a deep-seated fear of retribution or just the fact of reviving in print such a ghastly memory?

It had been a well-planned kidnap. They generally are in Italy. Clearly the gang had been watching him for weeks. He was a methodical man, a creature of habit, making the kidnappers' task that much easier. He followed the same route to work every day. On the morning of his abduction he had found the way ahead blocked on a narrow slip-road off a dual carriage-way by a car across the road. As he went into reverse, he found that another car had driven up behind. He was trapped. It was all over in seconds. They smashed his car window, dragged him out, threw him into their car in front, and drove out of Rome into the country. He was kept in an isolated house until agreement was reached on the ransom. During all that time the authorities never came anywhere near to finding him or detaining the gang. Indeed to this day the gang have not been caught.

This is his story:

I was kept in a cellar, two metres long, one metre twenty centimetres wide and only one metre twenty centimetres high. I could just about move around in a crouching position. There was no air direct; it came through a small door which opened on to a garage.

It was probably in a country house where people didn't go to stay in the spring, when I was first there. At first I got food in tins, not often warm, sometimes fried eggs. I got wine too. I was not chained and I had a small radio from which I could tell the passage of time. They probably gave it to me so that I couldn't hear noises outside. They were quite humane, if you can use the word about such people.

After about two months more people came to live in the house and they cooked for themselves. It meant I got hot dishes for the first time, sometimes spaghetti, sometimes meat. For a toilet, they gave me a twenty-litre bucket.

I wasn't beaten up except when I was actually kidnapped and nearly knocked unconscious. But I had no air and in August it got very hot. It was probably on a hillside, exposed to the sun—hot in the day and cool in the evening, so it must have been at a certain altitude. I said to them: 'You've kept me in good shape but now I'm dying. Give me a fan.' They always waited before giving me anything I asked for, perhaps to give the impression that they were part of a large organization. I had the impression that they had carried out three or four previous kidnaps. I even got the impression that Roberto Calvi was involved with them somehow. [*Roberto Calvi was the Roman banker who, during the scandal affecting the Bank of Ambrosiano in 1982, was found dead, hanging from Blackfriars Bridge, London.*]

They may have treated me in a decent way physically, but when they wanted to know about my money they were very tough with me mentally. At night they would come down and talk to me. Once they threatened to cut off my arm, another time they said 'You'll disappear'. They threatened to do physical harm if my wife didn't pay. 'We are a very strong organization,' they said. At first I thought the authorities would soon intervene. But as the weeks went by I began to lose confidence in them. It was the time the Red Brigades were at their height . . . Until July I was strong, but when I counted how long I had been a prisoner . . .

The gang kept me informed of the negotiations. My big dilemma was to decide after three or four months how much longer it was worth staying there as a prisoner, as I worked out that by then I had a possibility of paying their reduced demand. At a certain moment something must have happened and they came down to 2 billion from the 4–5 billion they had been insisting on. From then on I noticed they were easier in their dealings with me. Then came my release. I had the impression something went on inside the gang, that there was a quarrel over what to do with me. My wife, who was handling the negotiations, took a big gamble, because in other kidnaps they hadn't released the victim after the ransom was paid.

It's funny: in the last few days, I started to reason, 'It's worthwhile staying here another day. If my wife gives in [to their persistent demands for more] now, it'll cost me another 50 million lire.' I exploited the fact that she had heart trouble. I told the kidnappers: 'If she dies, there will be nobody to pay you.'

I had a strong faith in God. The radio was very helpful because it meant I wasn't so isolated. For exercise I would move about on my knees and count. If I had stayed there much longer, I don't think I would have lasted. I had fixed a deadline in my mind: September. When I think about it now, I think it's astonishing what a man can accept to survive.

My wife had thought we might be kidnap targets but I never did; we didn't show off or live ostentatiously, but they knew there was plenty of cash flowing through the business. When I tried to tell them that we had no money they would say, 'We see a lot of customers in your building.'

I wore the same clothes for the whole time I was imprisoned (129 days). When they had collected the ransom they gave me a tracksuit and tennis shoes and put me in the back of a car. They dropped me off in E.U.R. (a suburb of Rome) and told me not to move for a while, but I had been confined for so long in my little cell that I had difficulty even in walking.

I was so happy to be released. I think I recovered quite well. It's only when I talk about it, like now, that I begin to suffer again.

Am I afraid it will happen again? Well, there hasn't been a repeat kidnapping yet. But at night I can't go out by myself in a normal car. I drive in a specially equipped security car, and I am a little afraid to go out at night alone.

I had just enough strength and determination to survive —and the knowledge that I would be reunited with my wife did the rest. Between people who love one another there must be a silent understanding.

* * * *

The Via Condotti is Rome's most fashionable shopping street. Running from the Spanish Steps to the Via Corso it is closed to traffic —apart from the odd police car inching through the pedestrians. Every evening it is thronged with dawdling crowds, gossiping and gazing at the elegantly dressed windows of some of the world's most exclusive shops; but to stroll down the Via Condotti and on through the streets of Rome is to compile almost by accident an index to another Italian business which has made billions of lire for the people behind it: the kidnap business. The Italians have become world leaders in it and the Via Condotti contains the names of some of its most notable victims. It is the ideal place, after all, for a kidnapper to choose a target; a window on the Via Condotti is a sure sign of wealth.

As you walk down the street you will see the name Bulgari, the world's most fashionable jewellers, and a family twice hit by the kidnappers. The first time was in 1975, when Gianni Bulgari was abducted, held for a month and released on payment of 1.3 billion lire (£650,000)—the same sum that the Getty family had paid for the release of Paul Getty junior the previous year in the kidnap that had started the wave that was to sweep through Italy in the following decade. The second time for the Bulgaris was in 1983 when Ana Bulgari-Calissoni and her 17-year-old nephew Giorgio were seized, held for more than a month and only freed for a ransom of 3.5 miliardi (£1.75 million). The end of the affair was hastened by the arrival of Giorgio's ear at the family home in a macabre replay of the Getty case of a decade earlier.

Continue down the Via Condotti and you come to another elegant window under the legend *Piatelli*, displaying the best of men's fashion. In 1980 Barbara Piatelli was kidnapped, held for 342 days —still a record for Italy—and finally released for 1 billion lire (£500,000).

Stop for a meal and wash it down with a Sambuca liqueur; it will probably be poured from a bottle bearing the name Molinari. In 1981 Marcello Molinari was held for seventy-three days at an eventual cost to his family of 600 million lire (£300,000) . . . As you sip your coffee, reflect that the coffee beans the waiter puts in it may have been imported by the Palombini family, whose head, the elderly Giovanni Palombini, was kidnapped a month before Molinari but never freed despite several ransom payments by his increasingly desperate family, who, because Palombini was murdered during the course of his absence, unwittingly negotiated for his dead body which was eventually found buried in a lonely field . . . The list is endless.

The wave of Rome kidnaps started in 1975 when there were ten big abductions for a total of 5.6 billion lire in ransoms. There were a further ten in Rome alone in 1976 (2.5 billion lire paid), and a dozen in 1977 (5 billion lire paid). The numbers dropped in the following years but a steady average of around five a year in the capital was maintained.

Throughout Italy there was a total of 536 kidnaps between 1972 and 1984, which works out an average of a staggering forty-one each year (compared with, say, the United States' average of fourteen, and Germany's two). It was a plague that affected the rich alone. To be wealthy in Italy in that period was to feel oneself a permanent potential target for the *Anonime Sequestri*—Kidnappers Anonymous—as the Press dubbed them. Traditionally the kidnappers have been gangs of Calabrians—N'Drangetta (Sicilian Mafia), or Neapolitans of the Camorra—as their underworld is known—or Sardinians, where aggression, violence and antagonism towards society has long supported kidnapping as a way of life. All these criminals have spread their cruel 'trade' across the country, mainly to the big urban centres, like Rome, Turin, Genoa, Milan and other cities in the north-east.

The virus thrived in the conditions of the 1970s, above all on the slackness of the authorities, the poor quality of police training and methods, internecine warfare between the Polizia and the Carabinieri and also frequent corruption.

There was one development that rivalled kidnapping for its speed of expansion (and the size of its profits): the security business. Private security was the obvious answer to the failure of the official authorities, and the centre for it was London. There were various reasons for this, but pre-eminent was the combination of low pay and continuing defence cut-backs in the British Army. As a result high quality men left in droves (the Ministry of Defence were so worried at the losses that they wrote asking many officers back) and naturally turned to a career in a similar, but civilian field: the security industry. The massive explosion of terrorist activity in the 1960s and 1970s led to a demand for these services from all over the world. International companies and wealthy individuals frightened of attacks by political extremists or criminal elements could not wait for the official forces of law and order to overhaul their creaky mechanisms and get around to dealing with this new threat to lives and livelihoods. Private security was expensive but it promised to provide the quickest solution to urgent needs.

Another factor crucial to London's eminence in the field was that it housed Lloyd's, the centre of world insurance. As kidnapping mushroomed, Lloyd's underwriters and their brokers saw the potential for a lucrative new area of business: insurance against having to pay a ransom. Like any form of insurance, it could be tailored to suit particular needs: multinational corporations whose executives were regularly being whisked away in South America could take out a policy to cover all their employees in the risky areas, while rich individuals could insure their families too. It was extremely successful, not surprising in view of the enormous ransoms being demanded which were creating some horrendous problems for corporation tax advisors faced with accounting for huge pay-outs to criminals. In Argentina, the Bunge and Born Corporation paid a shattering $60 million-plus to the Montoneros for the release of the two Born brothers in 1975; while in El Salvador, in 1979, the Japanese company, Suzuki, paid $11 million, the giant electrical business, Phillips of Holland, paid $10 million, Lloyds Bank International reportedly paid $8 million for the release of two managers and $7 million was paid by L. B. Erikson; all to urban guerrillas.

Cover must match potential demands and $20 million is not uncommon for a large company, while for individuals cover will generally not exceed their assets. Premiums vary according to the risks in any particular area but may be 0.5% of cover for an individual, to as much as 5% for a family with a high-risk profile in Italy, which heads the league table in Europe. Some Central American countries rate even higher premiums. Lloyd's handles some 60% of the world market in kidnap for ransom insurance, worth $105 million worldwide. The other main competitors are three United

States insurers: Chubb Corporation, American International Group and The Republic Insurance Group.

In other forms of insurance, the insurance company reserves the right to employ a loss adjuster who ensures the company is not paying over the odds on a claim. But how do you check the limit on a ransom demanded by criminals? The answer is to use the services of a specialized sector of the security industry which provides consultants as kidnap negotiators. These men advise families, or companies, on how to negotiate throughout the kidnapping, and, if possible, reduce the amount finally paid out.

So, a scheme was introduced whereby those paying for the ransom insurance automatically had the services of a kidnap negotiator thrown in for good measure—though the insured had to pay his costs. Not cheap, but it suited the families for they badly needed objective advice to help them through such traumatic days, and not all ransom policies covered the whole amount eventually paid to the kidnappers; so, families were also keen to have the ransom reduced.

These kidnap negotiators also worked for non-insured clients and the biggest demand for their services came from Italy and Central and South America, where kidnapping had reached epidemic proportions. The market leader in kidnap and ransom consultancy (K and R, as it swiftly became known) was a firm called Control Risks, set up by two former officers in the Special Air Service Regiment (the S.A.S.), the legendary special forces unit of the British Army. The S.A.S. were catapulted into the limelight in May 1980 by their brilliant action in bringing to an end the siege of the Iranian Embassy in London, and following that by their involvement in the Falklands War of 1982. But long before they became the subject of films, a string of books and countless awe-struck newspaper articles, they had quietly established a worldwide reputation for excellence in the shadowy world of special forces, trained to perform the unorthodox. It was inevitable that many of the new breed of security consultants would come from the ranks of the S.A.S.

The links with Lloyd's were there from the start. Control Risks was in fact set up by the old-established insurance brokers Hogg Robinson, with another security firm called K.M.S. (standing for Keeni Meeni Services. *Keeni meeni* is from Swahili and means 'the sinuous secret movement of a snake through the grass'; it came to be synonymous for 'undercover'). There were others with an interest in this area: Lawnwest; Saladin; S.C.I. Ltd (all in London); Ackerman and Palumbo—ex F.B.I. agents working in the United States; Fred Rayne, an American working on his own; Risks International Inc.— with offices in Alexandria and Washington; Wynguard International; and Integrated Security Services Ltd.

The traumas were not only suffered by the kidnap victims. Control Risks found they could not always control the risks when, early on in the company's life, an operation in Colombia went disastrously wrong, and two of its founders, Arish Turle and Simon Adams-Dale, were held in a Bogotá jail for five weeks on suspicion of being accomplices of the kidnap gang. The charges were eventually dropped and the two allowed to leave Colombia without having to stand trial.

The activities of kidnap consultants have frequently been regarded with a great deal of suspicion and often outright hostility by the official authorities. This is perhaps partly sour grapes. If the authorities were doing their job properly, there would be no need for unofficial advisers to be called in, from another country, and in some cases from the other side of the world, to try to negotiate a satisfactory solution for the stricken family. But beyond this consultants are often accused of being no better than the kidnappers: it is said that they feed off the body of the family who have already been struck once by the criminals. This attitude surfaced publicly in Italy in 1981 when Rome's public prosecutor, Dr Ferdinando Imposimato, who had become famous for his hard-line posture towards kidnappers by trying to prevent the payment of ransoms (using Articles 219 and 340 of the Italian Penal Code which allow the blocking of a family's assets), adopted a similar attitude towards kidnap negotiators. He declared himself in favour of prosecuting them for the offence of 'favouring a crime' and the Italian Press took up the issue with gusto. Accusations that British consultants were behaving like 'jackals' were bandied about and life became very hot indeed for the few British kidnap negotiators who had by then successfully handled a number of big cases in Rome and Milan.

A particularly damaging charge was made by Valerio Ciocchetti, whose brother Sergio, a leading figure in the cement industry, had been shot dead and dumped in the River Tiber by his kidnappers. Valerio said an Italian had told him about an Englishman working in Rome who would advise in kidnap negotiations. The Englishman, he claimed, wanted three per cent of the final ransom figure, plus a daily fee of £450—over a three-month case and with an average ransom at the time of £350,000, that meant fees of £51,000—and he suspected the negotiations would be deliberately prolonged. He could not substantiate these allegations but, whatever the truth, it helped make life, already a delicate balancing act, even more precarious for Britons working in Italy at the time.

In fact, none of the major K and R security specialists would have dreamed of stipulating a percentage deal and they all stuck rigidly to a straight daily consultancy fee for as long as they were employed on a case. They were well aware how a family would regard rates linked to the final payment and that it would destroy their claim to objectivity; so prized was their stated aim of safely freeing the victim while, if the gang allowed it, keeping the ransom as low as possible. In cases of insured clients this minimized the insurance pay-out. In any event, business would have rapidly dried up if the consultants had acted in such an unethical way (if this adjective can be applied to the business). Furthermore, although the first connections in an area were generally made through lawyers or brokers who contacted stricken families to tout for business, almost all subsequent work came back to the security firm through a 'grapevine' of satisfied customers who had been established among the families of rich victims.

Instead of querying the motives of the British consultants, the Italian Press might have done better to investigate some of the Italians who acted as agents for the British. Of a dozen kidnaps that happened during a period in the late 1970s, all but one turned out to be insured at Lloyd's. If this was a coincidence then it was one of the most expensive that the City of London has experienced. When the British investigated, suspicion focussed on the Italian end of the business, but nothing could ever be proved. The families would not have been anxious to advise the authorities of the insurance, because this form of insurance is emphatically not authorized by the Italian Minister of Commerce and Industry. The only losers were the insurers—and of course the luckless victims who spent an average of three months in appalling hardship before a ransom was agreed and paid.

My own introduction to the K and R business was via one of the London security firms which I joined after leaving the S.A.S.—and the Army—in Hereford. An S.A.S. background equips a man well for this sort of work. What I had learned of military principles in training and on operations provided me with the knowledge that I subsequently found so useful when faced with the problems set by kidnap gangs. Wider research than my own has shown that the deeds and actions of revolutionaries and criminals are not remarkably different to those required of a modern professional soldier, and the S.A.S. has worked against, and studied, guerrilla and terrorist forces for many years. In spite of its glamorous image, S.A.S. work is hard, as recent campaigns in Oman, Northern Ireland and the Falkland Islands testify. All the time the regiment is learning about its enemies and improving its methods.

I had spent long periods studying the past form of various villains, in both rural and urban environments, and had acquired a good understanding of their motivations and of their capabilities. This work in the Army turned out useful in understanding the life of a kidnap gang. After all, ambush, seizing prisoners and covert movement through enemy-held areas—in uniform or in civilian clothes—are all subjects which make up standard Special Forces training. The principles of these aspects of military work are neither new nor exotic: they were taught in the last war and are still taught, but they are now far advanced and updated. It is fair to say that the principles of ambush apply equally well in the streets of a town as they do in the jungle; only the circumstances are different in each case. The kidnappers, who ambush their victim, must then hide him and negotiate the ransom, while taking care not to leave evidence for the police, and every time they make contact during the negotiation they expose themselves to the risk of being caught. They need to apply the principles of covert surveillance to avoid detection by the authorities and minimize these risks; on this subject too I was an expert. I was therefore well-trained to judge the kidnappers' activities, estimate what sort of problems they faced and draw the appropriate conclusions. Instinctively, I knew that this was the basis of good analysis in the negotiations ahead.

In the course of the kidnaps in which I became involved I evolved a series of strategies designed to counter the kidnappers' tactics and ensure the safe release of the victim for the lowest possible pay-out. The strategies had many sources. The backbone, as I have already stated, was my army training, with its emphasis on good intelligence based in turn on sound analyses and assessments of a situation, minutely observed as it develops; these are known by the military as 'appreciations'. The strategies also owed much to my study of the wide range of literature on the subject of countering terrorism and kidnapping, particularly specialist magazines such as the American publication *Terrorism*. From this I developed the concept of the Crisis Management Committee, a small group of hand-picked people from a kidnap victim's family and friends, who would handle the response to the gang and to whom I would make my recommendations for action.

Another subject to which I gave close attention was 'The Proof Question', to elicit evidence that the victim was still alive, and a common feature of kidnappings as far back as the Lindbergh case, but one whose importance could not be underestimated. Apart from these matters of professional technique, were principles common to any negotiation, from a game of poker to a labour dispute—the elements of bluff and counterbluff, of how much money to offer and when, of when to say there was no more on the table, of working out when to stand up to pressure and when to apply one's own.

Every case was different and called for its own on-the-spot analyses and decisions. The one common factor was that an innocent life was at stake.

I was called in as a consultant in a string of kidnaps in Italy, starting at the end of 1979. Each case had its own unique twists and crises. We have picked out the most interesting cases in the following chapters, highlighting the different strategies used in each one. In Part II we then show what is happening in the kidnap business around the world.

PART I

TWO

The Florida Gang

As my aircraft turned over the blue Mediterranean, for its final approach into Rome's Fiumicino airport, I wondered whether the brothers of a kidnapped man would behave differently to the other businessmen sitting placidly in the plane around me. Would desperation show in their faces? Or did they suffer their grief privately, beneath the routine of daily friendship and business? For Sergio Martinelli had been kidnapped four weeks before and I was on my way to meet his family. His kidnappers had demanded the huge ransom of 20 billion lire (approximately £10 million) and were threatening to kill him unless it was paid.

Some days earlier, the family had got in touch with us in London through an Italian lawyer in Rome. They felt completely out of their depth in the face of terrifying threats from the gang and had decided to accept a consultant to guide them through the traumatic negotiation for Sergio's release. I was to be the consultant. It was February 1980 and my first case in Rome as a kidnap negotiator. I was to learn how useful my military studies and firsthand experience of terrorists and their methods would be.

Sergio Martinelli was forty-seven years old. He came from a humble background and, working hard with his brothers, had built up a successful country-wide company. He was married with two daughters and was an outgoing man, popular and fond of parties, some of which were reported in the newspapers' social columns. A colleague and friend of mine, who had flown out as soon as possible to establish the first contact with the family, had put together a brief biography which also noted that Sergio was 'mentally very tough and capable of standing grief and pain in silence'. He would need all those qualities and more.

He had been seized from his car in the middle of the evening rush hour on a big dual carriageway through a smart residential area south-west of Rome. He was driving up the narrow road to his luxury house when the kidnappers blocked his way with a large metallic-silver Mercedes. Sergio tried desperately to escape, frantically reversing and driving across the busy traffic lanes pursued by the gang in the Mercedes. Suddenly one of Sergio's tyres burst on the kerb of the central reservation. He tried to make a run for it, screaming for help, but no one paid any attention. Dressed immaculately, like any successful businessman, it must have been clear that he was being attacked, but his screams were ignored by the commuters busily driving home. After a short chase on foot the kidnappers grabbed him beside the road. They gave him a thorough pistol-whipping, bundled him into their car and drove off at high speed. Days later, the Mercedes, which had been stolen in Florence and had French number plates, was found abandoned in Naples.

This pathetic story had little impact on the public. Kidnaps happened so regularly that the Italians had grown impervious to them. Tragically, kidnapping had become an unpleasant but accepted part of Italian life. In Italy throughout the 1970s, there had been no fewer than 435 officially reported kidnappings and many more that were never reported. There were to be another forty-nine in 1980. Most of those were long-term cases run by organized, and now highly experienced criminal gangs extorting ransoms of the order of £300,000 to £500,000 from each family. The situation has eased somewhat from a peak of ninety-three in 1983 but there are still as many cases every year in Italy as there are in a decade in Britain or Holland, where only a few of the Italian cases merit attention in the Press.

My first day that October in Rome was warm and humid, the air heavy with the oppressive threat of torrential rain. On my way from the airport, I wound down the taxi window, grateful that the fierce Mediterranean summer heat had waned. Relaxing back in the springy, comfortable seats, as I was whisked along the broad dual carriageway, I considered that being a kidnap negotiator had very definite advantages over lying concealed in some filthy, wet ditch in Northern Ireland, as I had done for weeks at a time during my army service. Rome, in the autumn sun, was a definite change for the better.

My colleague was waiting for me at the Hotel Quirinale, near the Piazza della Republica. 'There has been a further telephone contact from the gang this afternoon at half past three,' he said without much preamble, 'and we're expecting another call.'

'When?'

'This evening, about seven o'clock. We have to go to Casal Palocco, an up-market residential estate near Ostia. It's bloody miles away towards the coast but fortunately we have an Italian interpreter who drives, after a fashion, and he's going to take us there.'

'What time do we go?'

'About five o'clock.'

'Will we meet the family there?'

'We're going to a house belonging to one of the family company's managers. The victim's wife is distraught and the brother, who we'll see this evening, wants to avoid upsetting her as much as possible. He gave his manager's number to the gang as a safe place to take calls away from the Martinelli household.'

We walked through Rome, discussing the case, to a cafe in the Piazza Navona and chose a corner table where we could not be overheard. I wondered where Sergio Martinelli was being held. It felt unreal to be sitting in one of the world's most beautiful squares, casually enjoying a delicious cup of espresso coffee and dispassionately discussing a man whose freedoms had been brutally curtailed by vicious criminals, a man who had been beaten up and was being held in unspeakable conditions.

My colleague brought me up to date. He described how Sergio Martinelli had been kidnapped, pointing out that he had taken the same route to and from work for years and led a very conspicuous social life. He explained how the first contact from the gang had come ten days after the kidnap. The gang had telephoned and demanded a ransom of 20 miliardi (£10 million). The kidnapper's tone had been uncompromising, his negotiating attitude harsh. The family had since replied with two offers which now totalled 500 million lire (£250,000), a large sum but insignificant compared to the frighteningly high demand.

The story unfolded. The gang had threatened to kill their victim and attack his brother Matteo unless the demand was met. Near the start of the case a letter had been left in the lavatory of a cafe near the offices of the family's lawyer. It contained some of Sergio's personal effects. My colleague had explained to the family this move showed that they were almost certainly dealing with the criminals who had Sergio, but it did not necessarily prove that he was alive. As a result, he had advised Matteo to put a question to the gang to which only Sergio and the family would know the answer. Matteo had done this and everyone was waiting and hoping the gang could call back with the correct reply. The alternative was too awful to contemplate.

By the time our interpreter arrived in his small Autobianchi car the humid warmth had swelled and finally broken: the threatening air of the afternoon had gathered into dark glowering clouds and it began to rain. After introductions, we made a dash to the car and began the thirty-kilometre drive to the coast. The rain worsened ominously as we went.

My colleague pointed out the place where Sergio Martinelli had been seized as we passed through E.U.R., the neo-classical suburbs of Rome begun by Mussolini and now a smart business centre and residential area. I peered through the sheeting rain at the spot where Sergio had lost his liberty. I was amazed at the gang attempting to kidnap someone in such an open space, in the three-lane dual carriageway full of cars speeding home after work. It was not surprising that he had nearly escaped; the gang should have had another car to block off the target car and it was strange that they had given no thought to the numerous people who must have witnessed the attack (in fact very few came forward with evidence).

'No one would bother to help,' said our interpreter, shrugging his shoulders. 'No one would see.'

By the time we arrived at the house in the seaside dormitory town of Casal Palocco, the rain had become a torrent. Water splashing up off the pavement soaked our trousers to the knees as we ran to a gate in the high metal fence that surrounded the house. Attractive evergreen creepers had been allowed to grow over the steel-barred gate, which was visible from the house and controlled by an intercom, but the plants could not disguise the heavy security that is a common feature of the homes of wealthy Italians.

The manager took us downstairs to a bare games room,

underneath the villa. There, on that dismal rainy day, I met Matteo Martinelli, brother of the kidnapped man. He was a small neat man around forty, dressed in a grey suit. He looked drawn and worried. The whole work-load of the family business, normally shared with Sergio, had fallen on his shoulders; everyone looked to him for leadership, and the responsibility of negotiating his brother's release clearly weighed heavily upon him. It was our job to relieve some of that worry so that he could cope with the other, more usual, pressures of life that had been neglected since the kidnap.

He took off his glasses, in a gesture that was to become familiar in the weeks that followed, and welcomed us, a thin smile breaking the tired expression on his face for a moment. Through the interpreter my colleague asked if there was any news.

'No.'

The depressing negative needed no translation. Matteo had been waiting, on edge, by the telephone for the kidnappers to call. He knew that he would be abused and threatened, but he was hooked to them, like a fish, by the line that provided the only link to his brother—and his brother's life depended on it. He could wriggle and fight, insist that the kidnappers' demand was impossible, but he was caught. He was trapped by the strongest human bonds, of blood and kinship, into a macabre business deal from which he could not withdraw simply because he did not like the terms. He knew that he must bargain for his brother's life and the penalty of failure was Sergio's death. This fundamental truth of kidnap negotiations held him at the telephone for over one hundred agonizing calls with the kidnappers. He spent hours waiting for those calls. Every time, even on those countless other occasions when the gang never called, the tension rose inside him as the minutes crept by, drying his throat and straining his nerves to the limit. Each time he checked and re-checked his script, a few lines to guide his thoughts, which it was our job to provide. Under such pressures, it is hardly surprising that even the toughest businessman finds that his powers of objectivity desert him.

But now, after thirty-two days, Matteo had absolutely no idea how long the process would take. He and his family were grappling to understand what was happening to them. Not until the whole case was over would they be able to put their experiences properly in perspective. It was our task to supply the objectivity where it was lacking, to advise the family of their options at every stage, to recommend what to do at each new twist of the kidnappers' knife, and, like an 'Aunt Sally', take an endless bombardment of questions from the family. We talked over the same points time and again, hour after hour. In those joyless days, no single, simple answer would do.

My colleague had begun to explain the role of a negotiator in his first meetings with Matteo and the family, adding that by shouldering the pressure of assessing the negotiation we would release them for other things; otherwise the family business could get badly neglected. This was especially important at a time when the family fortunes were about to be stripped of a substantial sum. A great deal of business could be lost by neglect.

Ransoms have squeezed immense sums from families and their businesses over the years. The amounts vary: each area adopts a 'going rate', so that in the jungles of Colombia 5 million pesos (£42,000) is normal, while in the cities of Italy ten times that amount (850 million lire/£420,000) is average. My colleague had told me that he had begun to describe this idea of the going rate to Matteo. He had asked him to decide how much the family were prepared to offer for Sergio's ransom. This is the hardest decision. How can any family decide what value to put on the life of a person who is a loved father, a wife, a husband, a daughter or a brother? Yet they *must*. We knew that the approximate final ransom offer had to be chosen as soon as possible or the negotiation would lack shape and direction. Kidnap, like any negotiation, requires a thread, a plan, a strategy to link the beginning, middle and end. So far the flavour was purely commercial—the kidnappers had given no clue to a political motive which would complicate the affair—and it seemed that money was the bottom line. It was important to set the financial brackets in which to negotiate and to see that Matteo understood how the tactics at every stage would founder if there was no overall strategy.

As we stood about in the cold games room waiting for the gang to telephone, we discussed that strategy with Matteo. Two days before, my colleague had posed several negotiating options to the family. These options were estimates of how the ransom would increase by stages—depending on the circumstances as they developed—and showed how the extra money offered at each stage would tail off towards the end as they neared their maximum offer. Matteo had chosen one which would cost him 900 million lire by the end.

'Is there any way we can reduce the final amount during the negotiation?' Matteo asked through the interpreter.

'These scales are a guideline only,' my colleague explained. 'This figure of 900 gives us a target to work towards. We've considered your family profile, the going rate in Italy and the expectations of this gang as far as we can determine them at this stage. The problems arise when we try to reduce a gang's expectations from the average, or going rate, to a lower amount.'

Seeing Matteo's worried look, he added, 'However, 900 is a realistic ransom in your circumstances.'

A consultant negotiator ought never to conceal the unpleasantness of kidnap from a family: he should actually try to find the kindest way to prepare them for the worst of the harsh realities that might occur. However, I have generally found that there is always something encouraging in each new twist of a case and it does the family a power of good to hear something positive, though this may only momentarily lift the long depression of a negotiation.

The telephone rang. Its discordant sound echoed in the uncarpeted games room. Matteo waited nervously while I checked that the microphone (which we had given him) was firmly stuck against the body of the telephone. Satisfied, I switched on the tape recorder. He lifted the receiver. We watched Matteo's face closely, trying to read every expression, hoping to guess what was said and be ready to give advice for an immediate reply if the gang made an unforeseen demand. Then we saw his concentration relax. The caller was a girlfriend of the manager's daughter.

A temporary respite for Matteo. The anticlimax took further toll of his calm. His manager took the phone and quickly fobbed the girl off. I re-set the tape and checked the time. It was well past the hour—seven o'clock—when the gang had said they would call. We began to discuss whether to accept that the gang would not call that evening, and to gather our papers together to leave. Abruptly, at half past seven, the telephone cut across our talk.

'Hallo? This is Matteo. Who is it?'

'This is Florida,' said the caller, giving the code-name stipulated by the kidnappers in their earlier letter. 'The name you asked for is Carpi Paolo.'

'Very good, thank you,' Matteo replied, his relief obvious to us even through the barrier of language. The correct answer meant his brother was alive.

'So! What can you produce?'

'I want to tell you this. If you go on demanding incredible sums both of us will be in an impossible position.'

'Don't rattle on. Just tell me what you can produce.' The kidnappers voice was rough, his Italian bad and he sounded as though he came from the south of the country.

'But listen, Florida, we are ready to negotiate with you but on a logical basis. You have to come closer to our position.'

'How much. How much!'

'Have patience. We have already made two good offers.' Matteo was trying to make the kidnapper realize that the gang must reduce its enormous demand, but the caller had his brief too, apparently, and was sticking out for the family's next offer.

'Tell me your offer.'

'Listen Florida.' Matteo noticed us making urgent signs that the seconds were ticking away. Experienced kidnappers seldom spend more than a couple of minutes on the telephone, for fear of being traced, and we were afraid the man might end the call at any moment. He continued in a rush, 'I am making a big effort. I've already collected 420 million. I am finding the other 80 to reach the 500 I promised you. But I beg you to be realistic if we are to reach an agreement on this.'

Matteo had been following the script which was designed to show that the 500 had been a major first effort by the family and the speed with which it had been offered should not be taken as an indication that there would be more huge increases like that in the future. Our idea had been to split the 500 into 420 and 80 to show that finding enough money was hard even though it had been promised. It was the first of many steps we were to suggest in order to lower the ransom expectations of the gang.

'Listen,' said the kidnapper, his voice quiet and husky, 'can you produce 5 miliardi immediately?'

'What?' said Matteo, taken aback by the unexpected reduction in the gang's demand. 'No, listen, 5, 10 or 20 billion are all equally absurd demands.'

The kidnapper rang off.

Matteo put down the phone and slumped on the wooden chair, temporarily exhausted by the strain of the brief, tough conversation with Florida. This rough-spoken criminal was the only link with Sergio. It was likely that he knew where Sergio was being kept, whether he was well or sick, what money the gang expected for his release, and, perhaps, whether Sergio was to be killed or released. He was a gaoler, but more than any gaoler, he had absolute power over his victim's life. Matteo looked forward to each contact solely because it was the only way to help his brother, but these nerve-wracking few seconds were never long enough to say all the things he wanted, to convince the gang and bring the case to an early conclusion. But it drained him. The call had been only one minute and fifty-two seconds and he was thankful when it finished.

We were pleased with the way the call had gone, and said so, to encourage Matteo. The gang had given the proof answer showing that Sergio was alive at least until recently when the question had been posed. The kidnappers had kept him alive for over four weeks and this suggested that they might release him alive after all. It also suggested that they understood the essence of a negotiation: quid pro quo (something given for something taken), Sergio's life for the ransom. So far, they appeared to want a businesslike deal. The reduction was encouraging as it showed that the ransom offered was on the right lines: it was going some way to meet the gang's expectations and they had reduced accordingly. The trial of strength was yet to come as we further reduced those expectations from the absurd to the attainable, to a figure within the Martinelli budget.

We sat around a bare wood table to discuss the call and our interpreter began translating the text from the tape recorder. Matteo, who was worried by the kidnapper's harsh tone, relaxed more when we emphasized the two pieces of good news: the reduction and the correct proof answer.

'His wife will be very glad to hear this,' he said. 'Her daughter, Antonia, is looking after her wonderfully, but she is desperate with grief and we have to keep much of what happens from her.'

We talked on, picking out the salient facts and assessing the situation, just as I had learned to do on operations in the Army: in other grim circumstances against another kind of criminal. Coffee cups piled up on the table and the rain continued to pour down outside, drumming dismally on the darkened window panes. After the gang's reduced demand, I realized the family would have to make another increase in their offer.

At a quarter to nine, the telephone rang again. Startled and caught unawares we rushed about to re-connect the tape recorder to the listening device, careful to use a fresh tape. Ready, I nodded and Matteo grabbed the phone.

'Hallo? Just a moment,' said Matteo as my colleague handed him a scribbled note with his rapid decision for the amount of the next increase.

'This is Florida,' the kidnapper replied softly, and then there was silence.

'Hallo? Hello?' shouted Matteo, but the line was dead.

We could not tell whether the call was cut by the kidnapper or a result of the usual inefficiency of the Italian telephone system. There was an equal chance of either, but I favoured the former theory. The kidnappers had wanted to make sure we were still at the house and were likely to call again.

Matteo looked at the scribbled note and asked why we advised an increase of only 60 million. We explained that in the first call the gang had made a reduction, so an increase was required, but, since Matteo had said that he was still searching for 80 million to make up the 500 promised it would not be credible to offer a larger sum than about 60 at such short notice. Equally, an offer of less than 60 would be derisory at this stage and might cause the gang to become unduly aggressive. The time for much smaller increases would certainly arrive at the end of the negotiation; but not yet. We prepared a script for Matteo and waited.

Sure enough, shortly after nine the telephone rang again. After hearing the code-name Matteo asked whether the line had been cut off before. But the voice was that of a different man and he was furious.

'You told us you were going to make us a proposal. So do it!'

'Listen, Florida . . .'

'Don't start talking.'

'Please give me a second. I don't have much to say.'

'No! No! No! Immediately!'

'I say that your demand of 5 miliardi is absurd.'

'No! My demand is 20 miliardi! If you have 5 now then OK but otherwise it stays at 20. But if you don't care, you'll find him dead.'

'Have patience! You can't treat me so roughly! I think I'll be able to scrape up another 60 million.'

'What did you say?'

'Another 60. We will . . .'

But Matteo was cut short by the kidnapper's manic shouting. 'No! No! Listen to me! When you agree to give us the figure we want, put an appeal in the Rome newspapers.' A Sicilian accent crept in as the speaker became more and more excited. 'Put an appeal in the Press, and as soon as possible or the whole thing will go wrong.'

'Wait!' pleaded Matteo, but the line was dead.

I did not expect another call that night.

The early stages of a case, before the kidnap adviser gains the confidence of the family, can be difficult for both parties. However, the evening had passed off well, with two good contacts: the family had learned that Sergio was still alive and they had increased their offer, to keep up the momentum of the case. That meant they had improved their position in the only way that kidnappers really understand: offering more money.

Nevertheless, Matteo was understandably concerned about the threat to kill his brother, and that the demand had been increased to 20 miliardi again. He agreed the first call had been encouraging but was depressed and worried by the last. He was the victim of a tactic well-known to professional interrogators: the 'soft and hard' routine. The first call had been really no worse than a tough conversation in which the kidnapper pressed for an increase and made a reduction. The second was a verbal whiplashing: the demand was up again, the victim threatened with death. Carefully, through our interpreter, we explained the optimistic side: we believed the gang were genuinely annoyed not to receive another sizeable increase, like the last of 200 million; but at least Matteo had offered another 60 million which would take the edge off their anger. We did not believe that the threat to kill Sergio Martinelli was credible; after all they had kept him alive for so long and had the prospect of at least 560 million lire on offer. Matteo was reassured by our explanation. We went on to analyse the last call and re-make plans that had been changed by the second call.

For myself it had been a satisfactory start. Two calls, one 'soft' and one 'hard', in the first evening gave me the opportunity of establishing a relationship with the Martinelli family early on. I decided then—and every experience since has corroborated the belief—that any contact, of whatever sort, is encouraging for the family: the briefest contact indicates momentum and momentum means progress, which is impossible when there are long periods of silence. I knew that it was possible to wait for weeks without word from the kidnappers. Such silences are a complete waste of time for the family—they want to pay what they can as soon as they can—and for the kidnappers, who unnecessarily put off their payday. They also waste the kidnappers' resources and money (guarding and feeding the victim) which presumably could be better employed elsewhere, and prolong the risk of detection (as the police have time to analyse the evidence).

It was by now well past eleven o'clock, and dark outside with that intense gloom peculiar to terrible weather. As we worked on in the sparsely decorated games room, checking the translations of both calls for every nuance of tone and meaning, I reflected that throughout the world kidnapping is classified as a 'serious' crime and yet in this case I had seen no evidence of police assistance. Was it right that Matteo should be left alone at the very moment of contact with his brother's kidnappers? The Italian authorities had signally failed to protect their citizens (the statistics blazed their guilt) but shouldn't they redeem themselves, helping victim families with every contact? Straight from Britain where the police assist and advise to the point of interference, I did not think it good enough for Matteo and his family to know simply that the telephone in that cold games room was tapped by the Polizia. What comfort did this unseen eavesdropping provide? Strangely, the family were in constant touch with the investigating officer, liked him and told him everything. (Maybe the lack of police involvement is because in Italy the authorities do not enjoy a great measure of public confidence—so important to successful police operations—and they find it hard to communicate in these intensely personal situations.) However, I was deeply affected by an atmosphere of isolation in that room. Matteo was the focus of that sensation, sitting forlornly at the table which was by now covered in used paper, occasionally removing his spectacles with that familiar weary gesture and rubbing his tired eyes, listening to his own voice as we moved the tape back and forth over the two calls. Torrential rain outside beat against the black panes.

Before we left we provided Matteo with an outline telephone script in case the gang made a surprise call at his home or office. This safety measure was to ensure that our tactics in an unexpected contact fitted the overall negotiating strategy in case the kidnappers phoned somewhere without warning. It also gave Matteo confidence to have that scrap of paper folded in his pocket; he carried it everywhere and through every change of clothes—the paper got very worn but it did help.

We said goodnight, reminding Matteo of the encouraging aspects of the night's work, and arranged to meet at his lawyer's office the following morning. Then we ran for our car through the rain. It was well past midnight when we squelched into the hotel lobby on our way to bed. For me it had been a long first day.

The Martinelli case proceeded along normal lines, in so far as anything is normal during a kidnap, with the family making various increases in their offer. The gang generally treated these new offers with theatrical disgust during telephone contacts and kept the temperature high with the occasional threat to kill Sergio. The most dramatic of these was made public on Sunday 16 March three weeks after the terrible wet evening in Casal Palocco. One of the gang pushed a letter under the door of an apartment in Rome very early in the morning and the owner, finding it when he got up, followed the instructions he read inside and took it to the offices of the Rome newspaper *Il Messaggero*. The newspaper informed the Polizia and Matteo Martinelli. The letter contained a polaroid photograph of the victim, holding Saturday's copy of *Il Messaggero*, and a long letter written by him. The Martinelli family had used their influence to minimize reporting of the case by most of Rome's newspapers (a privately engineered media 'black-out'), but *Il Messaggero* could not ignore a scoop so cheaply obtained and the letter was published on Monday with a long article set round the photograph of Sergio looking drawn, exhausted and unshaven in his cell.

The family was very busy that Sunday with the Polizia and so it was not until past 11 p.m. that Matteo called a meeting to discuss the new situation. I had eaten and was thinking of bed when he phoned but I grabbed my notebooks and rushed by taxi across the city to a luxury apartment the other side of the River Tiber. There I was shown the letter, handwritten by Sergio Martinelli, which ran as follows:

Rome, 15 March 1980.
I am Sergio Martinelli kidnapped two months ago in Rome and until today still in the hands of kidnappers because my relatives have decided not to pay for my release. Maybe my wife and brothers do not want to know my present condition, because if it was known they would be in a hurry to pay the ransom, even if they had to sell everything, and even if they end up without a life, considering that it's my life at stake they are not going to lose anything except me.

I know from my kidnappers that my brothers continue to put announcements in the papers, begging and asking for new contacts with my kidnappers, but when they telephone they make excuses not to speak or to reach an agreement to free me. At this point the gentlemen who have me are very tired and they have no intention of going on with this, just yesterday they told me that everybody decided to kill me because my family doesn't want to pay. They told me they are not used to releasing any victims without any payment. They are going to kill me because they say they are ready for another kidnapping and they say they need the room where I am. After they told me these things I begged them to think about it and not to do anything crazy, but they don't want to know, so after my prayers they allowed me to write this letter as the last will of a person condemned to die. With this letter I speak to everybody, especially my wife and my brother, if you want me to come back soon I beg you to pay what they ask because these gentlemen know we can pay the figure they ask and considering what they said they showed me they are very well informed. For that reason I beg you to do your best to get me back, otherwise you can keep this as a memento of me. I am in your hands. I ask the Press to publish this everywhere so that if I do not come back the fault will be with my kidnappers but also with my family who prove they prefer money to me.

Martinelli, Sergio

The family group at the meeting was predictably upset by this letter, especially since it would appear in the Press. Nine of us sat round in the drawing-room of the modern apartment and an intense discussion of the impact of the message ensued, lasting long into the early hours of Monday morning. While we assessed the kidnappers' message, discussed every word, examined the grammar and looked for hidden meanings that his family hoped Sergio had managed to slip past his captors, the printing presses of *Il Messaggero* pounded out copies of the letter and photograph that all Rome would see in the morning.

The letter was designed to worry. It included a number of important points placed specifically to weaken the family's negotiating position and encourage them to pay up. The demand had by then come down to 2 miliardi (about £1.1 million). This was still a massive figure which it was unthinkable, indeed impossible, to pay. I believed the gang knew this by then, but they were tightening the screw to force the family to pay as much as they felt they could afford. Matteo's main worry was the threat to kill his brother and he had Sergio's wife very much in mind. We all knew how deeply she would be affected

that Monday morning, to see her husband's grim face staring out of
the page and read his familiar handwriting in the copy of his letter.
The threat to Sergio's life was the primary concern of everybody in
the smoke-laden room that night. Was that threat real? Would they
kill him? Matteo and the family desperately wanted reassurance that
Sergio would not be killed. They knew a ransom must be paid and
were prepared to do it but they craved what they knew they could not
have: promise of his safe return. This is the crux of every kidnap and
all kidnappers rub it in at various times during a negotiation. The task
of an adviser at these moments of psychological vulnerability is to
allay a family's worst fears. Here there was a let-out: the letter clearly
said that by 'doing your best' to get Sergio back all would be well.
This indicated that, in spite of their threatening language, the gang
were still in the business of negotiating for money. As long as that was
clear the family had a chance.

Principally, I was concerned to point out that their reaction was
exactly what the gang had wanted. It was the whole reason for writing
the letter. These kidnappers wanted to force the family to pay as
much as possible. Therefore they had instructed Sergio Martinelli to
write this letter which would bring tremendous private worry and, as
an extra twist of the knife, public pressure on his family.

I was at pains to highlight the factors in the letter and photograph
that I believed were cause for optimism. In brief these were that
Sergio seemed to be in good enough health, a view supported by a
graphologist who had examined the letter, and that his holding
Saturday's copy of the paper indicated that he had been alive at least
until then. (We were not to know of the example of Giovanni
Palombini whose corpse was taken out of a freezer to pose for a
similar 'proof of life' photograph, for that happened later.) The tone
of the letter, which was surely dictated by the gang, indicated that
they were still negotiating. The mention of another kidnap and their
plan to make room for a new victim suggested a certain professionalism which was encouraging, as was their assertion that the gang had a
good source of information on the family finances. One or two at the
meeting thought 'encouraging' an odd way to describe the kidnappers' threatening posture, until I explained that the more stable the
gang, the safer the negotiation. The converse is also true. The fact
that the gang was aware of the added pressure that could be brought
to bear on the family by making the letter public was a further
demonstration of their relative sophistication. Incidentally, their

willingness to go public showed the gang had little regard for the dangers of being caught, or for what the public thought of their crime.

Time and again Matteo or one of the others came back to the threats. We were all tired, but I could see that gradually they were beginning to accept that the letter actually changed none of the fundamental assumptions we had made about the gang. Indeed, they had given us a great deal of information which helped rather than hindered our position. By the time the meeting broke up at 3 a.m. I had managed to persuade the family that the letter and photograph were merely negotiating ploys. I gave Matteo an interim script in case the gang telephoned unexpectedly and we agreed to meet later the same day for another discussion, after I had had time for a full assessment (and a sleep) and could objectively recommend the next step. I left exhausted after fielding a barrage of questions and doubts, well aware that one of the most important roles of a kidnap adviser is to adopt the style of an 'Agony Aunt'. I got to bed as van-loads of *Il Messaggero*, Sergio's story in the headlines, were delivered around Rome in the dawn.

There were other occasions when the negotiating team met and talked into the small hours. There were too many people on the team to allow us to reach quick decisions, but the family had wide interests and these were not ordinary events. I was struck by a remark Matteo made late one night, at the start of December, as, once more, we talked round and round the latest development. He took off his spectacles in that neat familiar way and looked around the tired faces at the table.

'We are in a unique position. I feel we are ostracized by the rest of the world. Outside, they carry on their lives ignorant and regardless of my brother's fate.' He looked around his lawyer's smoke-laden office which was so familiar to him. 'In here, gathered round this old table, this should be just another business meeting, yet Sergio is missing.'

I realized that here was the answer to my thoughts about this family as I landed at the airport on the first day: Matteo and the others looked no different to anyone else. Of course, they were less cheerful than usual, and more thoughtful, but friends and businessmen alike could not see, nor begin to grasp, the awful sense of loss that the gap at our table meant to them. Their suffering did not end with the first shock of the loss—the nightmare continued endlessly. Yet there was nothing to show for it, nothing to see of Sergio's imprisonment, no marks of his pain, and nothing to see of his family's grief as they went about their daily lives. The family had been uniquely blighted and outlawed by this secret torture.

During any kidnap there is, inevitably, a lot of waiting around. During the Martinelli case there were long meetings every other day but that still meant I had a lot of free time. I spent it exploring Rome, against the exhilarating back-drop of St Peter's, the Forum or in the park of the Villa Borghese. As I wandered, I re-assessed my analyses of the case. I reviewed the various enemies (terrorists and criminals alike) I had learned to understand during my years in the army and tried to work out how they might behave as kidnappers. I assessed their capabilities against my own standards of operations in the Special Air Service, and then how I might behave if I were in their place. I considered tricks to get Sergio back quickly, safely and as cheaply as possible.

Occasionally, with the colleague who had been with me at the start of this case, I discussed what was the most flexible and realistic negotiating position, one that would serve the family's purpose but, at the same time, convince the most brutal of kidnappers. Between us, we came to the conclusion that a military style—hard, aggressive, confrontational and inflexible—was quite out of place and carried an unacceptably high risk to the victim. There is a terrible imbalance in kidnap negotiations: the family have the money, but the gang have the victim, who is always more important. No one but the criminals have control over the victim and no one has control over the criminals. All this is a complete contrast to hostage cases, military operations and routine police work. In our walks around Rome we conceived a more flexible strategy based on controlled compromise, dressed up to look like capitulation, but with very clear aims. These were to persuade the gang that the family could offer no more than the going rate (or less if possible), to reduce their expectations gradually, and to offer credible sums which achieved this purpose in a realistic time scale.

During my time in Rome, I had to take care not to advertise my presence. Kidnapping is a crime and being paid by a family to negotiate with criminals touches on some grey areas of the law. In Italy, my situation *vis-à-vis* the police was more than usually delicate. The minister responsible for ratifying insurance forbids kidnap ransom insurance and the Italian authorities view kidnap advisers with displeasure. Although insurance played no part in this case, I am sure (though I could not be certain at the time) that the Polizia knew of my involvement with the Martinelli family, so I took care to keep a low profile in Rome. I had no desire to provoke a test case and get locked up. I changed my hotels as much to confuse the Polizia's records of visitors as to avoid identification by the kidnap gang, and, on the occasions when a Polizia officer visited the offices where we met for our discussions, I waited silently in an adjacent room while the officer talked to the brothers. After he left, Matteo would tell me what had been said. I knew Matteo kept in constant touch with various police officers and he has since expressed his complete satisfaction with the help he received from the Polizia, but I cannot say that I was impressed.

During the case, the Polizia confidently forecast the gang would settle for 650 million lire, seemingly ignoring the facts of the case so far and the going rate in Rome at that time which was considerably higher. The family carried on offering increases in the region of 100–150 million, avoiding the central issue: it is no use saying there is no more, while you continue to offer fat increases at regular intervals—that is no way to convince them that your funds are limited.

So the gang stayed happy, their demands high and their threats few. Finally, the crisis management committee accepted that they had to start tailing off their offers (making the increases smaller and smaller) and the kidnappers' demand came down. From 5 billion lire, they reduced first to 1 billion, then to 800 million and, though they made a last ditch attempt to get more (a series of the usual threats), Matteo held firm and gave only tiny increases, as a sop, before agreement was reached at 716 million.

Suddenly, on 7 April, the gang started telling Matteo to 'prepare that money', and on 13 April, they finally agreed to the family's offer of 716 million lire, a figure nearly 200 million less than the ceiling allowed by the family at the start of our involvement and probably much less still than the figure first considered by them and their other business advisers.

This was the most dramatic moment for the Martinelli family. They were overjoyed. I was called to our usual meeting place in the lawyer's offices where the whole group was laughing and talking excitedly. I remember looking round the ecstatic faces and then glancing at Matteo; serious and considerate as always, he knew that though they had won a vital battle, their private war was not won until his brother had been released. Earlier, when he had turned from his last call with the kidnappers to tell four of his family that the gang had agreed, they had leapt for joy, oblivious of his cautions to keep calm.

The payment was a long-winded affair. For reasons that have never become clear the gang ordered the drop team to drive from Rome all the way to Milan. The authorities' surveillance effort was not distinguished, though the admixture of Roman and Milanese police forces cannot have helped. Matteo, who was left in Rome, found it difficult to keep in touch with either the man who was carrying his ransom money or the policemen who had been following. The affair was further complicated by the judge in charge of the case who also travelled north to Milan and ordered the Polizia to capture the kidnappers at the moment of the drop.

Since the Second World War, the Italian judiciary has been charged with control over the executive arm of the law. A judge is appointed in all criminal investigations and it is he, or she, who directs the operations of the Polizia and Carabinieri. In Italy, faced with a truly extraordinary number of kidnappings (compared with other European countries) and the inability of law enforcement agencies to control this situation, the Italian judges, desperate to catch the kidnap gangs, have chosen a hard, uncompromising attitude to the payment of ransom. They usually order the Polizia or Carabinieri surveillance teams to follow the drop and seize the kidnappers when they show up to collect the money. The judges explain this tough line by pointing to their legal guidelines in the *Procedura 219* (procedures laid down for application of the penal code), which states that the police must prevent the case 'becoming extreme'; including the 'death of the hostage' and the 'payment of ransom'. Unfortunately, this hardline refusal to condone the payment takes no account of the safety of the victim or the psychological effect on the family. Ironically, the Martinellis had developed a close, almost affectionate relationship with the investigating police officer in Rome which was seriously spoiled by the magistrate's instructions in Milan.

Solving a kidnap with due regard for the safety of the victim requires massive commitment of resources by the authorities and subtle police work—much of it skilled surveillance. The tough approach of the Italian authorities is both an excuse for the lack of commitment and a genuine, but crude, attempt to fight the crime. They seem to ignore the dreadful impact on families already suffering badly enough, the consequent effect on public co-operation with the police, and the fact that families everywhere have always found a way to pay ransoms when the life of someone they love is at stake. Perhaps the line is chosen to achieve the occasional dramatic success that can suitably portray the government's firm determination. It is cheap publicity. Many families, understandably worried that kidnappers will angrily kill the prisoner, make every effort to avoid the police during the payment.

Throughout the negotiation, I advised Matteo to keep the authorities informed of the development of the case, which he was content to do. There was no reason not to keep the police informed during the negotiation and I was sure that any half-intelligent gang, no matter how much they threatened the family not to speak to the police, would assume the police were ready to follow the payment run. I explained that the kidnappers would arrange some system of their own to pick up the money: a series of tricks to foil the police, grab the ransom and safeguard their freedom. The alternative, which is to give the kidnappers ideas of how to avoid police surveillance through telephone or letter contacts, is indefensible on moral and legal grounds.

When the payment was taking place, Matteo tried to keep in touch with the situation in Milan through the senior Polizia officer on the case in Rome, but, so complex were the various chains of command and control, this harassed official felt obliged to arrange to meet Matteo in a cafe, rather than his office—he believed that the Carabinieri were tapping his phone to find out what he was doing.

Twice, the kidnappers telephoned orders for the payment, and twice, while the Polizia, under orders from the judge, trailed after the ransom money, the drop was aborted. Matteo became increasingly frustrated at being so far away and unable to control the situation. I spoke to him from time to time, both of us using execrable French, and we met, together with his lawyer, to see if there was any more to be done. For the sake of Sergio's safety, I recommended that Matteo pressurized his Polizia contact to pull off the surveillance teams as it was clear from reports of the first attempts to make the payment that this gang, who had shown themselves to be well organized throughout the case, had men posted on counter-surveillance 'duties' to spot the plain-clothed Polizia officers.

The judge left Milan and finally, on 21 April, the ransom was handed over to armed men on a remote stretch of a main road in the Milan suburbs late at night. The kidnappers took the ransom money through a small maintenance door in a concrete wall running the length of the hard shoulder of the deserted dual-carriageway, and escaped in a waiting car along side roads behind and unconnected with the dual-carriageway.

Everyone returned to Rome. The family waited. The days went by and there was no contact from the gang nor sign of Sergio. In Rome at that time there had been some serious terrorist attacks, carried out by the Red Brigade, and the Polizia and the Carabinieri had road blocks on most of the main routes in and around the city. All the security forces were on the alert for other assaults. I told the Martinellis that this was not an atmosphere in which a gang could safely drive even a short distance with a kidnapped man. However, this assessment did little to reassure them. They had played their only card and were beginning to believe that Sergio had been killed after all. It was cheerless waiting. Matteo moved in with his mother, to keep her company through what is probably the most difficult period of every kidnap negotiation. He spent hours staring out of the window into the black night, wondering where his brother was, whether he was alive or lying somewhere dead and icy cold, and hoping that dawn would never lighten the sky before Sergio was released.

More than a week after the payment in Milan, on Wednesday 29 April, Sergio Martinelli was left by two of the kidnappers near a monastery in Rome. Filthy and dishevelled, he walked to the gate of the monastery and, after a moment's understandable hesitation, the guardian let him in. The Father Superior arranged for a monk to drive him home and, when they had left, rang his home. As the car made the last turn into the street where he lived, Sergio saw his entire family cavorting about in the middle of the road, shouting with happiness to see him back. It was the 104th day after his kidnap had started in the same place.

* * * *

The first time I met the family again was when I went back to Rome in June 1980, with the colleague who had worked with me at the start of the case. Keen as we were to learn from his experiences, we had not pressed to see Sergio on his release, though he was in very good physical and mental shape. We rightly guessed that the last thing he wanted to do at that time was to reminisce about the most uncomfortable months of his life. He wanted to be with his family, relaxing and enjoying the pleasure of being free after so long as a prisoner. However, after a period of rest he was perfectly willing to help us and talk about his captivity. We were interested to know whether our assumptions about the kidnappers during the negotiation had been correct, and wanted to know as much as possible about the gang to help us with future cases. I must admit that I was also more than a little curious about the person whose freedom I had helped negotiate for three months. The fact is that of all the people involved in the case—family, friends, business associates, and policemen—we, the consultant negotiators, were the only people who had never seen the victim.

The group met, in the evening, in the same offices where I had spent hours of endless meetings with the family group during the case. This occasion was more cheerful than the previous sessions. The sense of earnest desperation was gone, replaced by a tremendous feeling of family unity, achievement and victory; in spite of the fact that they had paid over 700 million lire (£350,000) to win Sergio's freedom. His daughters were there for the first time and the atmosphere was rather like the opening night in a theatre playing to a full house. Once everyone had settled down at the long table, with Sergio facing us in the middle, silence fell for the performance to begin.

Matteo's description of his brother had been entirely accurate. Sergio Martinelli is a neat well-built person, stockier than Matteo, intelligent, with a dry sense of humour. He gave us the impression that he had been well able to withstand the rigours of his incarceration. He admitted that he had been very frustrated at times, but we could see he possessed the strength of mind to cope with such enforced boredom.

The meeting went on for some hours, as Sergio described his experiences in response to our wide-ranging questions. His family listened rapt, and it occurred to me that perhaps Sergio had not so far had the opportunity to describe fully his experiences to his own family: three dramatic months when he had been snatched out of their lives. It was a fascinating interview and more so in retrospect because, when I returned to see him in 1985, researching this book, his story was still as fresh and detailed, and, astonishingly, equally unspoilt by thoughts of revenge.

The venue that second time was a total contrast to the traditional study atmosphere—the legal books and the painted ceiling of his lawyer's office in old Rome. This time we sat in an ultra-modern committee room, surrounded by glass-top tables, black leather and polished steel, on the top floor of the company's headquarters in a smart modern development in Rome. With Sergio were Matteo,

Franco and Sergio's daughter Antonia. As before, they listened closely to Sergio's story, adding pieces of their own at different moments. He began:

I was driving home in a small car, a Fiat 126, and approached the house along the side road over-looking the main road through the centre of our residential area. I took care to keep an eye open for trouble. Suddenly, a large Mercedes drew up beside me and I saw four men inside wearing masks and carrying pistols. I threw the Fiat into reverse and drove backwards as fast as I could towards the main road. To my right was the Hospital of Saint Eugenio [*where the bottle of Cesare Pagani's blood was left, see Chapter 3*] and next to it a Polizia station. But the Mercedes chased me and blocked my route to the Polizia station while the men fired shots at the wheels of my car, flattening a tyre. Desperate now, I changed course violently and tried to drive down the main road, but again the bigger Mercedes followed and rammed me against the kerb where my Fiat stalled.

I realized my car was useless and had become a trap, so I scrambled out fast and started running for my life, shouting for help as I went. But they were younger men, all under thirty, and they caught me. They beat me over the head with their pistols and fists, dragged me back into the Mercedes and stuffed me on to the floor behind the front seats. They took their hoods off once we started moving, but hooded me and secured my hands with metal handcuffs, like the police use.

I was sticky with my own blood from the beating and they continued to punch and kick me periodically during the journey, but, perhaps because of the shock of the attack, I preserved a remarkable clarity of mind. They were very agitated and coughed a lot but they did not speak very much, just a few brief orders from the man in the front passenger seat who seemed to be the boss. They drove at speed for about an hour. Once, we stopped and two of them got out while one stayed in the back threatening me with his pistol. A short while after that, maybe five minutes, we stopped again and we all got out. As far as I could tell, we were in a garage.

I was dragged immediately to the cell where I was to spend all my captivity. They dropped me down through a trapdoor into a round hole, then pushed me through a metal grille into an underground cell where they pulled the hood off my head and padlocked my ankle with a heavy chain to a wooden bunk. My cell was two metres long, by a metre wide and only one and a half metres high, so I could never stand up. I experienced the most frightening sensations as they slammed and locked the metal grille, leaving me in total darkness when they closed the trapdoor. I listened to the hollow sound as they scraped earth over the top of the wooden trapdoor and I felt as though I had been buried alive in a tomb.

They left me in darkness for four days and then, mercifully, switched on the electricity to a light in my cell. Fortunately, although they took all my personal belongings —wallet, credit cards and so on—they did not spot the tiny window of a luminous digital clock in my pen, which they left me, and I was able to tell the time and the date throughout. Even had I not had the pen, I could have counted the days since there were two tubes from my cell to the air outside, which served as a crude air supply. When the birds started singing I knew another day had dawned.

I had two buckets, one with drinking water and one to shit in, and every day they came with food and to change the buckets. I could hear them scraping away the earth which, I guessed, disguised the trapdoor, and each time I listened to that ominous hollow sound I had the most terrible fear of what they were going to do to me. I remembered Paul Getty's grandson had had his ear cut off and knew of other cases when the victims had been killed and I could not help thinking that they were coming to maim or kill me. Then they climbed down into the hole beyond the grille. They always wore tracksuits, training shoes, Balaclava hoods over their heads, rubber gloves to conceal their hands and they carried guns until I told them it was pointless to carry guns when I was locked behind the grille.

I tried to rationalize my position as much as I could, though it was very frustrating. I was worried about my family and decided that I couldn't do anything useful to resolve the payment of the ransom from my end, except to unsettle the kidnappers by telling them I had a bad heart and was ill. I had two main thoughts. Firstly, I decided to survive, and continually attempted to rationalize my predicament. Secondly, I knew my family would worry terribly about me and decided I would try to make some contact with them. Whenever I heard the kidnappers approaching, and the awful scraping above the trapdoor, I fought down my fears of what they might do to me and thought of what I could say to them about the negotiation. I talked to them every time and, though they did not respond readily, I established that the basis of the negotiations was commercial and not political. I realized that it would be very confusing for Matteo and my family if I were to try to negotiate my own ransom and I refused to discuss money with them. They tried to make me admit we were supernaturally wealthy and accused me of having bank accounts in Switzerland. I stared at my hooded captors and said, 'That's as absurd as if you were to tell that you are the Pope under that mask.'

Fighting the boredom was always difficult. They gave me Communist pamphlets, to annoy me, I think, because I don't think they were serious about Communism, and I refused to look at them. Then they gave me pornographic magazines which I tossed back through the grille into the hole. They asked me what I would like and I said I wanted a tape recorder and cassettes to learn English. I did not get them. Though I pretended to be ill, I exercised frequently, doing press-ups and bicycling on my back since I could not stand up in the cell. I would listen down the air tubes to the noises outside, of distant traffic, and aircraft high above in the sky. I also heard the sounds of small private aircraft at lower altitude, as if they were landing or taking off not far away. I knew when it rained because the birds stopped singing and there was less aircraft activity. Once, I heard a travelling salesman come to the house above my cell.

One day, early on, I nearly died of fright when I heard a deafening clatter in my cell. I looked at the tubes, where the noise came from, and realized that a bird was trapped, beating its wings against the metal sides of the tube. This happened five times during my captivity and my guards thought I was going mad when I told them I had birds flying about in my cell.

In the first fifty or even sixty days, I was constantly plagued by the thought that I would be killed once they had extorted the ransom money from my family, and the kidnappers kept these very real fears alight with threats to do just that. Gradually, and in spite of my physical surroundings, I began to accept the implication of a number of optimistic signs. I became convinced that the guards would not take such care to conceal their identities unless they planned to release me in the end. The floor of the cell was always damp and often covered with water and it was easy to pretend to be ill. I was heartened when my kidnappers gave me medicines: I believed it meant they wanted me alive. I began to test these ideas. I left the lid off my shit bucket and the smell grew so unbearable that the guards left the trapdoor open for a change of fresh air. I refused food, or would leave it uneaten, saying I felt unwell and my guards would stand in the hole outside my cell and, like concerned parents, order me, 'You'll eat your food and we'll not leave here till you do.' As time passed and evidence of their concern grew, I became more optimistic of my eventual release, but I was always afraid of the unexpected accident. I panicked that the air might foul up, or the tubes block so I would suffocate, or that the negotiation would go wrong and they would decide to amputate some piece of me after all to force my family to pay more.

The kidnappers were competent and clearly had good organizational backing. My usual guard was a tall, hard man with a Calabrese accent. He gave nothing away but was replaced in the last fifteen days by a smaller and far less impressive individual who was altogether sloppy by comparison. He left the grille unlocked once—on purpose I think—and undid the chain on my ankle so I could change the filthy pyjamas that I had worn for eleven weeks, since the second week in the cell. He left the chain undone, saying, 'They'll kill me if they find out.' I told him I would pretend to be chained when they visited, but I could not be bothered with this game and the others didn't notice. Later to my astonishment, this new guard even suggested that I escape. He said he would shoot himself in the foot and pretend to be attacked and overcome by me. I was very suspicious of this scheme, which, in addition to all the risks of what I would find outside, struck me as a trap—a way of providing the kidnappers with an excuse to kill me when I tried to run away. What made it especially suspicious was that this slack guard was quite out of character with the rest of the gang.

In the last week they told me they had made a deal and my family had paid the money. They were rather military and announced, 'We've had a summit meeting and decided to release you.' I was pleased but I admit I was afraid that they would demand a second ransom and the whole business would start over again. They must have been aware of the tension in me and my expectation of freedom because they gave me food only every two days in order to disguise the passage of time. Then one Friday night two elegantly suited men came down into the hole outside my grille. They studiously turned their backs on me so I could not recognize them and showed me cuttings from *Paese Sera* (a socialist and sensationalist newspaper in Rome) which said my family had paid a colossal ransom of 2,500 million.

'Rubbish,' I told them bluntly.

'O.K. We agree,' they replied coolly. 'Your brother, Matteo, has paid us 1,600 million.'

'Rubbish,' I said again. I was angry with their tricks.

They switched the subject to my release. 'We will set you free in two days.'

'Why two days? Why not now?'

'Because there are too many police check-points on the roads at the moment. There have been more terrorist attacks.'

I was visited again in the next few days and given a change of clothes. Then, I heard them scraping at the earth over my trapdoor for the last time. I was hooded and, as they took me out of the ground and put me into a car, one guard held the hood firmly down over my head. They drove off and I am sure they attempted to confuse me into thinking we were still in the country by driving sometimes on the verge and sometimes with two wheels on the rough roadside and two on the smooth tarmac.

When they ordered me out of the car they warned me not to look around and you can be sure that I didn't jeopardize my chances of freedom. They had given me a torch, since it was night. I looked about. I was in the street outside the monastery in Rome.

Our conversation turned over a mass of other points and I was impressed with Sergio's fortitude in choosing to leave the financial negotiation to his brothers. In other cases, victims who tried to strike their own bargains ran into trouble and were severely beaten up. What they also seemed to ignore was that they could not raise the money from within their prison, nor expect to convince their families outside that they had agreed to the sum.

Sergio was asked at the start how much he thought his family could pay and he stoutly maintained, against the threat of death, that the ransom could never be what the kidnappers demanded. He gave the gang a figure which was very much lower than the final payment. I am sure that his firm attitude helped considerably to bring down the kidnappers expectations of a big ransom. In this respect, he was the ideal victim from the point of view of the negotiator. Had he mentioned a figure as high, or higher, Matteo's job would have been much harder. Had he tried to negotiate his own freedom, he might have confused the issue and prolonged the case. In the event the gang appeared to have realized that whatever Sergio said about the ransom they had to negotiate with Matteo.

Sergio told us the two suave kidnappers wanted another payment after they released him. He lost his temper with them and shouted that they would not get another bean. A brave act and it worked. We had considered the problem after his release and came to the conclusion that further payment was out of the question, but the gang never pressed the point again.

It interested me that he had been irritated by the several proof questions that we gave to the gang to ask him. He said he did not see the point of these at the time and thought that the gang were trying to trick him again. They had asked him to write a number of letters and, since he was sure that they were not sending them all, he assumed the proof questions were some infuriating new ploy in the tactics of their negotiation. For their part, Sergio said the kidnappers believed that the proof questions signalled that the family was about to agree to their demand and finish the negotiation. They had been very annoyed when the case dragged on.

Sergio Martinelli coped well. He is a tough man with reserves of inner strength but he admitted to periods of terror, stifling frustration and an overwhelming sense of impotence. None of this is surprising, considering the appalling conditions in his underground cell, the fact that he never knew how long he would be held and the callous brutality of his captors who recognized no penal or moral code. When I asked him what gave him his greatest support, he replied simply, 'I am a Catholic. It was my faith in God.'

In the years since the kidnap the family has recovered from the tremendous shock and grown closer together. Under pressure of the negotiation, they found that the smallest personal idiosyncrasies, which they could ignore at other times, became irritations that assumed massive importance. But they persevered and began to rely on themselves, since friends were ready with advice that was not always helpful and often confusing. Now, Sergio spends more time with his daughters and is particularly attentive towards his wife who has taken the longest of them all to restore her shattered nerves. All the family shielded her from the worst shocks of the case but she seldom rested, tortured by her imagination. Considering the whole injustice, it is perhaps surprising that none of the family cherishes thoughts of revenge; but the kidnappers have not been caught. While the family assured me they were satisfied with the Polizia's support and advice during the kidnap, and their attempts to find the gang since, they did admit that they were frantic when the authorities were struggling in disarray during the payment in Milan.

Few who read this will have had such experiences. Few will know or appreciate the traumatic effects on the family of a kidnap victim. A powerful effort of imagination is needed to understand the terrific mental and physical pressures. Having seen the Martinelli family at close quarters throughout, I was surprised how well they survived. I looked round their faces at that last meeting and they gave no clues to the enormous strains of those three months. My first question was fully answered. Victims of kidnap show no outward sign of their conflict. I was struck at the ability of the mind to recover, but I wondered how deep were the scars under the façade. I thought too that it was time people knew how these injuries were inflicted; not all victims of kidnapping are as lucky as the Martinelli family.

THREE

The Bottle of Blood

Cesare Pagani is the thirty-six-year-old son of Alberto Pagani, owner of Pagani S.A.L., a successful factory just outside the ancient walls of Rome. He was kidnapped on 10 March 1981.

At 8.30 that evening he left the store with his uncle Arturo and they walked to a nearby underground car-park in a side street just off the wide boulevard that ran beside the building. There they said goodbye to one another and got into their cars—Cesare into his Fiat and Arturo into his Mercedes. As Cesare was manoeuvring to let his uncle out, a green Alfa Romeo pulled up in the street outside. A group of men, all with sweaters pulled up to their eyes and carrying guns, jumped out and ran down into the garage. They spread out, one covering the attendant and a witness with his gun while the others headed for the Paganis.

Cesare's driving window was smashed with a gun butt and he was dragged out. He put up a fight, twice breaking loose, until he was hit on the head with a gun and collapsed. Arturo, whose car window had proved altogether tougher than his nephew's and did not shatter when struck, watched horrified and powerless as Cesare was dragged like a sack into the Alfa Romeo. The gang drove the Fiat across Arturo's path, blocking him in the garage, and then escaped at speed in the green Alfa.

Only then could Arturo jump out, grabbing the gun he kept, like many wealthy Italians, for just such an emergency. It was a powerful weapon, a .357 Magnum and he fired one shot at the disappearing Alfa Romeo before realizing that he could just as easily hit Cesare as one of the gang.

The Carabinieri were soon on the scene. They discovered that in their haste the gang had dropped a bag in Cesare's car. It contained pistol bullets, shot-gun cartridges, sunglasses, a chain, a hypodermic syringe, tape and three locks: everything the modern kidnapper might need. But it contained no clues that might lead to Cesare's abductors. He was gone.

Cesare was described by his family as quiet, patient and with plenty of inner strength. He would need it all to endure the ordeal he was now undergoing. He was unmarried and clearly his father's favourite son: they ran the firm together. The family had discussed the possibility of a kidnapping. Cesare had said he would try to stay as quiet as possible if he were the victim. Unfortunately, the family had not thought to work out a simple code by which to communicate in the event of a kidnap. Fortunately, Cesare had been carrying only the usual personal documents, such as cheque-book and driving licence, and no business papers.

In this case, like the Martinelli's, our contact was through an Italian lawyer in Rome, and I flew out to start work building a relationship with the family. The case was to be more than usually stressful. The kidnap itself had been carried out quite efficiently, with lashings of violence making up for a lack of surgical precision, but as the case developed the initial impression of the gang's professionalism disappeared. It became clear that we were dealing with an erratic and possibly unstable group of people whose actions were frequently contradictory and bizarre. It did not make them easy to deal with or to anticipate.

Alberto Pagani was an impressive figure, cool and hard-headed during the whole ordeal of his son's disappearance despite the anguish he must have been feeling inside. His wife Anna Maria managed to maintain a calm and philosophical façade. I developed a deep respect for the Paganis. When Alberto decided on a course of action he stuck to it even though he well knew the awful possibilities.

I advised them to identify a crisis management committee which comprised Alberto and Anna Maria Pagani; Uncle Arturo for a while until he was excluded; the family lawyer Avvocato Leoni; another lawyer, Avvocato Rizzoli who liaised with the judiciary and the Press;

Dr Giampaolo Lucca, a family friend who was standby negotiator to
Alberto Pagani but was dropped eventually because of his gloomy
reaction to everything (and his attitude that the way to obtain the
release of the victim was to keep offering the kidnappers endless
increases in ransom); our interpreter; another lawyer; and Cesare's
brother Emilio who was a quiet man but occasionally asked pertinent
questions.

One of my first tasks was to convince Mr Pagani that he would have
to consider setting aside a sum high enough to satisfy the gang's
expectations, judged against what kidnap gangs had settled for in
Rome at that time. The going rate was in the region of 700–800
million lire (£350,000–400,000). He said he could not afford even
that. The family had a successful business but was not super-wealthy.
He placed his absolute ceiling at about 500 million (£250,000) and
his lawyer started with surprise when he heard Pagani name so high a
figure—though I had to tell him he would almost certainly have to
find or borrow more.

For a week after Cesare was taken, there was silence. On the eighth
day the daughter of one of the Pagani managers received a telephone
call at a nearby shop. A man's voice told her to tell her father to go to
the Montemario Observatory, on one of Rome's seven hills from the
top of which is a magnificent view of the city beneath. In a corner of
the statue there he would find a packet of Marlboro cigarettes. It
would contain a message for the Paganis.

The pack was where the kidnapper said it would be. Inside was
Cesare's American Express card and a letter in his handwriting:

> Dear Papa,
> I have been in this situation for a long time now and I really
> want to get out of here because it is really terrible.
>
> My kidnapping is entirely Uncle Arturo's fault because he
> wouldn't open the door to let me get into the car and then
> afterwards when we were driving away he put my life in
> danger by shooting at us. It is all his fault and I am really
> paying for it.
>
> I miss you all very much and unfortunately I am not very
> strong. I hope you can get me out of this situation as soon as
> possible, which has happened to me on behalf of all the
> family. The ransom required for my release is
> L. 2,500,000,000, two thousand five hundred million.

When you collect the money and are ready to pay, as a code signal you must place a star outside.

Afterwards we will get in touch with you.

Greetings and kisses to everyone.

Cesare.

PS. Be quick I can't hold out.

At the foot of the letter were a few words formed from letters cut out from magazines:

The money in 50 and 100 thousands.

I pointed out to the family later when we met that the letter had obviously been dictated by the gang. It contained the usual lurid references to the victim's circumstances and health, designed to upset and pressurize the family, and the reference to Arturo showed that the gang had been angered by the shot he fired, and were using the incident to make a veiled threat. There was some talk about whether Arturo had been the real target: the older man might have been popularly assumed to be richer, but the kidnappers found Cesare easier to grab when the Mercedes window would not break. This was speculation and, I pointed out, made no practical difference as they were both members of the same family.

But it was an unusual letter in some respects by Rome kidnap standards. Firstly, the ransom demand of 2,500 million (£1.25 million), although patently ludicrous, was in fact quite low by comparison with other first demands in Rome, which had gone as high as 10,000 million (£5 million). Secondly, it was unusual for a first communication to contain preliminary instructions about the drop—the amendment to the factory sign and the denominations of the banknotes to be handed over.

In summary though, it looked to us like a strong signal that the gang was prepared to negotiate. What followed was inexplicable and from their point of view totally counter-productive. The Pagani sign was duly altered four days later and could clearly be seen by any gang member walking or driving up the street safely hidden among the crowds. But, despite this signal of good intention from the family, there was no communication whatsoever from the gang for a further three weeks. It was a long, frustrating and pointless silence. The gang had removed the element of uncertainty by letting the family know they had Cesare and were now simply delaying the inevitable negotiation, which both parties wanted: the family as a step to Cesare's return and the gang to get the money.

The next communication, when it came, bore a strong resemblance to the first. A friend of Cesare, Vittorio Vencato, was telephoned at home by a man with a strong Sardinian accent. He ordered Vencato to pick up another Marlboro packet, this time from the base of a statue opposite the house.

It contained another letter in Cesare's handwriting, again obviously dictated. Clearly, the object was to increase the pressure on the family: 'I am really at the end of my tether . . . I don't believe I can resist for many more days . . . I beg you to do the impossible but get me out of here even if I alone should have to work my entire life to repay my debts . . . I feel I am going crazy, moment by moment, day by day.' Such language would be enough to place strain on the most stoical people. A vital part of our job as consultants was to show how the gang was playing on the family's feelings as a negotiating tactic. I believed it was a cause of optimism to see the further detailed instructions on how the ransom should be prepared and paid. The gang appeared willing to negotiate as far as the ransom. We could only hope at this early stage that they intended to return the victim afterwards.

The ransom was to be put in a canvas bag. Mr Pagani's white Talbot was to have the luggage rack mounted and a bicycle strapped to it. It is interesting that the kidnappers of Freddie Heineken in Holland used a similar instruction for the payment vehicle, and I believe it was so the gang would be able to pick out the car easily amongst the traffic. The man designated as bearer of the money was to wear all-yellow clothes and be ready between 4 p.m. and 7.30 p.m. every day. The signal that the operation was to be set in motion would be three rings on the telephone, followed by three more a minute later. The bearer would pick up the receiver and say: 'OK, the changeover operation will begin.' The Pagani sign was to be further amended when the family was ready to pay.

After this, another sixteen days of silence passed before the family had a chance to open the negotiation by making an offer, making a total of forty-seven days since the kidnap. I could not see how the gang could justify such a long silence at this stage of the negotiation, putting pressure on the family before they had had a chance to make an offer at all. (Pressure is logically applied when the gang are angry the family have not offered enough money.) Like many of the gang's actions, it was irrational.

It is true that silence can be an effective weapon for kidnappers, unless the victim's family has impartial advisers, like lawyers or police, to explain the tactic. It increases a family's anxieties, reduces their resistance to pay, and may be used for a short time—a few days—at the start of a case to soften up the family before the haggling begins. Short periods of quiet between contacts are common because of the sheer physical problems of passing messages between gang and family. Even in cities, using the telephone, it is rare to get more than two contacts a week in long-term cases. In rural areas, the contact can be more infrequent still. But over and above these practical limitations, gangs can use silence as a means of demonstrating dissatisfaction with the money on offer, with the pace of the negotiations—in other words the rate at which the offers climb towards the demand—or both. Experienced kidnappers don't mind how long the case lasts. They have the men and organization to wait. For them silence performs the same function as a threat of the more obvious kind. Nothing happens, no news and days of silence seem like a hollow vacuum which punishes the family's nerves and frightens them into raising their offer.

But silences can be a waste of everybody's time, including the gang's. In the Pagani case it is hard to see what was achieved except the brutalizing of the family—punishment before the family had been given a chance to annoy the gang—and the unnecessary spinning out of the case.

The first direct contact between the gang and the Paganis came in a bizarre telephone call which demonstrated the gang's strange behaviour well. Via a call to Vencato at 11.50 p.m., Alberto Pagani was directed to go to the Excelsior Hotel where a room had been booked in Vencato's name. The caller said he would ring there in fifteen minutes, which did not leave Alberto much time to spare. Unfortunately the hotel switchboard went out of action for nearly an hour which meant the gang could not get through and this raised their suspicions considerably.

But once on the line to Alberto the gang's spokesman, who said he wanted to be called 'Lugo', seemed reluctant to get off. The call went on for so long that in any country but Italy it would have been traced and the kidnapper caught. For the gang to take such a risk during the first conversation with the victim's family denoted either inexperience or over-confidence—in either case it was worrying.

There was a lengthy preamble during which Pagani demanded and got proof that the call was genuine (he asked the caller to describe where the second Marlboro pack had been left). Then he made his first offer, arrived at with our advice: 230 million and the hope of more in the following days. Oddly, Lugo did not reject it out of hand, which would have been the normal reaction. Pagani gave him a clean number—one not tapped by the Polizia—on which to call in future and Lugo laboriously insisted on getting the number right. In spite of the stupidity of the long call, the kidnappers showed they were willing to negotiate—at least as far as the ransom.

Events now moved quickly—more quickly than we anticipated after the long period of silence. But the gang's response was illogical. Within five days Pagani had increased his offer twice to 343 million lire, to raise the offer as fast as was realistically possible to a safe level (of the same order as the going rate), and a new negotiator on the gang's side responded by dropping the demand from 1,500 million to 1,000 million (£500,000). At the same time however he threatened to send Cesare back to his family piece by piece. This contradiction — reducing the pressure of the money demand while making savage threats normally used to get a family to pay more—made me seriously question the character of this gang. The Pagani family, beneath an impressively calm façade, were frantic.

One of the earliest questions you have to ask yourself in a kidnap is whether you think you are going to get the victim back safe and well, once the ransom has been paid. You constantly have to check the gang's seeming willingness to negotiate on the basis of quid pro quo, and build up a picture of their character. You have to feel able to trust the gang. This apparently absurd concept is the responsibility of the gang and the trust is won by the gang's businesslike negotiations showing there is a greater chance that they will fulfil their part of the deal. A gang with a political motive is much harder to deal with because their demands frequently involve more than money.

The erratic behaviour of the Pagani gang made it increasingly difficult for us to trust them. When this is the case it makes no sense to keep on making big increases in the ransom offer: there is no point in losing the victim and a lot of money. You may as well minimize your losses. In this case I felt justified in advising the family to tail off the increases in their offers once we had got the offer to a level that would be the absolute minimum figure acceptable to the gang.

Our analysis was confirmed by the next development. On day

fifty-five the family was ordered to pick up a parcel from outside St Alberto's Hospital, an appropriate collection point as it turned out. It was a brown paper bag, such as used to wrap bread. Inside was a dirty bottle containing about a third of a pint of blood, and two letters from Cesare, to his father and to his girlfriend. In the letter to his father Cesare confirmed that the blood was his:

> Hello Papa,
> Two months have now gone by and I am at the end of my strength. I'm sick in every way and have a wound in my head which is making my sight worse. Today they've also taken a lot of blood from me and I feel worse than normal, faint, sleepy and generally sick, and this is nothing compared to the general situation. I can't even remain sitting on the bed. I've stopped eating and can't sleep. Regrettably these aren't stories but the truth and my blood is the evidence. You must know that if you don't pay they will send you twice as much blood next time until I die from lack of blood. Now there is no escape. So I beg you father, I don't know how but pay, pay, pay. The 350 million you offered is absolutely not enough and they want what they initially demanded. Search for the money as you think best, asking whoever you want, put a mortgage on 'Pagani', on the house of Uncle Arturo and us, borrow the money—you can even go to Mr V......, the loan shark friend of Uncle Arturo. Don't listen to the wrong suggestions. Believe me this time I'm in trouble.
> So with your fatherly love and for the sake of our family, for our future together I beg you, pay immediately. I say again and unfortunately you have the first evidence, they are not joking and I am very, very bad, especially my morale which is destroyed.

There was plenty more in the same vein ending with a threatening postscript:

> You must know that after today they will not let me write to you any more and if the case goes on they will send you along with the blood a piece of my hand.

The family was naturally shattered at this gruesome evidence of

Cesare's predicament, but there was one lighter moment. We were called immediately to advise on this macabre development. The grimy bottle stood on the table in the lawyer's office which we used for meetings of the C.M.C. (Crisis Management Committee) and we sat round it discussing what to do until I thought it would be less awful, for Mrs Pagani especially, to put it in the fridge in the corner.

It was then 12.30 p.m. and we agreed to reconvene at two o'clock to decide on our response. It occurred to me at the time that many would think an hour and a half was not enough time to decide whether to change our entire negotiating strategy in the face of this powerful threat—an extreme example of frustration and anger—from the kidnappers. But, on analysis, it became clear to me that this latest move fitted in with the gang's erratic behaviour. In kidnap terms, in the local context, they had made an extremely violent threat at a very early stage. After forty-seven days of silence, two-way negotiations had been running for only eight days. We had not expected to be forced into a corner so soon.

Forensic analysis showed that the blood was from Cesare's blood group. It also revealed a high level of oxygen in the blood, which indicated a high degree of tension—hypertension—in the 'donor'. Given the circumstances under which the blood was taken, this was perfectly understandable—as we discovered later.

It is a common tactic for a gang disgruntled with the level of ransom offers to impose a period of silence or to threaten to mutilate or kill the victim. The taking of blood could be viewed as the equivalent of amputating a finger and sending that to the family. It was quite a cunning idea: an amputation runs the risk of septicaemia developing in the wound whereas taking blood is a lot less risky but just as effective in traumatizing the family. I wondered if the gang realized this. I also wondered if the gang included a medical student or someone with a knowledge of first aid. The more I looked at the problem, the less justification I could find for the gang taking such an extreme step. It seemed to me almost as though they had done this as a grisly experiment, and not as part of their negotiating tactics.

My conclusion was that Mr Pagani had to stick to his guns. The blood made us more convinced than ever that we were dealing with a bunch of lunatics who might not hand back Cesare alive. I recommended that Mr Pagani increase the offer to a level which ought to be just about acceptable to the gang: around 500 million lire (£250,000). In other words, the gang's aggressive stance had rebounded on them. It displayed a character that convinced us there was no point in offering more than the barest minimum compared to the going acceptable rate: we felt it was unlikely the kidnappers would return Cesare alive.

Mr Pagani was not a man who wanted to hear the processes that had led to my recommendation; he just wanted to hear the results. Despite the risk to his son, he agreed immediately. That most important decision taken swiftly and surely—and in this Cesare had reason to be grateful for his father's courage—we got to work at once on detailing what to put in his script for the next vital telephone call.

To encourage the gang to get in touch, the Paganis placed an advertisement in *Il Messaggero* on 10 May. It said simply: 'The deeply anguished Pagani family invite the kidnappers to make contact with them urgently.' It was prominently placed, in bold letters, at the top of page four, and naturally enough was the stimulus for the newspaper to run an article about it.

The next day Vittorio Vencato had another call. A man told him to be at the Bar Rosati in Piazza del Popolo in ten minutes, where he would get another call. Vencato rushed there with Alberto Pagani. When the phone rang, it was Lugo. Alberto took over the phone from Vencato and deliberately released his emotion.

'What d'you think I can do if you send me my son's blood?' he said, his voice choking. He pleaded with Lugo to tell him how Cesare was, insisting the kidnapper ring back with the answer to a proof question that would show Cesare was alive. This was vital after the bottle of blood.

The kidnapper agreed and said, 'He's OK, but how much are you offering?'

'Three hundred and sixty-nine,' said Alberto Pagani.

Lugo hung up.

I listened to the conversation later on the tape. I was deeply impressed with the stress, tone and intensity of Alberto Pagani's delivery of our coolly argued script. But he was emotionally shattered.

Two days later Vencato got another call at half past midnight. Alberto Pagani was to be at Vencato's flat at midday. Using a fresh script, he spoke again with extraordinary power, efficiency and heart-rending conviction. It was a virtuoso performance. He told them he was horrified at what they were doing to his son but in spite of that he had managed to scrape together some more money, to make a total of 509 million lire. He was almost in tears and so wound up

that he did not at first realize that Lugo was screaming at him, 'We
agree! We agree!'

The sudden deal took us all by surprise but only served to
strengthen our belief that the gang were behaving most strangely.
The pattern had been a long silence, a violent negotiating strategy
(two-way communications lasting only fifteen days from the first
meaningful contacts to the agreement) and a sudden, unexpected
agreement. What the gang obviously did not realize was that their
erratic behaviour and crude threats had led to the family offering the
minimal credible ransom—from the kidnappers point of view. This
amount was well below the going rate in Rome but the ironic twist of
fortune was that the family were hard-pressed to pay even that. The
kidnappers' brutal and irrational conducting of the negotiation had
destroyed the Paganis' initial willingness to pay what they could
scrape together. This was presumably quite the reverse of what the
kidnappers had planned.

The drop took place two days later. Vittorio Vencato agreed to be
the bearer. The instruction was to take the money and sit in the
Talbot in yellow clothes, as previously—in some of the first letters—
laid down by the gang, outside the Gran Cafe della Stazione. Alberto
Pagani had arranged for the money to be available twenty-four hours
a day at his bank, despite the fact that, early on, all his assets had been
frozen by the investigating magistrate in charge of the case. As in
every other kidnap where this crude financial control was made, it
proved to be unworkable: it upset the families, alienated them from
the authorities, and never prevented the payment of ransom.

The drop was arranged for a Saturday evening. When Vencato,
dressed in borrowed yellow clothes that were too small for him, got to
the square he found it crowded, and no room to park outside the cafe.
Anxiety about being moved on by the traffic police mounted until a
car pulled out and allowed him to park. He could not see anyone who
looked interested in him. After twenty minutes he was getting
worried: he was terribly conscious of the huge ransom on the back
seat and no less concerned that, lounging outside the cafe in tight
fitting yellow clothes, he would be taken for a loitering homosexual
and someone might foul up the drop by attempting to pick him up.

Suddenly, a tall man wearing a leather jacket and jeans, and a crash
helmet with a black, smoked Perspex wrap-around visor that
completely covered his face, appeared at Vencato's window which was
wound down.

'Give me the money,' the man grunted.

'Who're you?'

'I'm Lugo,' said the faceless man, with the same inflexion and tone that Vencato recognized from the telephone contacts with the gang. Vencato got out of the car.

'Hurry up,' ordered Lugo impatiently.

Only then did Vencato notice that Lugo had a small gun which he stuck menacingly through the open window. He hastily leaned across to the back seat for the money and handed it over. Lugo quickly moved through the evening crowds around the cafe to his accomplice, whose face was also hidden by a full-face crash helmet and smoked-glass visor, and who was waiting on a large motor bike at the corner. Lugo leapt on the back and they roared off down the crowded one-way street behind the cafe, against the traffic. Vencato took note that the bike was a large capacity Japanese make and then walked into the cafe to telephone Alberto and tell him the drop had been completed. It was half an hour before the Carabinieri arrived. Alberto Pagani had not told them of the drop because it had happened so fast. The kidnappers had phoned Alberto on the clean phone they had arranged earlier.

The drop was characteristic of the gang. They had taken a big risk in grabbing the money on the first leg of the drop run in such a public place at such a busy time. They obviously gambled on the factors of speed, the clean phone, and taking the authorities by surprise. If the Carabinieri had staked out the area of the cafe with a surveillance team, they had taken a chance on getting away on the bike through the streets packed with people socializing in cafes at that time of the evening. Were they inexperienced or just flamboyant? I think they simply decided to go for the quickest route to the money.

Possibly the worst period of a kidnap for the family of the victim is the wait between the payment and the release. There is no guarantee the victim will turn up alive. Almost as cruel is the possibility of another ransom demand, thus starting the whole agony again. There was a definite chance of this in the Pagani case, since the gang had agreed unexpectedly early to a ransom that was low compared to the average in Rome. This wait is all the worse for the family who have played their only card—the money—and have no further hold over the gang who still have the victim. It is a period of vacuum and anti-climax after the hectic worry of the negotiation.

In Cesare's case, the family had to wait for another four days. Then he turned up near Florence, ten kilos lighter than when he had been kidnapped eighty-two days previously but in surprisingly good shape. He sported a black eye but was in good spirits. He told the Carabinieri, 'They were like beasts. They drugged me and nearly every day they beat me.'

After resting at home and helping the Carabinieri he held a Press conference in a lawyer's office. During the kidnap itself, he had been knocked unconscious by a wad of ether pressed over his face and woke up to find himself on a bed with his left arm chained to a post. He was hooded and was to stay so for the whole of his ordeal; his ears were plugged with wax. On the floor was a basin with water. Virtually the only noises he could make out were the two doors opening and shutting once or twice a day. His food consisted of coarse pieces of mortadella, sausages, a cold soup with peas, or pieces of fat and beans. His captors spoke little and in low voices, with exaggerated foreign accents. Cesare described his ordeal:

> At first I tried to keep count of the days, then the noises, not to discover anything but just to keep in contact with life. There was always the effort of controlling myself. I thought that if I stayed good, did not lose my nerve, did not scream out, I would take my skin home intact.
>
> Only an hour before being released did my equilibrium break. They had told me that in an hour I would be freed. Then they gave me two injections to make me sleep, that did not have any effect. So, they put a pad of ether under my hood. It was then that I lost control; the fear, the feeling of being suffocated. I don't know; I reacted. The mark under my eye is the result of that reaction.

The Press gave a ransom figure of around 600 million lire. Mr Pagani would not confirm or deny it. He merely said that the bandits had first asked for an enormous amount and then slowly come down to a more reasonable one.

This brief account of Cesare's captivity sounds bad enough. It satisfied the transient curiosity of the public at the time. But it gave no real idea of the true situation, nor of Cesare's extraordinary courage in the face of such suffering. He gave us more details during an extensive briefing in 1985 when we were researching this book.

He sat in his comfortable but sparsely furnished office, neat, composed, good humoured and smiling. If there are any long-term effects they are certainly not evident. He had obviously thought about his time in the hands of the kidnap gang, but his story had not materially changed since the private briefing he gave us after he was released. His recollection of the pungent detail was just as sharp— such events would be hard to forget—but his emotions had mellowed. We listened as he spoke quietly:

I had little fear beforehand that I would be kidnapped because in Italy it is part of life and so I had ignored the possibility. We had not talked about it much. It was just a danger that existed for us. Everyone in the family knew the danger was there but we had been busy and had not discussed it with the others. It was, if you like, a minimal chance but not a real terror.

It happened to me on a Saturday evening after the factory closed. Uncle Arturo and I walked back to our underground garage where we kept our cars. When we got there we went to our separate cars, mine a Fiat and his a Mercedes. Suddenly a green car drove into the car-park at high speed, the brakes screaming. Five men jumped out putting on Balaclavas as they did so. I had a pistol in the glove compartment of my car but at that instant I realized it would be useless—there were five men outside with machine guns. I locked myself in my Fiat but one of them broke the window on my side, unlocked the car door from the inside and, opening the door, tried to drag me out. I threw myself to the other side of the car. They pulled me out but I managed to escape and started a hide and seek behind the other cars. I succeeded in getting out of their clutches three times altogether. I am not a big person or strong, but desperation gave me enormous strength I had not known I possessed. Finally, though, one of them hit me over the head with the butt of the gun and I was dragged by my feet to their car (the green Alfa Romeo).

One of them had kept Uncle Arturo covered all this time. They threw me on the back seat of their car and sat on top of me to hide me and drove off at high speed. Uncle Arturo ran out of the garage with his pistol and fired several shots at the car as it disappeared without any effect.

This time was one of the three worst periods of my experience. Lying on the back seat being sat on, I was nearly suffocating. We drove fast for maybe ten or fifteen minutes and I have no idea in what direction. The men on top of me and in the front were shouting frenetically at each other, arguing and yelling at the driver to go slower in case the car skidded in the wet weather. It was March and raining. After a time—maybe a quarter of an hour—I had the impression we drove into a large underground garage. It gave me the idea of a vast echoing space though it was absolutely silent. They shoved a sack over my head, tied my hands behind my back with a rope and we waited for about an hour, with me stretched out squashed on the back seat. They threatened me all the time because I had tried to escape so many times (in the garage). They were very nervous and were afraid they could have been seen by someone. They were scared and kept beating me in the stomach with a gun and saying, 'We'll kill you and feed you to the pigs.'

Another hour of this treatment passed, then they gave me three tablets to make me sleep. They forced these down with water and also gave me an injection which they administered by dragging me out of the car again, spread-eagling me across the boot of the car and jabbing the needle in my backside. Then they tied my feet, stuffed me in the boot of the car and slammed it shut. The next thing I knew was when I woke up lying on a bed. That period of the kidnapping and the drive was one of the worst times. They seemed highly nervous, possibly even drugged and certainly not very professional. So they made me nervous too. I was really scared. I thought they could have killed me by mistake. They argued continuously with each other and although I never saw their faces, I am sure they were quite young. The whole affair seemed as though it was the result of a sudden thought, an improvization.

When I woke up I had the impression that I had been asleep for a long time, maybe as long as two days. I realized the predicament I was in. There was a heavy chain on my left wrist holding me down and my whole head had been bound up while I slept, with three layers. The bottom one was thick Scotch tape, the sort that is used to pack boxes, then a sack and over that another layer of Scotch tape. The only hole was a cut in the tape and sacking over my lips so I could breathe. Under this head covering, my ears had been plugged with wax and so I could neither see nor hear anything. Because of the chain I could only move a little to shift my position on the metal bed which had no mattress; just a few blankets.

As I lay there, I sensed that the door had opened and someone had come into the room. I could hear nothing so I spoke. I said I knew what was happening to me and would behave as best I could and I asked them to do the same towards me. 'Shut up,' he snarled and punched me in the face.

For two days I had no water and I had no food for three days after they gave me something to drink. I believe they wanted to terrify me into thinking that I would not be given drink or food ever again. I could not move, because of the chain, so I had to piss and shit where I lay on the metal bed. When they gave me water it was in a large plastic bowl which I could not lift, so I had to go down and suck water like a beast. Finally, I got something to eat. It was left-overs: bits of fat, pieces of meat, spaghetti, even fruit peel, in a bowl. I did not feel hungry but I wanted to survive and I decided to eat whatever they gave me. This mess was the sort of food that I had for all but the last fortnight of my captivity.

I think they fed me once a day, but I guessed the passage of time by my sleeping routine and trusted in the metabolism of my body to regulate my sleep to five or six hours per day. I think they altered my feed times so my days were anything between twenty-two and twenty-six hours long and I am sure they did this to disorientate me. The first time I knew for sure how much time had passed was when I saw the dates I put on the letters they made me write to my parents. I realized that I had been held for fifty-four days when I thought it had been only fifty-two. When, at the end, I found out how long I had been held (eighty-two days) I was out by only three days.

After a week they let me get up to go to the toilet which was next door to my room. I never saw my room, but I got a sensation of what shape it was. Under the thick wrapping round my head I was cut off from all the normal sights and sounds we are used to and my senses, deprived of the usual mass of information passed through eyes and ears, began to develop extraordinary sensitivity. Now I know how the blind can understand so well what is going on around them, and how the deaf are aware too. Perhaps with the help of the tiniest sounds that reached through the sacking or from vibrations and touch, I was able to sense what was happening about me: people on the stairs, someone approaching me or how close they were. Later, I was put on a longer chain and could get off the bed and move about a little. I moved around the perimeter of my black world, the chain at full stretch, and could feel the walls and build a picture of the room. It was rectangular, with a chalky wall behind the bed and I felt a fleur-de-lis pattern on the floor tiles. There was probably a window at one end, behind a cupboard that I could feel. The room was very damp, with pools of water on the floor.

There was nothing to do. I had decided to survive and so my thoughts ran on two main issues. Firstly, how to survive, and secondly, thinking of what my family was doing to free me. One of my blankets was a tartan pattern type with tassels at the ends. I used to count each tassel every day and tie each one into a knot; there were seventy-two. I tied them up and untied them every day just to pass the time.

They took me out of the room and removed the bandages only twice. The first time was when I was taken out of my room and sat down at a table to write the letters. They took off the bandages from my eyes and immediately shone a bright light in my face. My eyes had been useless for so long that I was blinded, but they did not care for my problems; they just shouted at me to write the letter.

The other time was when they took my blood. They said they would take a litre every day until my family paid the ransom they had demanded. I was not worried about them taking blood but I was frightened that I would get secondary infections and then die of the resulting illness. I was sure they could not or would not be bothered to nurse me. They were totally inexpert. They had no idea that you have to find a vein to take blood, and just seemed to think that if you stick a needle in someone enough blood will come out. It took them two hours to fill the bottle; two hours of just sticking the needle in my arm. They did it hundreds of times.

After this I wrote the letter saying they would take a litre a day. I said to them, 'Let me write the way I know they will believe me. If I do they will pay.' They agreed. In the letter I was trying to leave messages, without letting the gang know, saying that I was well and trying to say things to help the negotiation. For example, 'Ask uncle to get money . . .' when I meant a bank that the family would know about. [*Without even the simplest pre-arranged code, it is extremely difficult for a family to be sure of hidden meanings. The Paganis hoped they could see messages in Cesare's letters but they could not have been convinced.*] At first the gang thought I was tricking them, but eventually they accepted the idea. I wrote three letters, but the third was never sent because the end came first. The first one I wrote with my head bandages on and it was very badly written. The second time, I wrote several letters together, one to my family, and one to a friend. They made me copy out the headline of that day's paper to prove that I was alive. [*This form of proof is not sufficient as the family cannot be utterly satisfied that the victim, and not a forger, wrote the headline.*] During these periods the gang constantly argued and shouted amongst themselves and hit me. One of them had a Sardinian accent and it sounded to me as though he was speaking through a funnel to disguise his voice.

The best moments were when my family asked for proof of life. It was proof to me that they were communicating with the gang and trying to negotiate my release. They asked two proof questions. Firstly, how did my sister break her leg twenty years previously? The answer was falling off her horse. Secondly, who had given me a cat that had died four years previously? These were the most beautiful moments. I have since advised other families suffering the ordeal of kidnap to constantly keep asking these sorts of questions, not just to get evidence of life but to keep up the victim's morale. [*The problem is not to devalue the importance of proof questions by asking them too often. Some kidnappers may construe proof questions asked during the negotiation as an indication that the family is about to capitulate and get angry when it does not.*]

The third worst time of my captivity was when I found out that my family had paid over the money. Now I knew I was useless to the gang and I was sure they would kill me. I knew

it was all over because they started to go through the same
process as when they had captured me. They gave me three
pills and an injection to make me go to sleep, but it had no
effect whatsoever. They saw I was still awake and gave me
another injection. I was terrified of what they intended but I
realized that I was helpless and must pretend to be
unconscious. But, crude as ever, they kicked me to check and
I instinctively reacted and they knew the drug had not
worked. They injected me again and this time I tried again to
lie quite still. But the awful anticipation of the kicking was too
much and I reacted once more. I had no idea what their plan
was but I was terrified they would simply kill me out of
frustration, so when they pushed a wad of ether over my face I
lay absolutely still controlling every fibre of my body even
though the vapour did not knock me out. I sensed their
presence beyond my mask and survived the inevitable kicking
this time without moving a muscle.

When they thought I was out cold, they undressed me, and
gave me a change of clothes (my first and only since being
kidnapped) and tied my hands and feet. I lay limp throughout,
straining to be aware of their movements around me through
my hood. They lifted me up, carried me down wooden stairs
and put me into a car boot which was much smaller than the
previous one. It was awful. I felt sick after the injections and
the ether and it was suffocating in the boot. I had an
overpowering desire to escape then, but I knew they would
not hesitate to kill me if I tried.

I was scared and, though I knew it was near the end, I did
not know whether I would make it. I felt so bad mentally and
physically. I was afraid I would not be able to breathe in the
stifling, closed boot, though by now only my eyes were
covered. I was wedged in tight and could not move at all. I
guess the car drove for about half an hour to an hour. Then it
stopped. I still pretended to be asleep. I was dragged out and
left on the ground, merciful for the fresh air and movement
but still frightened of what would happen next. Then I heard
the car drive away and the noise of the engine died away in
the distance.

I waited a moment and then, because my highly developed
senses told me no one was near, I got up and managed to

untie the ropes around my hands and feet. It was the middle of the night but I could see like a cat because I had been in the dark for eighty-two days. All the time, wrapped in my hood, I felt my senses had been operating at an extraordinary level of awareness and sensitivity, like a jungle animal. Now my kidnappers had disappeared.

I was in a country lane. It was pitch dark and I had, of course, a two-month-old beard, which had grown under the Scotch tape. I had no shoes. I heard a car coming a long way off, and, considering my appearance, it was perhaps not surprising that, when I gestured wildly as it passed, the driver put the headlights on full-beam and accelerated by me. I was nearly blinded by the lights but I watched it go and saw the tail lights turning off down a dirt road and that the road seemed to end at a house.

I ran after the car, shouting at the top of my voice, 'Call the Polizia, call the Carabinieri.' I reckoned that even if they thought I was a madman they would at least call the police. I ran for fifteen minutes down the road, finding some remarkable fund of energy to work my legs which were weakened by weeks of inactivity on that bed. [*For two months after his release, Cesare could not walk more than a few metres without sitting down again. Doctors diagnosed a low level of potassium in his body and he was, anyway, weak from lack of exercise, like a person who has been a long time in a hospital bed.*] Some mongrel dogs came running up to me, barking furiously, but I must have smelled so strongly that they followed me noisily at a safe distance.

Then I saw a light at the house. A woman shouted, 'Go away, go away.' But I carried on regardless. It was an ordinary country dwelling. Someone opened the door, and I jammed my foot in it and rushed inside. Fortunately, the light in the room was provided by only a low fire in the hearth, which did not trouble my eyes and I saw a table. I sat down at it and gulped down a glass of water standing there. The people of the house—maybe four or five—panicked at my dreadful appearance and rushed down the stairs and out of the front door, shouting at me to go away and leave them alone. They went on shouting outside the house.

I shouted back that I was a kidnap victim and asked them to call the Polizia and the Carabinieri who eventually arrived in great numbers. There seemed like a hundred cars, all flashing their blue lights and with their headlights blazing. Clearly they thought I might be a terrorist and were afraid that I might be the bait of an ambush. I shouted out who I was and would they turn out the headlights? Finally, I convinced them and they fell over themselves to help me. The Carabinieri Captain, who ordered everyone to turn off their headlights, even asked whether it would bother me if they used their sirens when we drove away? I said it wouldn't and we swept away in a massive convoy of cars along the country lanes to a military barracks where I was examined by a doctor. The Polizia wanted to ask me a lot of questions then but the doctor objected. I had been released near Florence and was soon reunited with my parents and family.

He paused, and after some thought, continued:

It is very difficult to understand the people who kidnapped me. I could not see them, and cannot find a proper explanation, even now five years later, of why they were so bad to me, because there was no need. Maybe it was sheer ignorance. Maybe they were people who had been mistreated by others and were wreaking their revenge on me. But there was too much hate there all the time. Compare them to bank robbers who, you could argue, show a certain 'nobility' of purpose, because they are risking something. But these were sadists. Only when someone was safely chained up would they dare to punch and kick out their aggression. It was torture, nothing less. Just for the sake of evil they would bang on the door of my room to scare me, threaten to cut off my ears, stick a pistol in my mouth and threaten to pull the trigger, or run up and down the house to create the impression that there were more of them than there really were.

I was certainly scared, because of the very real danger to me, but I did spend some of the time trying to put myself in their place. I tried to see their resentment as a social problem and I didn't react with hate. I am a rational man, but, for the life of me, I cannot see any meaning in what they did to me. My feeling is that they were too stupid to be the brains behind the kidnap.

How did I withstand it? Even today I do not know. If you had asked me before, I would say no one could last more than three days of that treatment. The Polizia and the Carabinieri told me it was the worst case of treatment they had come across. I was not afraid of the physical problems, but that I would emerge from the experience deranged.

I decided that my only hope of surviving was to accept the fact of death. Before, the worst thing that had happened to me was to be stopped by the traffic police for driving through a red light. And I compared my kidnap to spending several days in bed with a cold when you can't wait to get up. Then I assessed what might be the worst thing that could happen to me when I was already trussed up, sightless, deaf, chained to a bed and beaten up all the time, with little food. I decided that the gang might do anything at all to me and there seemed no particular hope that they would let me live after the ransom was paid. So my conclusion was that the next worse thing was to die, and I came to terms with my life and its limitations. I accepted the fact of my fragile mortality and the proximity of my death, but I fought to survive, telling myself, 'If death comes, then OK I have to die, but until then I'll go on fighting no matter what.'

There is no doubt that this experience was the worst thing that has happened to me but it has also been the most rewarding. I have suffered and survived and learned not just about myself but about other people and life itself. I learned that understanding is arrived at through suffering but that suffering is not the important factor; it is just a vehicle that brings the human condition around us all more sharply into focus, and sets our minds at rest amongst the pillars and walls of our own position in life's wider context. I consider this understanding is invaluable.

It was terrible not being able to communicate with anyone and, though I knew I would be beaten, I spoke to them when I became aware they were in the room just for the sake of talking. I felt I would go mad unless I talked to someone. I was determined to survive so I talked for my own sanity.

I tried to make a friend, since I am a dynamic person and I wanted to do something to help myself out of this situation. I tried to guess what was going on and learn about my kidnappers, by their gestures and beatings, by the way they spoke or gave me food, and after about twenty days, I realized one of them was kinder than the rest. He started to talk to me and to answer my questions. It became what I still call a friendship. He told me his whole story. He said he would escape if he could but they would find him and kill him. He devised a code: if he touched me twice, it meant we were alone in the house and could talk. He used to bring me fruit and other things that he had hidden and accompany me to the bathroom. For me this was another world.

This relationship started before they took my blood and I knew he would not be able to do anything if the others had decided on a particular course of action. But it was a gleam of hope. We talked for many hours. I had to consider whether he might be tricking me, taking me into his confidence and then relaying what I said to the others. It was from this man that I heard my family had paid the ransom and he told me what was happening outside. He talked about things I wasn't supposed to know. He told me that my family was working for my release and that somebody else was working with them. When the ransom was paid, he came up with two glasses of whisky and we drank a toast.

He helped me so much and I owe him a debt. Undoubtedly he was a criminal but, at some risk to himself, he showed me he had human values. Not only that but I thought he regretted his way of life. He talked about himself and his background. 'I'm your bandit friend,' he used to say. 'You should write a book about your bandit friend.' If they are ever arrested, I would denounce the others but not him. [*None of the kidnappers has been arrested for this crime at the time of writing.*]

I learned three things from this experience:

Firstly, I would never have thought it possible to make a friendship among such people. Even in that whole rotten set-up there was something good.

Secondly, I am amazed at finding how much physical and mental resistance exists in a human being.

Thirdly, I was overwhelmed by the support given by my friends and by people I had never even heard of. There were thousands of letters, from as far away as the U.S.A. offering help and sympathy. I knew that my family would care but I thought that my friends would lose interest after a short while and forget me. But it was not so; they were marvellous. And many of these people offered to help pay the ransom money; everyone from a rich industrialist who said he would pay it all, to my old nanny who said she would give the three million lire (£1,500) which she had put by in her savings.

As to long term effects, for two months I found difficulty in walking. I had stomach pains which still trouble me today. I did not suffer a big reaction after my release and fall apart psychologically, but I suffered gradually over a longer time later. I am happy to say I do not have nightmares about it. My father suffered much more than me. He had the terrible impotence of facing an invisible enemy and feeling no hurt himself.

We asked Cesare whether he took any new security measures. He shrugged lightly, and replied, 'No, I don't take any special measures.'

He continued: 'Such a shattering experience changes you deeply. It is a point of reference. After it, your scale of values is very different. It is something that is past and closed, but it is also something valuable that I will carry with me all my life.'

FOUR

Prisoner of the Jungle War

The Stendal family arrived in Colombia on 3 January 1964, from Minneapolis, Minnesota. Chad Stendal had given up a well-paid job as a senior engineer, building locks and dams on the Mississippi River, and, with the full support of his wife Pat, bravely decided to take their three children to join a missionary group working with the South American Indians.

The contrast was immeasurable. In America, Chad Stendal was a professional man on a good salary with a fine house and two cars. He gave up these and all the comforts and sophistication of the United States, for the chaos of the jungles and wild mountains of Colombia. For some years, he and his wife worked amongst the Kogi Indians, a tribe which fled the depredations of the invading Spanish in the seventeenth century and moved high up into the Sierra Nevada above Santa Marta, a bleached coastal port founded by Sir Francis Drake on Colombia's northern, Caribbean coast.

In the 1960s, when the Stendal family began to build a relationship with these Indians, whose history, handed down by word of mouth, made them understandably shy of white men, they found a society based on animism that had not changed for centuries. Isolated in the Santa Marta mountain range which rises to snow peaks at 19,000 feet only thirty-five miles from the baking Caribbean coast, it was a crime punishable with death by poisoning for a Kogi Indian to give information to an outsider.

The Stendals persevered and, with some luck, developed an embryonic relationship with the Indians. They eschewed the usual missionary practice of introducing western clothes and concentrated on medicine, to reduce the appalling death rate of children, and agriculture, to increase the standard of nourishment. Chad Stendal was made an honorary chief, a 'Mama', which gave him the chance to suggest essential new ideas, such as planting seed in season rather than at a time dictated by the unpredictable appearance of spirits from stones, trees or flowing water.

Russell Stendal, the eldest son, grew up in this environment. He was nine years old when his parents took him to Colombia and his formative years were spent with them in their work among the Kogi Indians, as he studied for school exams by correspondence. He trekked the jungles and barren hills with his father between the Stone-Age villages in the high Sierra, and hunted with these diminutive, but wiry Indians in the scrub and lush forests in his spare time. The contrast with his experience at school in the United States could not have been greater. Gone were the ice cream and apple pie. In Colombia, his school was life itself, learning from experience in the raw environment around him, with Indians who lived at subsistence level.

By 1975, Russell's father had been given charge of all the missionary groups in Colombia, but, when he started to raise money to help and employ local people, the missionary rules obliged him to leave the mission and obtain a visa on his own account. With the money he raised he bought a large tract of cheap land in the south-eastern part of the Amazon basin, on which he encouraged local people to become self-supporting. Russell, who had just returned from studying agriculture at the University of Minnesota, was given the job of managing this untouched 'farm' while his parents worked on with the Kogis.

The task was formidable. Russell had to struggle against the peasants' centuries-old habit of 'cut, burn, grow and move on to the next piece of jungle', the corruption of the Colombian bureaucracy and the jealousies of other missionaries of all denominations. And against the ever-growing menace of Marxist guerrillas.

The Eastern plains and jungles of Colombia are perfect breeding grounds for lawlessness. The region is remote, its people and terrain are tough, and roads are insufficient. Access to this vast rugged area is best by air. The police and army have little control on the ground they fly over, from one dilapidated township to another, landing on rough laterite airstrips hacked from the ever-encroaching jungle.

In the early 1970s, marijuana was grown in the Sierra Nevada de Santa Marta, on the foothills of the Kogis' refuge. When Russell moved south into the Llanos region, marijuana, bulky and expensive to deliver to Americans who increasingly grew their own in the States, was fading in popularity. Cocaine was more profitable: it was lighter, the returns were greater and it was easier to smuggle to America. And coca plants grew fast in the humid jungles, in small clearings alongside the myriad rivers which flow into the huge arteries of the Orinoco and Amazon. Best of all, the area was so vast, some three quarters of a million square kilometres in Colombia alone, that the authorities could not compete.

One group of guerrillas thrived in particular: the *Fuerzas Armadas Revolucionarias de Colombia*, (F.A.R.C.). The numbers of guerrillas grew as men and women became increasingly dissatisfied with the incompetencies of governments that were frightened to act radically against serious social inequalities. As the F.A.R.C. expanded its influence across the Llanos region, it controlled disgruntled members with the ruthless discipline of Cuban-trained leaders, and it made money by extorting 'tax' from the local farmers or growing coca plants for the cocaine trade. And from kidnapping.

Russell Stendal was well aware of the cocaine trade. In 1978, his aeroplane had been attacked and fired on by two Colombian air force T33 jets in the mistaken belief that he was a drug smuggler. Fortunately, the skill he had been forced to learn quickly to survive as a jungle pilot saved him, as he dodged the tracer bullets. His passenger at the time was the local police commander, and the terrified man never forgot how he had been saved by Russell's superb flying. Later, when Russell got embroiled with the local, drug-smuggling mafiosi, he helped him out of trouble.

However, for people in trouble in this region there is no fall-back on the police, the courts or even the army. The F.A.R.C. claim that they have over 13,200 men operating in military groups, called *frentes*, and the drug-smugglers have innumerable coca growers spaced along tributaries of rivers like the Guaviare and Vaupés. Criminal attacks are commonplace: Chad Stendal had been machine-gunned one day in San Martin. Fortunately he escaped unhurt but neither the gunman nor his motive were discovered. The lesson was learned: Russell always carried a pistol in an ankle holster, hidden beneath his trouser leg.

However well-prepared the victim may be, there is no substitute for surprise in an attack. On 14 August 1983, Russell had flown to Cano Jabon, a small jungle town on the river Guaviare to discuss the fishing trade. As he chatted with friends in the store, several armed men ran up the street and he heard shooting. Someone remarked that it was the army, but, by the time Russell's suspicions were fully aroused and he had realized that it was in fact an attack by guerrillas, his chances of escape were cut off by men with assault rifles. Reluctantly, he assessed that his double-barrelled 20-bore shotgun was useless.

What happened next is best described in a letter I received from Russell's parents:

> Russell disappeared inside the store, but when they asked for him by name and threatened to shoot the store owner and other bystanders, he came out and gave himself up. Meanwhile, other guerrillas damaged three aircraft which were on the airstrip, one of which was Russell's. They broke the windshields with an axe, tore off the doors, shot up the fuselage and wrecked the radios.
>
> Russell was marched off into the jungle with his hands over his head, and that was the last we heard of him.
>
> At the time of the kidnapping, Russell's captors left us a message demanding ransom. Since then we have reason to believe that he is alive. It looks like the motive was to obtain ransom money.

Russell had become well-known in the jungle area, flying consignments of fish from the remote river settlements to the towns, like San Martin, nearer the centre of the country. He had become a target. Though he spoke Spanish fluently, helped the local people, and had lived in Colombia for years, he was still a 'gringo'. He was a blond, well-built American. It did not matter that his family were missionaries: all Americans are wealthy, according to the standards of jungle life. Americans are also the sworn enemy of Marxism. Russell Stendal was a perfect target. The F.A.R.C. had heard Russell was coming to Cano Jabon for a meeting and planned his kidnap.

I received news of this disaster by post. My wife and I knew the Stendals. We had met Chad and Gloria, his daughter, in Colombia in January 1983 by chance in Bogotá airport, as we were waiting in a check-in queue. The officials were typically slow to start business and we got chatting. Gloria was to go to college in the United States and we agreed to look after her during the flight and see her on to her connection in Miami. I said nothing at the time, but I recognized the name of Stendal as that of a pilot who occasionally took Americans from the U.S. Embassy on flights over the jungle. These flights were innocent enough but I knew that they would have been construed by guerrillas and others in Colombia as help to the capitalist Americans and to the Drug Enforcement Agency, and I decided it would not have been wise to reveal my knowledge. On our plane, Gloria told us more about her family, and unwittingly confirmed her brother Russell was the embassy pilot.

Later that year, shortly before Russell's kidnap, Chad and Pat had visited us in England. Our meeting at the airport and friendship was providential, since I could help when Russell was kidnapped, but in this case, with the involvement of my friends, my objectivity, on which I prided myself, was put severely to the test.

I wrote back to Russell's mother and gave what advice I could based on the information she had put in her letter, and in the course of the weeks that followed we corresponded often. In view of the distance between such contrasting countries—the neat fields of England and the jungle chaos of South America—and the communications by letter, it was certainly the most bizarre case in which I have been involved.

All countries have their rough social spots but it is fair to say that Colombia is a violent country. Its raw society is different in so many ways to Europe and the United States. The Stendals' letters to me are refreshingly direct, describing the situation as it is, unspoiled by understatement or embellishment. So, I shall continue the story of Russell's kidnap partly through the medium of his parents' correspondence with me, outlining the course of the negotiation, and interspersed with the story of his ordeal that finally emerged from the jungle.

* * * *

As soon as the guerrillas had Russell in the street with his hands up, they marched him into the jungle. Once out of the little town and in the shelter of the trees, he was ordered to lie down. Reluctantly, because he thought they would shoot him out of hand, he lay down on his stomach. A guerrilla called Manuel pulled Russell's arms behind him, slipped a noose over each wrist and another round his neck and secured all three with a slip-knot at his back. No one saw the .38 pistol in the holster strapped to Russell's ankle. When he stood up again his trouser leg fell back over the gun.

After a further ten minutes walking, they came to the Guaviare River where they were met by the group leader, Jaime. He announced that the kidnap was to raise money for the F.A.R.C.—he had left a message for Russell's family demanding $500,000—and that if Russell behaved he would come to no harm. Then a nurse appeared and gave the captive a medical examination. While she checked his blood pressure and heart, another guerrilla, searching through Russell's flight bag, found some .38 bullets and demanded to know where the gun was. Russell struggled to think of an answer and the nurse, puzzled at his racing pulse and high blood pressure, accepted his sudden statement that he suffered from a weak heart. After a moment of panic, he explained that he had some bullets but the gun was his brother's.

The F.A.R.C. guerrillas loaded a dug-out canoe and put Russell in it, wearing a green poncho and a Fidel Castro hat as a disguise. Five armed men sat behind him and three in front. A second canoe followed. They had been travelling down the wide grey river for an hour when a speedboat suddenly appeared, swinging round the greenery which hung over the bank at a bend in the river. It was the police. Instantly, the guerrilla leader shouted orders for the boats to make for the bank, where they beached in a banana patch. The guerrillas leapt out of the boats and took up firing positions along the bank to ambush the police.

Manuel, who had the job of guarding Russell, led his captive to the back of the bananas where they crouched and waited. Russell pretended he wanted to shit and acted embarrassed, squatting low and wrapping the poncho about him. Manuel, who was more interested in the chance of action on the river, ignored him.

It was the best opportunity to escape. The guerrillas' attention was diverted, and, close to his own farm, Russell was still on familiar ground. (It is a fundamental rule that the longer a captive leaves the opportunity to make a run for it the more difficult it becomes; as he is taken deeper into enemy territory, the physical and mental coils throttle his will to escape.)

Russell pulled out his .38 revolver and, because he was looking into the muzzle of a machine gun, fired at Manuel without hesitation. The sudden movement caught the guerrilla's eye and he turned as the bullet struck him full in the chest. The force drove him over backwards but he did not let go of the rope. The cord tightened the slip-knots around Russell's hands and neck, choking him. Desperately, Russell fired at the rope in Manuel's hand. Then he fired at his head. Blood and froth poured from the guerrilla's mouth and across his chest but the rope was fast in his hand.

Confused by the jungle canopy and concentrating on the river, the other guerrillas thought for a moment that they were being fired on from the police speedboat. One, nearer the captive, suddenly realized where the shots came from and ran to help his comrade. Coming through the banana leaves he saw what had happened and immediately aimed his German G3 assault rifle at Russell twenty yards away. The hammer fell on a dud cap. He dived into cover on the ground and frantically began to eject and re-load. As he did so Russell, aiming at the guerrilla, ran out of ammunition. He flopped back behind another banana tree, trussed helpless like a turkey for Thanksgiving, and waited to be shot.

* * * *

His parents had their problems too. No one knew where Russell was held and there was nothing the authorities could do to help in so vast an area. If he was still alive, Russell was captive somewhere in the jungle.

Eventually they heard some news. In October, his father, Chad, wrote:

> We are now having regular contact with the guerrillas, trying to negotiate Russell's release. The guerrillas are apparently short of money and that seems to be the reason they kidnapped Russell. The whole situation is very complicated. The lives of the five people involved in the negotiating are in constant danger. I cannot give the details here, but each negotiation involves airplane flights and dug-out canoe trips on the river.

This is a far cry from the simple telephone in Rome. Kidnappers-to-family communications in rough rural areas are quite different to the sophistications available in cities. I wrote back that even in Colombia's capital, Bogotá, one gang had avoided using the telephone and, on each contact, instead ordered a member of the victim's family to drive a circuitous route until stopped by someone with a pre-designated sign. This unknown person would quickly pass the message before disappearing into the crowds.

There can be few more complex situations than those faced by the Stendals—and other victims—in rural South America. The sheer physical problems of reaching the kidnap gang through the jungle are immense. They were obliged to use intermediaries; but were these intermediaries really in touch with the men who had their son, and might they not take the ransom, or a proportion of it, for themselves? The area buzzed with rumours about the kidnap and local people had no scruples about taking advantage of the Stendals' predicament.

Whereas families in cities might expect to hear from the gang within a few days, or within two weeks at the outside, the Stendals did not hear anything from the F.A.R.C. group until 11 September, four weeks after their son had been seized. This letter was dated on 24 August, three weeks earlier. A second letter arrived two days later, on 13 September, before the Marxist guerrillas had had time to receive a reply from the family. Clearly, the difficulties of communication through the jungle affected the guerrillas as much as the Stendals. All these delays added weeks to the negotiation. Russell Stendal was in for a long period of captivity.

A letter in November explained the problems in more detail:

> In these first weeks after Russell had been captured, when we still had had no contact from the kidnappers, an acquaintance of Russell from a nearby town came to offer condolences. He said that since he had connections with people who interacted with the main group of guerrillas in the Llanos region, he could arrange a contact for us. At this point we thought Russell was being held by the small group of Chinese Communist oriented guerrillas, but this friend was sure that the larger group would know about it. Since we were at absolute zero at this point in our knowledge of what was going on we decided to go ahead. We even had illusions that maybe this larger, more established guerrilla group—the F.A.R.C. —would be incensed that the smaller group had kidnapped someone right in the area which they considered to be theirs and rescue him for us.
>
> A few days later a contact was established. We tried to cancel the other effort but it was too late.

The issue was not simply that the family would lose their money by paying it to the wrong person. They needed to establish contact with the gang that had Russell to show that, yes, a ransom might be paid, but only if the kidnappers would return their victim. Negotiations are vastly important, not simply as a means of paying a proportion of the demands, but to make the kidnappers realize that the deal is on the basis of quid pro quo. Such negotiations oblige the gang to consider the safe return of the victim at an early stage.

To the Stendals, surrounded by the chaos of their environment, proof of life was essential, for their own peace of mind and to cut out the problem of false intermediaries. It was one of the most important points in my first letter to them:

> Have you demanded proof of life? For example, a photo of Russell with a daily paper, or better still, tell the gang to ask him some question that you know only he will be able to answer. Make the question short, unambiguous, easy to explain to an idiot bandit, and easy for an idiot bandit to understand when Russell gives the answer. Pre-arranged codes, if you have them, are Utopian.

Fortunately, in November I read that they had received pictures of Russell and letters through a real contact with the guerrillas. The guerrillas had suggested that the family send a piece of clothing so they could take Polaroid photographs of Russell to prove he was alive and in their hands. This shows the kidnappers had a clear understanding of the necessity of proof in a kidnap negotiation. Instead, his parents sent him a Bible and the guerrillas photographed him with that.

The guerrillas' understanding of the necessary requirements for satisfactory proof of life indicated a degree of professionalism that was encouraging, for it was therefore likely that Russell's eventual release had been considered as an integral part of the kidnap negotiation. However, I believe that this degree of organization among guerrillas in the depths of the jungle is not possible without some outside help and training. I do not decry it, because the more professional the gang, the more likely the victim is to survive, but it strongly suggests the guerrillas are receiving training specifically for kidnapping. Perhaps that is not surprising; the guerrillas do everything else strictly in accordance with their Marxist training in Cuba.

*   *   *   *

Russell's attempt to escape had failed. As he lay waiting for death, Jaime, the guerrilla leader, ran through the bananas to re-establish control.

'Throw down your weapon,' he shouted. Russell obeyed. 'And stand up.'

Russell could not move against the cords that bound him. Two other men hauled him to his feet, while a third grabbed the rifle from Manuel who was still trying to get his finger around the trigger to shoot his captive. The wounded guard got little sympathy.

'Why didn't you search the prisoner thoroughly like I told you to?' screamed the leader at Manuel. 'This is what you get for failing to obey orders.' Then he whipped round on Russell. 'Why did you do this?'

There was several moments' tense silence. The guerrillas had murdered men for much less than this.

'Put yourself in my position,' Russell said bravely. 'If you had a weapon with the chance to escape, wouldn't you try?'

The F.A.R.C. guerrilla leader looked at his bound prisoner thoughtfully. Suddenly he said, 'You're right!'

The guerrillas were impressed with Russell's attempt to escape, but their reactions were predictable: they increased their control over him and never left him alone. They strapped him up with more rope and threw him in the bottom of the canoe for the rest of the long river journey to their camp.

The guerrilla group left the river and walked for two days. Bound by the slip-knots with the end of the cord held by one guerrilla, Russell was marched along in the middle of a column of six men. Once, in the darkness, they had to hide in the scrub at the side of a track when headlights appeared. It was the vehicle that had come to pick up the wounded Manuel and take him to the guerrillas' field hospital, where an operation was performed to remove the bullet. Later, the squad climbed into a Russian Gaz 66 jeep for an hour's ride along another track. Finally, they reached a campsite near a stream in virgin, primary jungle.

The nylon cord stayed tied around Russell's neck in the camp; and an armed guard twenty feet away held the other end at all times. Though Russell knew the jungle well, his chances of escape had been reduced to virtually nil. And he was a long way from help.

His guards made him a place to live in the jungle camp, chopping wood and palms with their machetes. He was provided with a bench and a table of freshly cut poles and split palm, all tied together with vines and lianas. His bed was a hammock slung between two trees, over which the guerrillas tied a large black tarpaulin. They even gave him a mosquito net to hang under the tarpaulin and, though it was stuffy lying under the net in the jungle where there are no refreshing currents of air, he was free of torment from the jungle's myriad insects, especially the ubiquitous and infuriating mosquitos.

As far as is possible in a semi-permanent camp in the jungle, Russell's living conditions, and those of the guerrillas, were comfortable. Certainly, the average soldier would be grateful for such luxuries in the jungle theatre. His food was adequate too: breakfast often consisted of eggs, sausages, corn patties, and coffee. Clearly the guerrillas were trying to keep their victim in good health.

If his physical welfare was well catered for, the mental pressure was considerable. Jaime commanded a squad of eight, whose job it was to guard Russell, and three guards covered the day on eight-hour shifts. Each handed over the end of the nylon cord that was now tied around the captive's neck with a slip-knot. The guerrillas had learned their lesson and gave Russell absolutely no privacy. At six o'clock, when the evening sky darkens the green world beneath the jungle canopy to pitch impenetrability, they took his shoes away and made him lie in his hammock. There he sweated in the warmth of the evening, in the wool hammock under the mosquito net which was made of a thick cloth material, attentively guarded by an armed guerrilla. Sometimes they tied a string to his hammock to check he was still there at night—by pulling the string they could feel his body's weight. Russell would lie awake, unable to sleep, waiting for the guard to tug the string or shine a torch into his eyes any time he moved in the hammock.

Night in the jungle is long and Russell spent more than twelve hours a day in his hammock, lying awake, tired but sleepless, usually until past midnight. He lay staring up at the black tarpaulin, terrified that his guerrilla guard would shoot him in the mistaken belief that he was attempting another escape. Night in the jungle is also full of noise, of nocturnal creatures feeding and hunting, of leaves disturbed or rotten vegetation falling. At each sudden noise the guard would jump and Russell would hear the metallic click of the safety catch as the man made ready to fire.

Captivity, with no end in sight, is utterly depressing. The rope tied to his neck dragged on the ground and mud caked everything; the thin jungle soil was regularly soaked by torrential rain, and constantly churned up by the guerrillas' boots. Thoughts of escape, which

tormented him constantly, were dampened by the extra precautions
the guerrillas took to restrict him to his hammock, the fear that he
would be shot as he ran away and the worry that, should he escape, he
would die anyway, lost in the jungle with no shoes, matches or food.

* * * *

The slowness of communications hampered his parents' negotiations,
already tough enough in the face of the guerrillas' impossible
demand. Chad, and Russell's younger brother Chaddy, had been
increasing offers little by little, against the initial demand. It was
encouraging to read, in Chad's letter in October, that the kidnappers
were actually negotiating, but the family had more fundamental
worries. Extracts from our correspondence perfectly describe, in the
words of the victims themselves, the heart-searching that every family
goes through: whether or not to pay any ransom at all.

> Our initial reaction was that we should not, though Pat has
> come to the conclusion that we should pay the ransom if we
> can. She feels that if we could get him out for less than an
> astronomical amount, his life is worth more than the benefit
> of the money to the enemy. She feels that we should
> negotiate, thereby providing a means of communication with
> the kidnappers. Both Chaddy and I felt that if it were us
> personally being held that we would prefer to give our lives
> instead of paying a ransom. However Chaddy pointed out
> that it was fine for us to say that, but we could not make that
> decision for Russell. So we asked the kidnappers to let
> Russell write what he thought.
>
> We received a letter from Russell, but it is very difficult to
> decide what they made him write and what he really means.
> However it appears he wants us to get him out.
>
> Russell's wife, Marina, and her family want to ransom
> Russell. They are selling some of their few possessions to
> raise some money to help. They would not understand
> sacrificing Russell for a higher cause.

The last sentence says it all: the victim's family cannot contemplate
sacrificing the one they love. Russell was kidnapped because the
Colombian government cannot control the huge areas of the country
in which Marxist guerrillas do what they please. Government failure,

so much a feature of the Stendal case, lies at the root of most kidnaps. So, is it fair for any government to turn round on the victims and order them not to pay the ransom? Is it an honest claim that non-payment of a few thousand dollars will deter kidnappers from acting again?

My advice was to pay the ransom. In November, Russell's mother Pat returned to the theme. Clearly the arguments and doubts persisted:

> Marina (Russell's wife) has been handling the situation very well, trusting in her faith for his safe return. However she is not at all prepared to cope with the eventuality of his not returning. When I tried to explain to her that some people felt that it was morally wrong to pay ransom money, she got hysterical and started to cry and scream that we were terrible people if we loved money more than our son.
>
> After the first contact with the kidnappers (we were) asked to make an offer, (but) Chad was inclined to refuse. This caused Marina to lose control again. She and her father both made it very clear that their sons' lives were also being risked (in the role of intermediaries) and that we were expected to go along with the custom to negotiate.
>
> I decided this was right. After all, Russell's testimony in the future would do more harm to the cause of Communism in the world than the amount of money would benefit the guerrillas. It is not as if the F.A.R.C. would collapse if they didn't get this ransom money. And it didn't seem to me wise to cut off the only means of communication with Russell and the kidnappers. Negotiation also gives us the opportunity of dialogue with the guerrillas.

Again the last point is most important. It once more shows the difference between a hostage situation, in which the authorities surround both the criminals and their victims, and kidnapping, in which the criminals derive their advantage because the location of both is unknown. Negotiation is vital. It gives the family, and the authorities, the opportunity to learn about the kidnappers. The greater the dialogue, the more the kidnappers give away about themselves, and, in countries more organized than Colombia, the greater the chances that the gang will eventually be caught.

Furthermore, dialogue increases the chance that the kidnappers will return the victim.

The ransom negotiation had been going slowly but along predictable lines. The F.A.R.C. were demanding a staggering 40 million Colombian pesos ($500,000). Chad Stendal had replied with an offer of only 500,000 pesos ($6,250). What could he do? They were not rich owners of a successful family business, like the classic targets of European or urban kidnapping. Chad and his family were missionaries with no available capital, though the terrorists saw them as wealthy Americans.

Hampered by the slow jungle communications, Chad negotiated through Marina's relations who, living out in the jungle areas where the guerrillas were hidden, acted as intermediaries with Russell's kidnappers. I had explained in my first letter that it was important to analyse the guerrillas' actions in detail:

> This is the most valuable exercise you can do. Write down all the things that have happened, all the things that they have done, and the way they have done them, the demands, the method of communications they have used, their threats, periods of silence or inactivity between contacts, and what they say—lies, bluff, threats—in their contacts.
> Analyse the bandits and then choose your strategy to fit.

Chad had been gradually increasing his offers until he was at 1.4 million pesos ($17,500). By this time the family were being helped by donations raised by their mission contacts in the United States. The guerrillas responded with a reduction of their demand to 15 million pesos ($187,500). This was still absurd but it was an encouraging step in the right direction, and showed the F.A.R.C. were willing to continue the negotiations.

Pat Stendal explained that Chad had been making every excuse for not offering more money. The family had limited resources and the cattle were in hock to the bank—letters from the bank were sent to back this claim. Chad had explained that even the house and farm would not attract offers with the added chance that the new owners would suffer the same fate as Russell. They had even sent copies of the family's Colombian income tax returns.

The guerrillas finally responded to this endless barrage of excuses with a classic response typical of all kidnappers. Pat described their exasperated plea:

In their last letter they said they don't want any more letters from us; only the money.

The mental pressures on both the victim and the family are tremendous. Some people cope better than others. During long months, the assault on the mind is exhausting for both sides. The victim agonizes about his eventual survival, asking himself over and over what he has done to deserve such maltreatment, questioning the very essence of his life, while, 'on the outside', the family is obsessed with clues to the health of the victim, worried about the amount of money they have to find, and whether they will ever see the one they love again.

The kidnappers turn the screw tighter and tighter on the family's mental control, with huge demands, deadlines, doubling their demands, mutilation, suggestions of ill-health and threats to kill. They hope all the time to break the family's will and open the floodgates holding down the ransom. All these, and the moral pressures of whether to pay at all, prey constantly, insidiously persuading the family to capitulate.

The Stendals, both Russell and his family, coped better than most. They were missionaries with a strong religious faith. They took risks in everyday life—that the Kogi Indians would poison them if medical treatment given to an elder failed, or with the banks to finance farms to make the local people self-sufficient—but they knew what they were doing. Their faith had not blinded them to practical issues or to the penalties of failure. Nor did their Christian belief make them soft. A letter from Pat describes how Chad Stendal wrote to the F.A.R.C. in October:

> Chad told them they made a bad mistake to kidnap the son of a missionary, for two reasons:
> 1. We don't have money.
> 2. We are not afraid to die.
> And Chaddy wrote ... encouraging them to repent and get right with God.

On 4 December, having outlined various threats that the guerrillas might use against the family, I finished my letter to them as follows:

> Of all the families I have seen suffering through kidnap, yours

is the best equipped. Not the money, for you haven't that, but you have the strength of your faith to hold you steady when desperate hopes are shredded in pieces.

I came across only one other person, the father of Cesare Pagani, who demonstrated the same firm resolve. His balanced self-control, concealing great inner turmoil, was a major factor in the eventual safe release of his son from the hands of a group of erratic and murderous kidnappers.

The Stendals needed their faith. Their kidnap negotiations did not prevent the F.A.R.C. from continuing their attacks on the people. Insurgent Communist guerrillas are particularly aggressive against people whose job or lifestyle sets them in competition with the Marxist 'ideal'; examples are local leaders and businessmen, families farming their own plot of land, and, of course, Christian families. Pat Stendal described one incident in her letter of 23 November:

> Last week two of our neighbours—that is, people who have a farm in the general vicinity of ours—were shot in cold blood right in front of their families. Their bodies were brought to San Martin, and they were buried last Saturday. They were told before being shot that they had been sentenced to death for talking too much. These were young men in their twenties, both married with small children. They had been complaining in town about the 'protection money' which they were being forced to pay. Also one of our friends in the area was killed. One of the reasons that was given for killing him was that he was a friend to the gringos.

Chad adds to this story, in his letter of 8 December:

> When the family brought the bodies to San Martin for burial, the guerrillas returned to the farm and stole dishes, blankets, and everything they had.

His letter went on to describe another case that shows how close the Stendal family were to the violence:

> Eduardo and Margarita had a little farm downstream from us. A Communist sympathizer had a quarrel with Eduardo about

a few head of cattle and told the guerrillas about it. The
guerrillas came for Eduardo to kill him. I found out about it
just before they were able to get to his place and dropped a
note from the airplane telling him they were coming. But he
decided to stay and defend his farm and property.

The guerrillas caught him and another man, tied them to a
tree and shot them both in the stomach and in the head.
Then, they contacted his wife who happened to be about an
hour away and told her he had been executed by order of the
people's court, and if she or her family gave any further
resistance, they would all be killed. She requested the body
but was refused.

Later, the body was discovered in an isolated area,
abandoned where he had been shot. Chaddy sent someone to
attempt a proper burial. Eduardo had been one of Chaddy's
friends for many years. When Margarita returned to her little
farm, she found a note written by her husband before he was
taken away: he said he wanted her to be sure the children
grew up to be real Christians.

How did Chad Stendal hear of the impending attack on this family?
In spite of, or perhaps because of, poor communications, rumours
spread fast in the jungle areas. Each 'grapevine' informs interested
parties in different social and business groups, while gossip and
conversations overheard in cafes, stores or between people passing on
remote roads ensure the jungle 'grapevines' are truly tangled. For
example, Chad told the F.A.R.C. in one letter to them that he would
have to sell an old red Toyota car to raise more money. He never
mentioned this to anyone else and yet, a few days later, a man in the
local town told Pat Stendal that he had heard they were about to sell
the red Toyota. Rumours abound and stories thrive, like plants, in the
humid jungle.

So it was that the Stendals heard what happened to Mrs Kirby,
another American who lived with her husband in the area near the
Stendals. She was over sixty years old and her husband, aged sixty-
five, was crippled by arthritis. In April 1983, she had been kidnapped
and rumour had it that she was held by the same group that had
Russell. The authorities had been alerted as soon as she was taken
and there was considerable publicity arising from the apparent co-
operation between the Colombian authorities and the United States

Embassy. The Colombians were clearly embarrassed and felt they should make some show of releasing the kidnapped woman.

Understandably, the resulting Press coverage presented the F.A.R.C. in a bad light. Their response was simple. They broke off all communications with the family, and publicized statements that their victim had been 'liberated' and was already back in the United States. The F.A.R.C. hate bad Press: it counters their efforts to present themselves as freedom-loving liberators of the people from the capitalist yoke. Pat Stendal wrote that they had murdered several hostages whose cases were closely followed by the Press. The Stendals were aware of this and the first reports of Russell Stendal's kidnap appeared from statements made by the F.A.R.C. themselves in local papers, giving the story in a suitably rose-tinted light.

Control of the media is an important theme for insurgent groups and the guerrillas' sensitivity to newspaper coverage is one aspect that makes political kidnappings so much more complicated than ordinary 'commercial' cases. In Italy, for example, gangs are not so sensitive to critical newspaper articles—'commercial' kidnappers do not kill their victims in revenge for bad Press—though they will often refer to them in future letters or telephone calls (which is encouraging for the family). Articles appear regularly, written either by journalists following the case, or sponsored by the family in order to create a specific image that will enhance their negotiating strategy.

Each area, each kidnap group and each motive creates its own criteria and it is important that the family understands these local characteristics. The choice of negotiation strategy and the ultimate safe return of the victim depends on it.

The F.A.R.C. remained quiet about Mrs Kirby for months until their negotiator mentioned it to one of Marina's relatives who was acting as the intermediary negotiating for Russell's release. The guerrillas, who saw their opportunity to renew negotiations for her ransom through the Stendals, threatened to kill the intermediary if word of the new talks about the woman got out on the jungle grapevine.

This placed further stress on the Stendals' negotiation but, in choosing this course of action, the F.A.R.C. provided considerable information through the medium of the Kirby case about their own tactics and about Russell.

The guerrillas had gradually reduced their vast demand on Mr Kirby to 5 million pesos ($62,500) and set a deadline and ultimatum for the ransom payment on 25 October. The next developments gave away valuable information about Russell's situation.

Mrs Kirby's husband agreed to meet the demand and her release was arranged through the Stendals' intermediaries. Since the F.A.R.C. had already publicized Mrs Kirby's 'liberation' they were obsessive about secrecy and threatened to kill Russell should any word of the actual release leak out.

Two days after her husband agreed to pay, the F.A.R.C. brought Mrs Kirby downriver and hid her close to the intermediaries' contact rendezvous in the jungle. They held her there for a week while the money was collected and then, so eager were they at the handover, they took it without counting it and freed Mrs Kirby. She told her story of captivity, details of which directly helped the Stendals. She said that she had lived out in the jungle in a hammock, under a tarpaulin with a mosquito net and her basic physical needs were met. She was, she said, kept 'decently' like a 'valuable animal'. The F.A.R.C. disregarded her emotional requirements and gave her no writing materials, though she was allowed to read her Bible. She spent seven months reading it. So what came out of all this? Mrs Kirby's case provided most encouraging information for the Stendal family and I felt able to write back in December:

> She seems to have been well treated from a physical point of view, and that, for thinking people like Russell who can find ways of coping mentally, is a great thing. Her reports about how she was held tell us about the attitude of the gang to their kidnap victims. They appreciate the need to keep their victims alive and well.
>
> The other bit of good news was that they released Mrs Kirby for $62,500. This means that they are prepared to come down to this level. [*Chad Stendal had assumed early on that the kidnappers might be persuaded to come down to $75,000 or 6 million pesos.*] The 'going rate' for ransoms in an area seems to be a concept (unconsciously) accepted by gangs. Indeed they don't like going beneath that rate. In Italy at the moment it is about $900,000. A gang has certain expectations that result from the particular circumstances of the area. You can get below this 'going rate' (i.e. reduce the gang's expectations) but you have to be prepared to be very tough with yourselves at the end of the negotiation when you tail off the amount of

the increases in your offers (as you reach the final ransom figure). Then the gang usually puts the pressure on with more threats (like the deadline and ultimatum ploy). They are testing you and convincing themselves that your offers are all they are going to get.

All this may have been obvious to the Stendals in Colombia but it is my experience that, however astute the family, it is tremendously encouraging for them to hear the optimistic side to their case from an outsider. They are immersed in gloom which threatens to stretch out to eternity. There is no yardstick of time, dependent as they are on the whim of the kidnappers, and no end in sight. Their view is entirely subjective, masked by threats from the kidnap gang and natural despondency, and they need to have the good news spelled out or they will miss it altogether.

During the delicate negotiations for Mrs Kirby's release, the Colombian authorities became involved. After reading Russell's earlier letters sent out by the F.A.R.C., Chaddy mistakenly believed there was a code concealed in the text that gave the location of the guerrillas' hide-out. He believed he was able to pinpoint the location of their camp by relating it to an expedition he and Russell had made many years previously. Father and son contacted the local army unit and spoke to the General commanding the area to discuss the feasibility of a rescue attempt. The General assured Chad that he would pursue his investigations.

After several days, during which, no doubt, the army collected rumours—or 'sources of information', to use official terminology — and after flights to reconnoitre the jungle area, the General agreed to mount a rescue attempt.

The attempt posed a number of problems, all of them considerable. Firstly, the participants' lives would be at risk: Chaddy, because he had to lead the army into the jungle; the army lieutenant, who was to be recalled from leave and from his fiancée to whom he was to be married in two weeks (hardly guaranteeing his enthusiasm for such a dangerous task); and the intermediaries, some of whom were Marina's relations. Secondly, the location of the hide-out had to be known to the nearest tree (to avoid blundering about in thick jungle where visibility may be as short as three metres) and the attack team would have to search about in an area of jungle—not an easy military exercise with the best troops—without alerting the enemy to the patrol's presence or intentions. And, finally, the greatest concern was that failure might cause the F.A.R.C. to kill Russell.

Furthermore, the negotiations for Russell's ransom payment were going quite well. The F.A.R.C. had reduced their demand from 40 million pesos to 15 million ($187,500). At this stage, it seemed to make no sense to embark on a rescue attempt with such slender chances of success.

Finally, the dilemma was resolved by Mr Kirby. Chad Stendal felt it was his duty to tell the old man that the army planned a rescue attempt since Mrs Kirby at this time was still held captive. At first Mr Kirby was in favour of the idea; but, after he had agreed to pay 5 million pesos and meet the deadline of 25 October, he was worried that any move on the part of the army, especially one so risky, would jeopardize the safe return of his wife. Chad Stendal informed the army of this and the attempt was called off. By the time that Mrs Kirby had been released and the family had considered the rescue again, rumour from the jungle spoke of Russell being moved into the centre of a much larger guerrilla encampment. This presented a quite different challenge and the idea was shelved completely. It was galling to have missed an opportunity but doubtless there was genuine relief all round.

In her letter about the murders locally, Pat Stendal wrote that 'the Communists are taking over the area around and the only thing that is keeping the army out is the fact that the F.A.R.C. have Russell.' This may have been a good reason for calling off the attempted rescue, but is it a *carte blanche* excuse for not protecting and helping people against the wider depredations of the guerrillas?

If the overall picture of the Kirby episode was encouraging, the negotiation for Russell's release took an apparent turn for the worse after Mrs Kirby was set free. Pat Stendal wrote to me:

> Since I wrote the enclosed letter (dated 7 November) we have had one more contact, bringing a hand-written note demanding 30 million by 2 December. They say, 'Don't you understand that this is an *ultimatum*?' They do not say what they will do if we don't meet their demands. Let me translate that into dollars: at an exchange rate of 80 to 1, 30 million becomes $375,000 dollars. Before this kidnapping, a million pesos seemed like an immense amount of money to us. Now it seems like nothing.

This deadline was an exact replica of the threat used in the Kirby case. Perhaps its repeated use indicated that the F.A.R.C. guerrillas negotiate all their kidnaps along similar lines. Perhaps this lack of flexibility —which is an essential ingredient in kidnap negotiation —was due to the rigid thinking typical of Communist ideology. Whatever the reason, the F.A.R.C. should have known the Stendals would know about the deadline threat; maybe that is why they threw in the doubled ransom demand as good measure. Both are classic tactics used to pressure the family.

Imposing a deadline is a standard ploy. Kidnappers, airplane hijackers, and all kinds of terrorists use it. The power of this threat is not so much in its credibility but in its shock effect. The family suddenly face an ultimatum. This is the family's underlying fear all the time but, as the days pass interminably, nightmares are pushed to the back of the mind, rationalized, or plain ignored. Suddenly the horror is focused with blinding clarity: the victim will die on a certain date.

The F.A.R.C. did not say what they would do when the deadline was passed; but the underlying threat was that they would kill Russell (this threat almost goes without saying in every kidnap). But then what? Did they seriously expect the Stendals to pay any money at all if they killed their only hostage? I wrote back that, under the harsh light of objective reasoning, the F.A.R.C. could not expect the family —missionaries at that—to increase their present offer from just 1,400,000 pesos to a staggering 30 million.

The guerrillas had learned of the intermediaries the Stendals had first used—and then rejected—and they decided to employ these men in the future. It seems these men who had volunteered their services as contacts in the beginning had offered no less than 20 million pesos ($250,000)—only half the original demand—to the F.A.R.C. on the Stendals' behalf. They said they thought they were doing the family a favour.

Perhaps that accounted for doubling the ransom. But, as a tactic, this trick served no useful purpose because the guerrillas had already reduced their demand to 15 million pesos ($187,500). This clearly indicated that their expectations of ransom were at 15 million, not 30 million, and, by the very nature of negotiation, were probably below that.

The kidnappers' chief mistake was that they had already used up the novelty of these tactics for it was the Stendals' intermediaries who passed on similar deadline threats to Mr Kirby. While the threat to Mrs

Kirby was credible, because $62,500 was an attainable demand, doubling the Stendals' figure was not: $375,000 was clearly quite unreasonable. Fortunately, I was able to write to the Stendals and put some of these points.

However, the kidnappers were certainly increasing the tempo of their negotiation. This was encouraging in one sense, because it suggested that the end of the negotiation was drawing closer; it is a common feature of all kidnap negotiations. The F.A.R.C. had put Mr Kirby under pressure at the end. It did not make life any easier for the Stendals who, apart from the negotiation to free Russell, felt they were under tremendous pressure from the guerrillas to leave the area for good.

The Kirby ransom, their own ultimatum for 2 December and the murders locally caused the family to re-think their ransom level. Chad decided he had to borrow more money. Marina went herself to see the new contact and increased their offer to 4 million pesos ($50,000). Then they settled down to an agonizing wait as the days slowly passed towards the deadline of Friday 2 December.

* * * *

Russell was suffering too. While the guerrillas negotiated to break his parents resolve, they had different reasons for making their victim miserable. Like many kidnap victims—Mrs Kirby, and Sergio Martinelli in Rome—Russell fell back heavily on his faith, and had been absorbed by reading his Bible. He had put his thoughts on paper describing the experience of captivity. This in itself did not pose a threat to the guerrillas but gradually they realized that their victim was making his guards question Marxist ideology and, since they all came from a staunch Catholic background, reconsider Christianity.

At first the leadership allowed Russell's notes to be circulated among the guerrillas, so they would appear fair-minded. When they saw that the guerrillas instead began to question their own ideology, they gradually made life worse for Russell. One guard intimated that Russell's wife had also been seized by the guerrillas. He slyly suggested that she was being brainwashed and trained as a fighter herself. Russell raged with thoughts of revenge, until he calmed himself with the thought that this was most unlikely and only part of a plan to shatter his mental balance. Other tricks were less subtle. They told him horrifying stories of wild animals and the terrors of the jungle to intimidate him and put him off any ideas of escaping. One day, Arnuval, a guard in Jaime's squad, shot a monkey through the stomach and tied it to a stake to die by Russell's bivouac; quite in view but just out of reach of Russell who was still tied by the rope round his neck. The screaming monkey was female and a tiny baby clung frantically to its chest. He watched helplessly as the wounded mother took all day to die.

The routine in the guerrillas' camp did not change during the period of his captivity, though Russell was indeed relocated, from the small campsite near the river to a large headquarters area of several hundred men on higher ground, a few days before the deadline for Mrs Kirby ran out on 25 October.

The guerrillas' day started at 4 a.m. when each man rolled up his bedding—the tarpaulin, hammock, wool blanket and mosquito net like Russell's—and made up his back-pack ready to leave at a moment's notice. Weapon cleaning was encouraged at all times and the guerrillas, because they were obsessed with guns, kept their rifles immaculate. It is likely that Russell's lucky escape in the banana patch—he was saved by a dud bullet—was due to poor-quality ammunition supplied to the F.A.R.C.

Perhaps because he was less trouble in his hammock, Russell was allowed to sleep on until six o'clock. Then, Giovani, the man who had tried to shoot him with the dud bullet, would come to wake him with a cup of coffee and some water to brush his teeth. Breakfast followed at seven.

Russell took every opportunity to talk to Giovani and his other guards about their lives and answer their bitter questions. American capitalism and Christianity, the foremost enemies of Marxism, were the main topics and, before moving to the larger camp, Russell made a considerable impact with his arguments. It was during these chats that Russell noticed Giovani's accent was foreign: he was Cuban.

Russell was in the grip of an organized, if rigid, machine. Every morning there was a two-hour indoctrination session for all the guerrillas not on guard duties. Reflecting the orthodox manning of the Russian army, the F.A.R.C. guerrilla units were controlled by two types of commander: one was the military commander, the other responsible for political affairs. It was the latter who supervized the indoctrination sessions each morning, when instruction was carried out using a large black tarpaulin, stretched taut between two trees, as a blackboard. The United States was always the object of their hatred. In Russell's small squad, Jaime was the military leader and Giovani was the political officer.

Propaganda was not restricted to the guerrillas alone. The F.A.R.C. leadership arranged meetings for the local peasants to impress them with the excitement of being a 'freedom fighter'. They sat around fires in the night, their faces glowing in the light of the flames as they listened to presentations specially prepared by the leadership. They were shown video films, run on a generator, of suitably edited material designed to vilify the American way of life. Once they showed *Apocalypse Now* to a fascinated audience who were told, and believed implicitly, that they were watching a true documentary of the Vietnam war. These meetings ended with rousing songs to uplift the revolutionary spirit, and Russell lay in his hammock listening to the hundreds of raucous voices echoing through the dark forest. He was not allowed to attend these presentations—it would not have done to spoil the guerrillas' image by showing a kidnap victim right in the camp—but he mended the generator and Betamax video when they broke down.

Clearly the guerrillas were unworried by the amount of noise they made. They were kept occupied throughout the day with military training. Shooting went on for hours at a time, both in daylight and at night, as the guerrillas prepared for jungle combat against the Colombian army. Drill instructors shouted out their crude rhythms of movement and counter-movement at squads of male and female recruits sometimes a hundred strong. There was no shortage of weapons: about a third carried modern assault rifles, the German G-3 or the American M-16 and AR-15, while the rest had American M-1 carbines and the inevitable motley collection of bolt action rifles. They were well supplied with up-to-date rockets and .50 calibre machine guns, but they had few hand grenades or anti-aircraft weapons. Some of this equipment had been stolen from the arsenals of the Colombian army itself, the rest was supplied, like the edited films, from Cuba.

There was one other major task for the freedom fighters every day: to tend the coca plantations around the camp area. The drug traffic in cocaine provided another important source of income for the guerrillas. They were employed to plant little coca cuttings, at about a metre spacing; to prevent weeds growing between the rows, with paraquat spray (which, ironically, the Colombian government refused to allow the anti-drug-smuggling agencies to use); and to harvest the leaves for processing. Russell found himself at one time held next to a cocaine laboratory, with all the necessary chemicals stacked nearby. For the first stage of the process there were drums of kerosene, bags, of sodium bicarbonate and ammonium hydroxide, and for the second stage they used potassium permanganate, sulphuric acid, and more ammonium hydroxide. These chemicals were either ferried quietly along the jungle rivers concealed from aerial view by overhanging greenery, or flown direct into dangerous and secret landing strips hewn out of the forest.

Russell guessed that he was about twenty-five miles from a small town on the Rio Initida, and that put him in the main cocaine-producing area in Colombia. The guerrillas were forbidden drugs, and Russell asked Giovani why the F.A.R.C. did not try to prevent narcotics abuse altogether, since it caused such social misery. With a twisted grin, he replied, 'The revolution is being financed by Americans who use cocaine. If the corrupt capitalists in North America want to buy cocaine, we'll produce and sell them all they need. We will destroy your corrupt society with its own money.'

Russell developed a close relationship with Jaime, the guard squad leader, and other guards. Arnuval eventually apologized for shooting the monkey, and said he wished he could be a Christian, like Russell, but that he had made a serious agreement with the organization when he joined.

'If I go back on my oath of allegiance, they can kill me,' he said sadly. 'For the time being I will have to continue to be a guerrilla. It's too bad I didn't meet you before I joined.'

But Giovani stubbornly refused to yield. He became violent and threatened to kill Russell on several occasions. When Russell remembered that he had met Giovani before, the guerrilla's hatred intensified. Giovani had been on a 'fishing trip' with a professor and a group of school children in the jungle when Russell had landed his plane nearby. It was Giovani's accent that had stuck in Russell's mind and given him away. Giovani was furious that the true purpose of the 'fishing trip' had been discovered: he and the professor had been recruiting the students into their organization.

There are plenty of reasons to criticize Colombian society, and recruiting thrives among the disaffected. There are social inequalities, wide wealth differentials, injustice, corrupt officials, misappropriation of money for roads, schools or hospitals, and police who extort money from both drug smugglers and ordinary citizens passing through road blocks. It has been claimed that police officers bribe their own superiors for postings to drug smuggling areas. The bribe is taken on credit and paid off once the newly appointed officer strikes his own lucrative deals with the smugglers. Colombia is the most Catholic of South American countries, where it is forbidden to get married except as a Catholic, and yet over fifty per cent of children are born illegitimate.

Recruiting into the F.A.R.C., therefore, is largely a matter of perspective. The potential recruit asks himself: 'If this is capitalism in Colombia then surely it is the same in the United States? In fact, since America is the home of capitalism, conditions there must be infinitely worse.' The potential recruit, who has no other experience, eagerly listens to Utopian Marxism and is prepared to suffer some discomfort before enjoying these visions. He is not told that he might have to . spend years in the jungle, 'fighting against the State.'

Another guard explained that new recruits are sworn into the F.A.R.C. with the words: 'We will fight unto death against the Yankees, the enemies of all mankind.' This oath is made over Simon Bolivar's sword (which was stolen from a Colombian State museum) and is included in the Sandinistas' Nicaraguan national anthem. Once in the F.A.R.C., the soldier of freedom finds it harder to leave than it was to join.

Discipline is harsh. However much they despise the Colombian army—and the overt routine of their camp reveals that they do—the F.A.R.C. are in enemy territory and the leadership has to maintain iron control. Time drags, even though the days are deliberately filled with training; guerrillas get drunk, use the drugs they grow themselves, or, a more fundamental crime, question Marx himself. Punishments for first offences are swiftly given and typical of any military unit: no cigarette rations, no trips to town and therefore no women, and extra guard duties. Punishment for repeated crimes marks the difference: death. The guilty man is executed in front of the rest of the guerrillas. This severe code exerted a strong grip on the minds of the guerrillas. However much they came to doubt their situation, and some evidently felt intense loneliness, they dared not speak, for fear that another would report them to the political leaders, nor could they ever leave, for they would be breaking their oath and would be shot if they were caught. Besides, this lush but hard land is their home; where else could they go?

The guerrillas in the jungle were not completely cut off from the world. They had radios which kept them abreast of world events, but even their listening was controlled. On 1 September, Russell had tuned in his guard's radio and was listening to the Voice of America when he heard the news of the shooting down of the Korean Airlines jet by Russian fighters. The guards were as shocked as Russell and a little group of them crowded around the radio to hear a Press conference by President Reagan.

The next day the F.A.R.C. leadership issued orders to tune into Radio Moscow or Radio Havana only. Russell noted that the Russian and Cuban broadcasts differed according to their audiences: the reports beamed on the higher wavelengths at Europe and the West admitted shooting down the plane in self defence, but the announcements for Central and South America flatly denied shooting down an airliner at all.

If Giovani, the political disciplinarian, was virulently anti-American, Russell had more success in establishing a rapport with Jaime and Arnuval. One day in November, 110 days after his kidnap, he was pacing up and down beside his hammock, constricted by the rope tied to his neck, and idly swatting the tarpaulin over his bed-space. Suddenly, from a little pile of dead leaves on the tarpaulin, a snake (a Fer-de-Lance, notorious for its aggression) struck furiously at his neck, missing by inches. Russell moved smartly away as far as his rope allowed and Arnuval, his guard at the time, walloped the snake with the flat of his machete so as not to damage the tarpaulin. The snake fell to the ground and launched another attack on Russell with Arnuval hot on its tail. Russell dodged the snake and, in the panic, tripped over Arnuval and they both crashed to the ground. As they rolled about trying to escape the snake, Russell's hand fell on his guard's bayonet, in his belt, and for a moment he considered escape. He could draw the bayonet, kill Arnuval, grab his G-3 rifle and run off. But Russell found he could not go through with it. His long period of captivity, his earlier attempt and wounding of Manuel, the thought of getting out of the bigger camp and finding his way through the jungle, and, perhaps most tellingly, his friendship with Arnuval all held him back. The opportunity had suddenly presented itself and as suddenly had passed. Arnuval killed the snake with his machete, they dusted themselves off, and drab normality returned.

He continued to spend the hours they guarded him talking about passages from the Bible and discussing them in relation to the guerrillas' Marxist teachings. One day, after Arnuval had listened to

Russell's explanation of Proverbs 25:3–6, the guerrilla exclaimed that
he agreed there was real wisdom in the little verse. He noted it down
enthusiastically and said that, since he was in charge of the indoctrination period the next day, he would reveal to everyone the good sense in
the lesson from the Bible.

The following morning started as usual, with the guerrillas going off
to the ideology class. But by the afternoon Arnuval was gone and so was
Jaime, the squad leader. Giovani had been reporting their weakening
commitment to the cause and Arnuval's public attempt to link Proverbs
with Marx had been the last straw. Russell's two most amenable guards
had been removed, and Eleizar, another Cuban, took over as squad
leader. Eleizar was a hard-liner and immediately imposed on Russell a
regime tougher than before, designed to break him down completely.

* * * *

Under different but equally tiring emotional stress, his mother and
father sat tight through the deadline of 2 December and it passed
uneventfully. The Stendals decided to send another letter and
meetings between the intermediaries and the guerrillas were arranged
for the end of the first week in December. The family offered 5.1
million pesos, up from 4 million, but inflation was playing havoc with
the real value of the offers: the rate of exchange had gone up from 80 to
102 pesos to the dollar, so that the two offers, apparently different by
1.1 million pesos were the same: $50,000.

The family's letter crossed one from the F.A.R.C. dated 5
December. The guerrillas told the Stendals' intermediaries that the
demand was now 12 million pesos (approximately $120,000 at the new
rate). They had reduced it again from the doubled amount, but the
relief of this was lost in the shock of another deadline. The Marxist
guerrillas said they wanted their demand paid in full by 25 December,
Christmas Day. Perhaps it was a subtle twist of the knife to choose a day
so important to this family, because of the trouble that Russell had
caused them with his subversive religious efforts in their camp. Or
possibly, the guerrillas were employing the same tactic as before, which
is quite a usual trick of kidnappers, to keep the family wriggling on the
hook as the end draws near. Or maybe, they wanted to disguise the
embarrassment of having to reduce their absurd demand. Whatever
the reason, in his letter of 8 December Chad Stendal wrote again,
using for the first time what I considered to be massive understatement:

It looks like this is going to be a difficult Christmas. We appreciate your continued prayers.

I wrote back before Christmas. Once more I was hit by the contrast between the two countries: the mechanized happiness of our Christmas in England and theirs in the tropical confusion of Colombia.

I am very sorry to hear that the guerrillas are killing so many people and among them good friends of yours. Marxism and human rights are all too casually understood, even by educated people, in the West. Russell's human rights have taken a beating since 14 August, and yours are under attack all the time.

You have my greatest sympathy for having your lives blighted by this form of politics, and my greater regard for your commitment in having stayed so long under pressure. It is one thing for a soldier to volunteer himself to leave home and fight, but an infinitely greater demand is made upon parents who commit themselves, their family and their home. You all have my enormous admiration.

I was encouraged by the news in your last letter (of 8 December) that the gang had reduced their demand to $125,000. I presume this had happened in the period of the deadline of 2 December, when in the same period I understood their demand to be increased to $387,000. All this seems to show they are simply haggling their way down to what they consider an acceptable sum, using a variety of threats, deadlines, periods of silence, etc. to weaken your resolve not to pay their demands. The good news is that they are coming down to realistic levels. This is a sure sign they are lowering their expectations towards the time when they must meet the actual offer you are making.

You have offered now what they have been prepared to accept in the past (Mrs Kirby), and I would say that you are drawing to the end of the negotiation. You have made some quite sizeable offers in the past two months, and I believe you must begin the process of 'tailing off', as I described in my first letter, in order to signal to the gang that you have no more to add and have reached the end of your tether. This is

essential, for the gang must be convinced that a family will not
offer any more. Or they keep the victim and wait ... These
tailing-off sums must be very small increases, so that your
intention and message is clear, so the gang recognize you are
'finished'. The only reason for making any increase at all is to
take the edge off giving nothing more at all—though that has
been done and worked before, and you might consider it.
The amount of these little increases at the end very much
depends on local circumstances. Since these F.A.R.C. types
are just sitting in the jungle anyway, their costs of keeping the
case going (guards, food, etc.) cannot be much different to
times with no kidnaps. You are the best judges of what is an
insignificant sum in your area, but make it really tiny.

In summary, I should have thought they will make a new
demand of $100,000 soon before finally agreeing to your
offer, which, still within the bounds of safety (*vis-à-vis*
Russell) might be no more than $68,750. The encouraging
thing is that this gang seem ready to release their victims very
soon after getting the money. In other places it can take quite
a while. I would hope that the gang will return Russell mid-
January time, but I am guessing now and that I should never
do. One never knows what swine like these will do next and
it's wrong to raise your hopes. However, unlike most caught
up in kidnapping, I know you have a strong faith which helps
you through the bad times and the disappointments.

Pat Stendal had written to me to tell me that my advice had been
helpful, particularly in assessing threats, like the deadlines, doubling
the ransom and second demands, which had badly worried them
before they were introduced to the objective view. However, they
were in the thick of it and, naturally enough, the worries persisted.

They had other problems besides wondering if the guerrillas would
really kill their son. The intermediaries said that the money had to be
paid to a go-between in Bogotá and the Stendals suspected foul play:
the Kirby payment had not been made like this and it seemed highly
likely that the go-betweens were planning to take some of the money.
So how big an offer was actually being passed on to the F.A.R.C.?
They worried, all through the long days up to Christmas, that the
guerrillas had been told a much lesser sum than 5.1 million pesos and
that this was the sticking point. So just before Christmas, Chad

decided to increase the offer to 5.5 million pesos. He wrote 'Stay alive with 55' on a white T-shirt, using the slogan for the 55 m.p.h. speed limit in the United States. In his letter offering the new amount, he asked the guerrillas to write their latest demand below the slogan and then take a Polaroid photograph of Russell wearing the T-shirt. This ingenious idea would bring the offers and demands of the negotiation out into the open and provide proof he was still alive (the guerrillas had sent Polaroids of Russell before). The scheme caused Marina's relatives some trouble contacting the F.A.R.C. go-betweens who became very active but with little result.

On Christmas day the Stendals set a plate at a vacant place at the table and spent the day praying and worrying about what might happen.

* * * *

The Stendals' worries were justified. Ever since the American invasion of Grenada, the guerrillas had considerably toughened their treatment of Russell. They were incensed that their Cuban comrades had been attacked and defeated by the 'imperialist Yankees'. When news reached them that the invasion troops had seized a shipment of arms destined for the F.A.R.C. some of the guerrillas wanted to kill Russell out of hand. Fortunately for him, the leadership, doubtless aware of his value to them, restrained their men.

Eleizar, the Cuban who had taken over from Jaime, seemed to have been given the task of reducing his captive charge to a psychological wreck, to show him to the other F.A.R.C. guerrillas as a gibbering religious lunatic, and to discredit him. His measures were thorough, though hardly subtle.

A typewriter Russell had been allowed to use earlier, making his notes, was removed and taken apart. The pieces were given to the F.A.R.C. gunsmith to repair weapons, and, though they left him with his Bible and notebooks, Russell was ordered not to do any more writing. His drink was spoiled. In spite of the airless heat under the canopy of jungle trees, he was given a special mixture, tasting like lemonade, instead of water. He developed migraines and was convinced that they had drugged the sour-tasting fluid. His guards threatened to kill him. They said they would do it only at night, by firing a bullet into his head as he slept. Then in the inky darkness, they woke him time after time by suddenly flashing their torches in his eyes.

Lying in the stifling heat, under the claustrophobic wool mosquito net in his hammock, for hours on end, Russell felt his control slipping. He was tired of green leaves, trees and the mud. He felt smothered and oppressed on every front. He wanted to scream, to tear his way out of the bivouac, throw off the awful nylon cord from his neck, to be out of the jungle and to see the blue sky. He wanted to be free.

But he took a grip of his exhausted emotions and went on the attack, speaking to each of his guards as they came on duty and telling them they were misled. Their lives were, he said, un-Christian. His own serious predicament lent his words extra force and even Giovani was impressed. He listened carefully as Russell told him it was never too late to admit mistakes. Giovani admitted that his mother had been deeply religious and, pulling aside his combat shirt, showed that he, the hard-line Cuban-trained political officer, wore a heavy gold crucifix around his neck.

Russell searched for an example that might parallel their own situation and reminded the guards of the urban guerrilla movement called the M-19. The M-19 had been spectacularly successful, their most famous operation being in 1980 when, on 27 April during a diplomatic reception, they seized twelve hostages, including eight ambassadors, inside the Embassy of the Dominican Republic in Bogotá. They demanded the release of 311 prisoners and $50 million. After two months, sixteen guerrillas were flown safely to Havana, with eleven of their hostages who were released from Cuba. Later, they kidnapped a businessman called Chet Bitterman and killed him. Within a month the M-19 group suffered unprecedented reverses by the Colombian army which killed or captured hundreds of guerrillas. The F.A.R.C. guards brushed this off as bad luck, but Russell, reacting bravely to his worsening treatment, told them bluntly that 'God lowered the boom on them after they killed Chet Bitterman.'

* * * *

The Stendals' Christmas was not a happy one. There had been no word from the guerrillas and it looked as though the T-shirt plan had foiled what appeared to have been an attempt to hijack the ransom. They worried that perhaps Russell had been killed long before and the negotiations had been kept going by the intermediaries for the money. Then, on New Year's Eve, a letter in Russell's handwriting dated 28 December arrived from the F.A.R.C. go-betweens: the guerrillas accepted the offer and wanted to release Russell immediately because he was sick.

As had happened in the Kirby case, the guerrillas wanted the payment made as soon as possible. Russell's letter explained all the details. Chaddy was to bring the money with the F.A.R.C. intermediary to a rendezvous deep in the jungle where Russell would be handed over in direct exchange (in a guerrilla-held area with no danger of the Colombian army following). They refused to provide proof with the T-shirt but the family studied that letter minutely and were convinced that it was indeed Russell's writing.

On Tuesday afternoon, 2 January, Chad and Chaddy met the man who was the F.A.R.C.'s intermediary and, taking the money with them, flew over the jungle to the secret meeting-place. The intermediary told Chad where to go only once they were airborne and, under his directions, they landed at an isolated airstrip where just two men waited with several small children, who were present to discourage any shooting, in case the Colombian army had come too. Chad was told to return the following morning at 9 a.m. and the guerrillas took Chaddy in a boat downriver to the exchange rendezvous. Chad had no option but to leave, though he was terribly worried: he left behind the ransom money and two sons in the hands of the kidnappers.

* * * *

On day 142 of his captivity at 5 p.m., Russell was surprised to see Giovani and two other guards rush over to his bed-space in the campsite and begin to take his hammock and tarpaulin down at top speed. 'You are going to be released,' they told him in excited tones. 'The order has just come over the radio.' (Another indication of the level of sophistication of the guerrillas' equipment and therefore of the extent of their control in Colombia.) All the guards in the platoon that had held Russell were delighted with the news.

In less than fifteen minutes they marched him off and, half an hour later, they came to a stream where they blindfolded him and put him in a boat. They travelled for five hours through the night, along secret waterways known only to the guerrillas—swift supply routes to their camp through the impenetrable jungle. They stopped once in a while, leaving the silver moonlight on the middle waters to hide in complete silence under the shadows of the trees overhanging the banks.

Finally after 10 p.m., they pulled in to an island and one guard untied Russell's blindfold and then the rope binding his neck and hands. He ordered the captive to get out on to the bank. Russell climbed on land and looked up. There was his brother, Chaddy.

Chaddy had arrived on the island over two hours before and, having handed over the ransom of 5.5 million pesos (about $55,000), had been talking to the guerrilla commander and the intermediary. Now he introduced Russell to these two men, whose features were unclear in the soft moonlight. The commander said he wanted them to pay another million pesos to the intermediary for his hard work. Chaddy protested but the commander snapped, 'I think your two lives are worth another one million pesos.' Alone on the island, Chaddy agreed to pay when they could.

The commander informed them that they were free to go and that the ransom was a 'bargain price'. He announced, 'You must not talk to the Press, and we will not cause you any more trouble if you pay the additional money within thirty days.' (They paid only 400,000 pesos, as surety while they stayed in the area.)

Russell shook hands with all the guards who had been with him for so long and found he was in some way sad to leave these men who had committed themselves to a life in the jungle. In their turn, the guerrillas had developed a curious friendship with and respect for their captive.

Chad Stendal flew the Cessna 170 back to the airstrip the following morning and, glancing apprehensively down, saw Chaddy waving up at the plane from the side of the strip. Beside him was Russell. He landed and his two sons came running over to the plane. Suddenly, Chad noticed two rough-looking men approaching the plane, so they cut the greetings short and took off. The Cessna landed at Lomalinda airstrip where a crowd of family and friends were waiting. It was a marvellous occasion for celebration. After 142 days as a prisoner, Russell was free, on 3 January, the day when, exactly twenty years before, the Stendals had first arrived in Colombia.

The next communication to me from Colombia was a telegram. It was dated 4 January 1984, and read simply:

Russell freed unharmed. Pat Stendal.

FIVE

The Green Canary

The Brunelli family are well-known in the hotel and restaurant business in Rome. They own and run two establishments in E.U.R. (the El Dorado Hotel and a restaurant), a holiday complex known as the Centro Brunelli at the seaside thirty kilometres from Rome, and another restaurant in the centre of the city. The business is run by three brothers, Marcello, Stefano and Renato, whose father established it. Under their shrewd management it had prospered. The Centro Brunelli was the biggest seaside complex in the region, with a swimming pool, chalets, shops, a night-club, beach and restaurant. The El Dorado was big and successful and in 1981 had just been enlarged substantially; the hotel and its restaurant were extremely popular among the large commercial and wealthy social communities in E.U.R. All these businesses, by their very nature, gave the family a high security profile. The Brunellis were known to the public, locally and nationally. Indeed, their prosperity depended on this, together with their good reputation. The other side of the coin was that such a high profile would, in Rome at this time, inevitably draw the attention of kidnappers, who would not necessarily know, or care, that 1981 was proving a difficult year financially for all the Brunelli businesses after a long period of prosperity and expansion.

On the evening of 10 April 1981, Giuseppe Brunelli, twenty-

year-old son of Renato, was attacked by five men as he rang the
bell on the automatic gate at his family's home in E.U.R. He had
driven up in his Fiat Ritmo and was still inside it when the men
materialized. They had been waiting for some time inside a van
parked nearby, in the quiet street which ran between the walls of
exclusive gardens in the rich residential area. Giuseppe put up a
struggle as the men tried to grab him, one of them smashing the
windscreen of his car with a pistol butt. Alerted by his son's screams
for help, Renato Brunelli grabbed a gun, ran outside and fired several
shots in the air. The gang panicked, and abandoned their kidnap
attempt. They fled to their van and drove off. The police discovered
that the van had been stolen three days previously. Fortunately
Giuseppe's only injury was a damaged hand, where he had been
struck with a pistol.

It was a warning to the family that they were kidnap targets. But, if
they thought they had escaped, their relief was short-lived. Three
months later the kidnappers had a go at them again. Their target was
Giuseppe's thirteen-year-old sister Nicola and this time they were
successful.

Nicola could have passed for a girl several years older: she was tall
for a thirteen-year-old and good looking. She was friendly, talkative
and extremely bright, but her family, perhaps expecting more from
one so seemingly grown up, thought her naive as well.

Oddly, the first kidnap attempt had not persuaded the Brunellis to
employ bodyguards. The only security ploy they introduced was that
Nicola should not go out unaccompanied by another member of the
family. As it turned out, it was a useless rule.

In July, Nicola went with her family to the seaside holiday complex.
At 11.45 p.m. on Friday 17 July, Nicola, her mother and two of her
friends, escorted by an uncle, left the restaurant to walk to their
chalet. They found they had left the key in reception. Nicola
volunteered to run back and fetch it. She went back alone, and, as she
came out again, she was grabbed by a man. Like her brother, she
struggled fiercely but another man appeared and they manhandled
her into a car, which was driven off at high speed by a third man
waiting at the wheel. A pistol shot was fired into the air as they
escaped, presumably to deter rescuers.

Giuseppe Brunelli had been sitting in his car, talking to some
friends, only a few yards away. The abduction happened so swiftly
they were powerless to prevent it, but Giuseppe's presence gave rise

to the thought that he may have been the intended target, for the second time. The kidnappers' car was driven across the road from where it was parked to a position between Giuseppe's car and the front door. The kidnappers may have been surprised by Nicola's sudden and unexpected reappearance and decided that she would do as well as, or better than, her brother. The getaway car was found abandoned the following Monday at Campverde, thirty-five kilometres away. Some children near the Centro Brunelli reported having seen it the day before the kidnap.

Six days after Nicola's abduction there was no word from her kidnappers. At that stage British negotiators were brought in at the suggestion of a friend of the Brunellis who had been helped by them during a previous case. The British firm sent John Seton, an experienced negotiator who had worked with me at the start of the Martinelli case. He met the family and explained his background before they made a decision to employ him. He had worked on eight cases in Rome alone and many others elsewhere. He briefed them on the adviser's role, on why and how to organize a Crisis Management Committee (C.M.C.) and the need to be prepared to 'invest' money when considering a negotiating budget for the final ransom amount. He also outlined briefly the sort of tactics used by kidnappers—to warn them against future shocks—and the counter-tactics open to the family.

The whole of a kidnap is a frightful ordeal for any family. They suffer as much in their way as the victim from the initial shock of the capture. One of the worst times is probably the first days before communication with the gang is established. The longer the silence, the worse the situation appears. Is the victim still alive? In what conditions is he, or she, held? How much money will we be expected to find? What sort of people are the kidnappers? As the silence drags on, the family's morale dips. Kidnappers know this only too well and use silence as a potent bargaining tool to soften up the family so they accede more readily to demands when contact is finally established. Seton's cool advice was valuable in rationalizing these problems.

Seton revealed a tactic with which the Brunellis might be able to force the kidnappers to end their silence sooner than they wanted. He advised them to place an advertisement prominently in a newspaper which would appear to be a coded message. The real kidnappers would, it was hoped, assume that the family were communicating with hoaxers who had already got in touch with them. They might even be preparing to hand over the ransom which the real gang would reason was 'rightfully' theirs. So, it would be in their own interest to contact the family, and start negotiations.

The message that Seton recommended was a cryptic one. It read:

'Spigola [*sea bass*] on the menu today at our previous price.'

The C.M.C. consisted, on Seton's advice, of the three brothers plus Maria (Nicola's mother); Massimo (Stefano's seventeen-year-old son who spoke English and acted as interpreter; his understanding was beyond his years and, coupled with his position inside the family, was a tremendous help to Seton); and Carlo Storchi (Stefano's brother-in-law) who was suggested as negotiator on the telephone. They agreed to Seton's plan and the advertisement was placed in *Il Messaggero* on 29 July. One unforeseen consequence of this was that the Carabinieri arrested for questioning the person who placed the advert. He was released when the family explained what was going on. Seton noted that he should have anticipated this. While they waited for a reaction from the gang, Massimo took Seton around the family's establishments and briefed him on their financial situation so that he could get an idea of the family's profile, and try to see it from the gang's point of view.

On 27 July, a telegram arrived at Centro Brunelli. It was addressed to the Trunelli (*sic*) family and advised of 'important news'. It gave a Rome address and presumably was a hoax. The following day it was forgotten, because, twelve days after the kidnap, the real kidnappers finally made contact.

The means they chose were two letters written by Nicola herself, one to her parents and one to her uncle Stefano. The dates on the letters were 19 and 20 July respectively but they had not been posted until 23 July, from Mondragone, Casserta. (Seton's ploy had not been needed—these messages were on their way before the advertisement appeared in *Il Messaggero*).

Nicola's letter to her parents contained plenty for the family and their new adviser to chew on. It read:

> Dear Parents,
> It is not easy to start a dialogue in circumstances of this sort
> . . . When I think that it is because of me that you are
> suffering, especially Papa who is very ill, I feel I am dying. I

don't think it's a good idea to describe the conditions I am being kept in . . . I just tell you to offer what is necessary for my release, in particular I beg you to get hold of cash quickly before the magistrate freezes your assets, otherwise I believe my captors will keep me for a long, long time. They are not treating me badly but time doesn't pass without me thinking of all the difficulties of this restriction. I have been told that for my freedom we need 7,000,000,000 lire. I hope you can do it quickly although I know of the difficulties.

When you are sure of the payment put an advertisement in *Il Messaggero*, in the *Cronica di Roma* section, with the following message: LOST CANARY IN TORVAJANICA, GREEN EYES, BIG REWARD. The kidnappers will identify themselves through the words THE SEA IS WARM TO BATHE IN. I love you very much and please excuse me. Goodbye,
Nicola Brunelli

The second letter, to Stefano, read:

Dear Uncle Stefano,
I am Nicola. I am writing this letter to reassure you about my health and state of mind.

I have already written a letter to my father about contact with the kidnappers and I believe he has received it. The days are passing slowly for me but in spite of everything they are treating me quite well. I greet you with all my heart and please try to keep my Papa calm.
Nicola Brunelli
(They will identify themselves with the phrase, THE SEA IS WARM TO BATHE IN.)

The next day a third letter arrived, posted from Mondragone on 23 July. Again it was from Nicola, this time to her uncle Marcello, who lived next door to her parents. It read:

Dear Uncle Marcello,
I am Nicola, and at this moment I am in the hands of kidnappers who are not treating me badly. However I must say they are looking after my health. They have allowed me to

write a letter to Mama and Papa in which they indicated their instructions for my release and how contact is to be made. Here every moment of the day passes slowly and with all sincerity I cannot see when I will return home. Please do all you can to keep my parents' morale up and tell them, please, to pardon me for my mistake if they can. Many, many greetings,
Nicola Brunelli
(They will identify themselves with the phrase THE SEA IS WARM TO BATHE IN.)

Armed with this material John Seton could make his first appreciation. He concluded that the gang was experienced and professional and that Nicola was unlikely to be harmed in her cell, wherever it was. But there were significant references to time which meant that the gang was prepared to sit it out, if their demands were not swiftly met. There were many similarities with ransom letters sent by the kidnappers of Giovanni Palombini, an eighty-two-year-old industrialist, kidnapped on 17 April of the same year. There was still no sign of him more than four months later. It did not augur well for Nicola's swift release. The information about the letters in his case came from Aldo Palombini, Giovanni's son, who was conducting the negotiations for his father's release and who briefed the Brunellis about his case. So too did Micol Incardona who had been kidnapped himself earlier in the year (Silvia and Micol Incardona had been seized on 13 March and released on 11 May after a ransom of 500 million lire [£250,000] was paid).

Seton calculated that the Brunellis should be prepared to budget realistically for a final pay-out of between 700 and 800 million lire (£350–400,000) which he reckoned, on the basis of the going rate in Rome and the family's profile, would be acceptable to the gang. A well-balanced first offer could be 275 million (£137,500). The repetition of their contact phrase: 'The sea is warm to bathe in', was a clear indication that the gang was prepared for regular communications which, coupled with their acknowledgement that 7 billion was a difficult sum to collect, implied that the gang was prepared to negotiate. The gang was apparently influenced by the actions of magistrates in other cases by their reference to the possibility of the sequestration of the family's assets (under Articles 219 and 340 of the Italian Penal Code); indeed, the Brunelli assets had been frozen.

Seton noted that there was a letter to each of the brothers; he thought it possible that the gang might try to split the family later during the negotiations.

He reasoned that the family should aim to project an image of helplessness and confusion, thus giving the gang the illusion that they were in total control (a difficult negotiating strategy for any gang to see through, whether they know advisers are helping or not, because it accords perfectly with real reactions of a family whose daughter has been kidnapped). Seton drew up some guidelines as to the negotiating scale. They envisaged a fairly rapid advance to around 650 million, to minimize the time of the whole case, and then a gradual tapering off to the final amount of about 750/770 million, the increases lessening all the time. But he knew these could only be rough guidelines. As the case developed new elements could come into play. He reasoned that there was no need to delay in placing the advertisement the gang had ordered and getting the negotiations started.

The first 'Canary' advert was placed on 30 July and drew an immediate response. A brief telephone call to the manager of the seaside complex, using the code phrase, told him to warn the family to be ready for a call later that day, at 9 p.m. At 9.02 p.m., very punctually, the call came through and was taken by Nicola's father. It lasted for two minutes thirty-eight seconds. The caller, a man, sounded confident and said several times, 'Tell me!' (i.e. 'how much can you offer?'.)

'280 million,' replied Renato Brunelli near the end of the call. The other laughed, but he did not ring off. He instructed Brunelli to place the advertisement again.

'We are not a Sardinian gang, or a bunch of chicken thieves, or rabbits,' he said. 'When you are ready with a conspicuous amount, place the advertisement.'

Seton's analysis was that, as the gang's spokesman had made no attempt to keep to a higher demand, he was admitting that the price was negotiable. There was therefore a good chance of keeping up the momentum with a reasonably good second offer. He looked at the different options—increases of 120 through 170 to 220 million—and settled for the middle one. That would take the total on offer to 450 million (£225,000), a sum that should keep the gang happy with the course of events; and be a tempting amount to prevent the gang doing anything drastic should the negotiation turn nasty. But they should not be too hasty, or they would give the impression that such money was easily available (which, in truth, it was not) and that there was therefore a lot more. The ad should not be placed for another five days.

Seton was also concerned with taking the initiative against the gang with the aim of lowering their expectations of the amount of ransom they would actually get. The gang had to be persuaded that the family had less money than they thought or that they had lost large amounts. It was no good telling them directly: the most effective way would be through the Press, either with planted stories or with trumped-up actions which would be faithfully reported. Using ruses from past experience and his imagination, Seton came up with the following possibilities:

1. The family would attempt to sell one of the four restaurants to raise cash for the ransom—but if the employees demonstrated against the sale they would prevent it. Press reports would show the family doing its best to raise money but running into impossible difficulties of labour disputes.

2. A member of the family could be arrested for illegally importing money and be suitably publicized (understandably the brothers were not too keen on this idea). Alternatively, a family member could be arrested leaving a bank or a friend's house with a large quantity of money. This could be staged with the Carabinieri's co-operation and would be hailed in the Press as a new drive by the judiciary to prevent ransom payments. It would mean the family could claim that the confiscated money was no longer available to make up the ransom total, and persuade the gang to settle for what they could get. (Seton had successfully used this ruse before; it is strange that the very antagonism between families and the authorities, caused by the judiciary's hard line, could be turned to the families' advantage; but only at the families' initiative.)

3. A 'robbery' involving a large sum of money could be reported from one of the brothers' houses or the hotel.

There was potential too for less dramatic themes to be exploited in the Press. These included the recession in the restaurant business over the past two years and poor investments recently which had left the family over-extended financially.

On 5 August, day twenty of the case, the 'Canary' ad was placed again in *Il Messaggero*. As with the first time, it elicited a response the same evening, starting with a call to the house of a friend, Juan Domenico Audano, telling the family to assemble there at the same time as before, 9 p.m. (the switch of venue being made presumably to avoid the attentions of a police phone tap). It came through at 9.13 p.m. and was taken by Marcello. After the code phrase, it turned out to be a long call. In reply to a query from Marcello, the kidnapper said his name was Alphonso. Marcello played his role well, persistently inquiring about Nicola's well-being and asking the kidnapper to tell her not to blame herself for her capture. Alphonso referred several times to the family's ample income from interests outside restaurants, and at one stage went into a lengthy diatribe against the police in which he demonstrated his utter contempt for them: 'That lot only have dealings with robbers, idiots and chicken thieves,' he shouted. 'Here, you are dealing with something very different.'

Marcello spun out the conversation before revealing the latest offer, taking the total up to 450 million lire (£225,000).

'You are a long way away,' Alphonso replied eventually, and told Marcello to get a bank loan, or the kidnap would go on for a very long time. They should place the usual ad when they had a better offer.

John Seton was not disheartened. The reference to a bank loan indicated that the gang realized there were limits to what the Brunellis could raise in cash by themselves. He reckoned the gang was happy with the way things were going or they would not have been in touch so soon after the second ad appeared. He also felt the gang's spokesman's tone would normally have been more aggressive at this early stage. Alphonso had implied a substantial reduction and might have excused this to himself by thinking that Marcello's pleading, distraught, tone indicated that the gang was in full control. In fact, Marcello was sticking closely to the script drawn up by Seton at the last meeting of the C.M.C.

Seton felt the momentum had to be continued with another increased offer, this time of 120 million making a total of 570 million (£225,000 plus £60,000, totalling £285,000). It would keep the gang's expectations in check while nearing the area of what he hoped would be the final settlement. Again the placing of the 'Canary' ad should be delayed for a few days to avoid the impression of the family being able to collect extra money easily.

On the offensive front, the restaurant workers went on strike on day twenty-six, in a move agreed by them to dupe the kidnappers. Before the ad appeared the family also managed to place a friendly article in *Il Messaggero*, stressing their anguish at Nicola's disappearance. The ad appeared in the same newspaper three days later, on day twenty-five, and again drew an immediate response. A phone call the same day to the house of Domenico Audano told the family to be there the next day.

Marcello took that call, again from Alphonso. Keeping to his script, Marcello demanded proof that Nicola was still alive: he asked Alphonso to find out what her father gave her for her last birthday. Alphonso raised no objection. Marcello then pressed for a photograph or a tape. 'Later, later,' came the reply. Marcello went on to raise the offer to 560 million (10 less than Seton had suggested at the C.M.C. meeting, and approximately £280,000), but he said he had felt able to offer this sum only with the greatest difficulty. It was not enough, said Alphonso. Marcello stressed the problems the family was encountering in raising the money. They had already been to the banks for loans and were not paying their suppliers. Alphonso claimed to know plenty about the family's finances (which Seton doubted), but at the end of the conversation (again prolonged) he told Marcello to place the ad when they had raised 1 billion lire (£500,000). It was a significant decrease from the kidnappers' initial demand of 7 billion lire.

The indications were that the gang was reasonably satisfied with the progress of the negotiations. They were not piling on the threats, they appeared to be ready to settle for less than 1 billion and to want to keep up the momentum of the talks. But Seton was suspicious. Was it all going too well? The family had, on his advice, demanded proof. He had to warn them that the gang might turn aggressive when providing it, calculating that the impact would be greater on a family whose hopes had been raised by the comparatively smooth progress of the negotiations so far. But was there a deeper motive behind the gang's actions? He re-examined the gang's tactics, which showed a casual disregard for the Polizia and the Carabinieri: their main calls had lasted four minutes thirty seconds, and six minutes, very lengthy by kidnap standards. The gang had not been aggressive: they had reduced their initial demand dramatically, telephoned as soon as the ad appeared and seemed genuinely concerned that the family got word about the victim.

It is worth quoting Seton's conclusion at this stage of the negotiations in full:

> It is not impossible that the gang is experienced and extremely professional and they are deliberately giving the family the impression that they want to reach a quick and painless settlement in order to take a first payment and then demand a second.

Uppermost in his thoughts was the knowledge that in the Palombini case a second demand had been made after a first payment, of 350 million lire, on day seventy of the case, two months previously in June. There had been a three-week silence after the payment which was followed by the second demand, for another 650 million. That family's negotiating method had been somewhat novel: they offered a figure, and then reduced it as time went on. Seton's view was that this must have infuriated the gang whose expectations would naturally settle on the higher amount, and accept nothing less. The Brunelli case had been better handled, but there was no escaping from the probability that the two kidnaps had been carried out by the same gang. If they could demand a second payment once, they could try it again.

Seton recommended that the gang be allowed a week to furnish proof of Nicola's well-being. The family should react with a suitable display of grief and anguish (genuine enough) and offer an increase over 560 million of only 70 to make a total of 630 million (£280,000 plus £35,000, totalling £315,000); but it should not be made too quickly. He did not want the family to see a photograph or hear a tape by way of proof: these would contain no extra message but could upset them so much that they might be put off the course of their negotiating strategy.

The Brunellis decided on the rise of 75 million to 635 million and the 'Canary' ad went in again on 15 August, day thirty of the case. This time there was no response so they put the ad in again two days later. Again there was no response.

Two members of the Palombini family, the victim's son Aldo and his daughter, then met the Brunelli C.M.C. and brought along tapes of the latest telephone calls from their gang. All agreed it was the same voice as the Brunellis' caller, the man who called himself Alphonso, but John Seton reassured the Brunellis that he did not think Nicola was in the same danger as Giovanni Palombini, who was elderly and would suffer more the physical discomfort of captivity. Besides, he believed the other case had been mishandled.

The Brunellis worried as time passed and the 'Canary' ad was published twice more before the gang made contact again in the usual way: a warning call in the morning and a fuller one in the evening with the C.M.C. assembled to listen. It was Alphonso. The only reason he gave for not replying to the ad when it first appeared was 'technical reasons'. But he provided the correct proof answer to Marcello's question: Nicola had received 30,000 lire (£15) on her birthday. The conversation moved on swiftly to somewhat higher figures. Marcello pleaded that 1 billion was as impossible as 7 billion, and then, under the instructions of his script, he carried out a long stalling manoeuvre and avoided talking about exact figures at all. He said it was impossible to raise further loans from the banks but indicated that some friends might be able to come up with something, and all without specific promises. Marcello pressed the kidnapper to talk again on Saturday evening (this was Wednesday) and the matter was left there.

Marcello had not mentioned the next increase. That could wait until Saturday. The family agreed to Seton's first suggestion of a 70 million rise, to make a total offer of 630 million. The important thing was that they should get proof that Nicola was alive; at least until recently. Her parents were naturally desperate and suffering badly under the intense psychological strain, which especially affects parents of a captive daughter. Nicola was young, too young, but her grown-up appearance might lead to dangers that were all too easy to imagine. Maria somehow managed to keep her feelings under control, at least as far as Seton could tell, but Renato wore his heart on his sleeve and was more demonstrative with his grief. The others in the family were not so affected and were able to maintain a form of objectivity; they were not so close to the problem as the parents. But the continuing events absorbed all their thoughts and every available moment was spent discussing the case. In the restaurants and hotel the family went about their normal work—they could not discuss the matter with strangers—but as soon as they sat down together their conversation was once more dominated by the traumatic affair. What especially worried the brothers was the massive loss of capital which all three of them were facing and which none of their businesses could stand at that time.

Seton's analysis was that the gang were fighting for further offers. This was not the hallmark of a gang going for a second ransom. The silence of the previous few days had been a deliberate ploy to pressurize the family but the kidnappers appeared to recognize that the Brunellis depended on loans and credit to raise the money and were indicating that they wanted to get on with the negotiation.

Before the Saturday contact, two of the Brunellis visited the family of Cesare Menasci, who had been released a few days before after an eighty-six-day kidnap in Rome on payment of 800 million lire (£400,000). Seton thought it had little relevance to the Brunelli case. He was certain that it was a different gang (and, incidentally, thought the Menascis had paid 100 million more than they need have done).

On Saturday, 22 August and case-day thirty-seven, Alphonso rang as agreed; but his tone was sharp and he kept the call brief. Marcello again demanded proof that Nicola was all right by asking the kidnapper for the name of the family's ginger cat. Alphonso assured him she was well.

'She's more of an adult than you think,' he said, casually.

After some prevarication Marcello said that with the help of some friends he had managed to scrape together 630 million (£230,000). Alphonso's response was simple.

'We'll speak again in a month,' he said, and, repeating the chilling threat of silence, he cut short the call.

The suggestive comment about Nicola 'being older than you think' upset her father. He probably read too much into the remark—kidnappers are not noted for the subtlety of their phraseology and threats, and an attempt to play the line of sexual harassment would have been couched in blunter terms. However, it was enough to upset his already shaken nerves. (Rape is probably the least of a female victim's worries if statistics from Sardinia are any guide: in ninety-two cases, only one was raped. But ill treatment in some degree is general.)

More to the point, the call contained the first threat of a long period of silence. Seton noted that this was a customary ploy when gangs thought money was running out. It pressured families to produce that little extra. He thought that the threat could be countered by the family convincing the gang that they could get the same result in seven to ten days. He felt the family strategy should be adhered to: the projection of deep anguish and apparent willingness to do anything because a child was involved. They should stick to their idea of getting the ransom up to seventy-five per cent of their target in the first five weeks and then take about a month to get to the final amount. They were on course for that. If the gang stayed silent, the family should run the ad continuously. If that did not produce results, they should consider amending the ad to indicate that they had a new offer. But this new offer should not be made for at least another ten days, and should be in the region of 60–80 million.

An article linking the Brunelli and Palombini kidnaps had recently appeared. This could influence the gang's thinking: perhaps they would suspect that the Brunellis would be reluctant to pay up because of the double ransom that had complicated, and appeared to have prevented, Palombini's release.

Captain Ragusa, head of the Rome Carabinieri anti-kidnap squad, had come to the C.M.C. meeting after the last call. He believed there would be a fifteen-day silence but that negotiations were going well.

In fact the gang's threat of silence was an empty one. They were back in touch only three days later, after the 'Canary' advertisement had run twice. It was an inconclusive call: Marcello repeated that the family had no chance of finding 1 billion lire (£500,000), to which Alphonso replied with veiled threats, 'We know how to play tough . . . you will get reprisals later.' Marcello again emphasized the difficulties of any more loans and they agreed to talk again on Monday.

When the C.M.C. assembled the following day, 26 August, there were two main topics for discussion: how much to offer next time (they settled on a 70 million increase) and the possibility of a double payment being demanded. Seton's view was that the family had made no attempt to withhold money, had reached 630 million in a relatively short period (thirty-seven days) and that double payments only seemed to happen when the first offer was too small.

In the light of what was to happen, the question has to be asked: was Seton's strategy mistaken? Although he did not dismiss a double payment entirely, he felt he had done enough to prevent it happening in this case. With hindsight it could well be that 630 million was reached safely—relative to increasing the danger to the victim, for example by being stingy—but too quickly. And thereby it fuelled the gang's hopes that there was a lot more to be tapped from this particular source.

A couple of hours afterwards the C.M.C. was forced to meet again by a new development: the arrival of the fourth letter in Nicola's hand, accompanied by a photograph of her. She appeared to be well. She was sitting on a clean-looking mattress, to which she was chained. The chain looked light; Seton thought it might have been put on her just for the picture. Her blouse was half undone and her hair a little dishevelled but her overall appearance was encouraging.

In her letter the gang were again speaking through Nicola. It was dated that day, Wednesday 26 August. The kidnap was now forty days old, she wrote. (It was actually forty-one.) The letter went on with the following main points: the sum demanded was 'not astronomical', it was surely not too difficult to amass; Nicola couldn't understand why agreement was a problem; the gang did not want to continue negotiation with Marcello, but with her parents; she might even be sold to another gang; she felt ill, could not wash or 'do her personal things' and felt like killing herself; then, contradicting that, she continued with a promise to repay the ransom to her parents. But there was an optimistic note: a postscript told her parents to insert another advertisement in *Il Messaggero* when they were ready.

Seton's analysis was that the gang probably expected between 750 and 800 million and the next increase would be still less than the last one. 'The chances of a double payment have reduced although they cannot be dismissed,' he noted. The next offer should be 70 million but it should not be offered for at least a week. A new advertisement should be used, based on the old one, but adding a phrase like, 'it is hoped to increase the reward as soon as possible'. The 'Canary' ads had been spotted by the Press and the tabloids prominently featured stories on Nicola's abduction. More similarities in the communications with Palombini's gang had also been noticed and given further publicity. Nicola was known from now on as the 'Green Canary' when the Press wrote about the case.

At this stage the authorities started to make their presence felt for the first time since the early days of the kidnap. Captain Ragusa told Renato that in future he would block the line after each call from the gang in an attempt to trace Alphonso.

Seton thought this new interest might be because of Ragusa's success with the Molinari case. In that case the family had been talking to the kidnapper on the telephone when Ragusa had indicated that if they could keep him chatting, he would be able to trace the call. It was something of a challenge to produce suddenly a twenty-minute script, but the family's negotiator did his best to hold the kidnapper's attention. Then the kidnapper rang off, saying he would call back; presumably he had run out of coins because he did not ring again for several minutes. During the second call, as the Molinaris crowded around their phone, they heard strangled cries, silence and then the cool tones of Captain Ragusa inquiring whether all was well; he had raced to the phone box and arrested the kidnapper in the act. The strange comedy of this case continued when Captain Ragusa took the arrested man to a forest in the south of Italy where the kidnapper said others were holding Molinari. Leaving the back-up force some way behind, Ragusa and his prisoner advanced through some woods and suddenly came upon the gang, who jumped up and vanished deeper into the wood. Then, Ragusa, with his prisoner, began a conversation with his unseen opponents, who were hidden away in the trees, by banging rocks together and whistling. The kidnappers finally agreed to release Molinari who scuttled instantly to cover, unsure what was going on but determined not to be caught again. For some hours, he crept about the forest in hiding, watching a number of rough-looking armed men stalking about and unaware that many of these were Carabinieri in plain clothes chasing the kidnappers. Eventually, Ragusa gathered Molinari and all his men together and returned to Rome.

The Brunellis were alarmed that the Carabinieri thought they could repeat this coup, and decided to offer the gang a new number next time they called. Despite their pleas for him to lay off controlling the telephones, Ragusa went ahead. There was also a change in the attitude of the investigating magistrate, Judge Maria Cordova. Through an intermediary, a high-ranking policeman who was a family friend and had offered to help, she had at first assured the Brunellis that she would not interfere with their negotiating arrangements. But she changed her tune, accusing the family, via another intermediary, this time a lawyer, of condoning kidnapping by trying to pay a ransom. She was to take a still tougher line in the days ahead.

Meanwhile the family were trying to get the gang to resume contact, using the new advertisement. The first read: 'Lost Canary: we are making all efforts to increase the reward as soon as possible.' The second, two days later, emphasized the problems, somewhat bluntly; but one rule of negotiating is never to make your messages so subtle that the other side cannot understand them: 'Lost Canary: be assured despite the difficulties, we are continuing to try to obtain an increase in the reward.'

Two days later, came a further call from Alphonso, to a new number arranged with the family, at the house of Alessandro Di Terracciano, manager of the Centro Brunelli complex, in an effort to avoid police wire-tapping.

The call was taken by Renato, who was keen to take over from Marcello as demanded by the kidnappers; and he turned out to be brilliant, in Seton's opinion. It helped that he was not acting: the grief that he displayed was genuine. As the weeks had passed he had become more and more emotional about the loss of his daughter and his performance on the telephone was all the more effective for being genuine. He had asked Seton to prepare, not a complicated script, but a few headings and keywords. This was done and the script consisted of the headings:

1. **Anguish about Nicola:**
   What have you done to her?
   Chained like an animal
   She is terrified
   Terrible conditions
2. **Offer:**
   We have done our best
   If we fail not lack effort
   710 million
   No more

These were refined even further to read:

1. **Nicola—Anguished:**
   Molested
   Chained
   Terrified
   Conditions
2. **Offer:**
   Tried
   Failure
   710
   Finished

They worked brilliantly, Renato insisting on knowing how his daughter was and pleading, or rather demanding, that Alphonso treat her well. He even drew the revelation that she was provided with a radio and a television. Finally, he got around to the offer of 710 million, an increase of 80 million, (now approximately £355,000) to which Alphonso reacted brusquely with a renewed demand that Renato go back to the banks, and an oath. Then he hung up.

Seton's analysis was that the negotiations looked as if they were in their final sequence and there was a strong hope of concluding a deal in two to three weeks. The chances of a double payment were receding all the time. He thought the gang might resort to silence, which they had suggested though not used, but, whatever the threats, it was clear that they expected a good deal less than 1 billion. The next offer had to indicate there was very little left: 20 million to be revealed in about a week's time, for a total of 730 (£365,000).

Captain Ragusa telephoned soon after the call, demonstrating that the Carabinieri had been listening in. His verdict was that there was now no chance of a double payment being demanded.

The next day, 2 September and case-day forty-eight, Nicola's parents visited the Judge who made it plain that she expected total co-operation from them, particularly at the drop which the authorities knew was close. Renato returned depressed and thought the case could drag on for a further three months. He had already been in a state of anxiety before the kidnap because of the condition of the business and was being treated for it by his doctor, who was now insisting that he should not be the telephone negotiator: the strain was too great. But Renato still asked Seton to prepare him a draft script for next time. It was on the same lines as before: how was Nicola? It had a proof question thrown in, plus an attitude of total despair though they had managed to rustle up a further 20 million (another £10,000). In reality, credit was now exhausted and Renato was deeply worried about a double payment.

The usual pattern of advertisements and short calls from the gang ended with a call from Alphonso a week after his last substantive communication. Aware that this man was the only link with his lost daughter, Renato broke down several times during the call, while raising the offer to 740 million. To calm the distraught father (kidnappers are always ready to say anything to allay the fears of their victims when it suits them), Alphonso casually assured him Nicola was 'excellent'.

'Help me . . . help me,' Renato shouted tragically, 'Help me . . . help me,' sobbing uncontrollably.

'Shit yourself. Go shit yourself,' Alphonso replied brutally, before hanging up. Clearly he thought Renato had been over-doing the 'act'.

That was at 1 p.m. At 8.45 p.m., Mrs Di Terracciano received a call at home. After giving the code-phrase Alphonso said he had a message. 'We have had a meeting of our organization,' he said. 'Instead of 1 miliardo, we want 870 . . . until Friday . . . if they don't pay we sell the girl to others . . . the ultimatum finishes on Friday evening.'

Seton concluded that the threat to sell Nicola was not consistent with a double payment plan. The gang's reduction to 870 million (£435,000) indicated that they would probably settle for 800 and if the family stuck to 760 million (£380,000), as he thought they should, the gang would only agree after more pressure tactics, such as another threat to sell Nicola.

All factors considered, it was time to prepare the drop. Seton explained the ground rules of preparation. The team should be on one hour's notice to go into action after a thorough briefing from Seton, depending on what instructions the gang gave. Dr Mauro Colombo, the family doctor and long-time friend, volunteered to be a member of the team; the other would be Mario Kinski, the tall and angular head waiter of the family restaurant in the El Dorado Hotel.

The tensions were testing the whole family severely, not least because the three families had had to find an enormous amount of capital together, for one of their children, and family disagreements, which had been insignificant in happier times, had been exaggerated quite beyond their true importance. The brothers did not fall out, for their sense of family duty held them together, but they were shaken. Renato, always the most emotional of the three, felt the situation slip temporarily out of his control. He decided his health did not permit him to play the role of telephone spokesman again and handed the job over to his wife Maria.

But, as the preparations got under way for the drop, Judge Cordova wrote to all the banks asking them to inform her at once when the Brunelli ransom money was withdrawn. This hard-line attitude scarcely encouraged the family to support her, or the authorities, as their main concern was the safe release of Nicola, not the arrest of criminals or even the recovery of the money. The family was deeply worried because they did not trust the Carabinieri to carry out surveillance operations successfully (without being spotted by the gang during the drop). And then one might imagine that the kidnappers would get very mad indeed. The link between this case and that of Valerio Ciocchetti, who had been murdered after a payment of 450 million, was only too frightening. What particularly upset the C.M.C. was that the authorities did not discuss these moves with the family who, after all, stood to lose most. Indeed the posture of the authorities is all the harder to understand in the light of a report made out by the Rome Carabinieri, dated December 1980 and classified 'secret', in which it is admitted that 'a decision to block the goods of members of the family . . . represents an additional difficulty to the negotiations between the family and the kidnappers.' Why make things harder for the family without discussing matters with them first?

Some 450 million of the ransom money had been photographed already and the rest was due to be recorded shortly; this was current practice—and still is—in Rome. It is done in the hope that finding the notes later might lead to the arrest of the kidnappers. Transport arrangements were made, setting aside cars and ensuring they were fully fuelled and ready. Finally, three new telephones were identified and people briefed to man them.

The gang did apply a little pressure as Seton had forecast. Two days after the last contact, a strange call was taken by Massimo's mother. All she could hear was what sounded like a girl sobbing and a chain rattling. She called the Carabinieri to see if they had been monitoring the line, but they had not. Seton decided it was certainly the gang but the news was kept from Renato and Maria in order not to upset them further. However rational an explanation there may be, such persistent psychological brutality can be very disturbing and exhausting. Having an outside adviser to analyse the horrors does help, but his advice cannot entirely salve a frenzied imagination.

The next day was Maria's début as telephone negotiator and she performed well, adhering to the script Seton had prepared for her. As advised, she begged Alphonso not to sell her daughter and projected a convincing picture of anguish (perfectly in accordance with her true feelings) pleading repeatedly, 'Give me back my daughter . . . I want only my daughter.'

At the end of the call, she let slip the new increase of, 'perhaps 10 or 15 million on Sunday evening.'

'You must get more than 800,' was the brief response.

   This last reduction to 'more than 800' was further evidence in
Seton's view that the case was near its conclusion and that the final sum
would be 760 million. Among the encouraging signs was the fact that
the gang had called exactly when they said they would and had made no
threats. Also, they had made this reduction in less than forty-eight
hours since the previous one.

   Seton's chief concern now was to convince the gang that 760 million
was the final offer. The next script for Maria emphasized this. Indeed,
they decided to make it 755 million on offer and to continue to project
an image of complete despair. When Alphonso called back again two
days later, Maria stuck steadily to her lines. But so did the kidnapper,
never deviating from his demand for 800 million. His tone was calm
and relaxed and he uttered no threats, merely demanding that the
family try the banks again for more loans. Seton took some comfort
from this calm attitude.

   It was now a critical moment. Would the gang stick to 800 million, or
would they come down some more? Seton assessed the betting as
evens. The family had for the first time indicated that there was actually
no more available, and he thought the gang should be left to chew on
that and decide if they would stand firm as well. Seton thought that if
Alphonso had really believed he could get 800, he would have
employed more aggressive tactics with Maria on the last call.

   While speculation and discussions continued in all three Brunelli
households, Judge Cordova had been busy again. She instigated the
rigorous application of a new law which laid down that anyone
depositing or withdrawing 50,000 or 100,000 lire notes (£25 or £50)
had to provide identification and a legitimate address. This measure
was designed to catch kidnappers laundering their ransom monies
through the banks. A similar law tried the previous year had proved
unworkable and had been hastily shelved. Judge Cordova called in
Nicola's parents, who were very much on edge with the agreement
imminent, and interrogated them about the state of the negotiation.
She wanted to know who was going to carry out the drop, where the
money was and numerous other details. The Brunellis answered
truthfully and asked for the co-operation of the authorities to save their
daughter: the fact was they did not care about the money or catching
the gang.

   So, to the call which the family hoped would clinch everything and
ensure Nicola's return. Nicola had been kidnapped sixty-three days
before, in mid-summer and now it was 17 September and the

Mediterranean summer heat was fading into autumn. At last it seemed there might be a deal:

'I know your organization wants 800 million if I'm to get my daughter back,' said Maria. There was a pause.

'Tell me, how much?'

'800 million. Is that right? . . . Now I'm finding . . . Look, because this amount is a lot, I'm trying to reach that amount.'

'All right. Listen,' replied Alphonso, and continued as though with great reluctance. 'Anyway . . . we want . . . eh . . . we can, we can have a conclusion.' It looked like a deal—at last.

'I'll have it in a few days,' said Maria.

The next day, 18 September, the agreement was confirmed with a call to a new telephone number, that of Giorgio, Marcello's son-in-law.

Seton could see problems for himself with the active Judge Cordova looming in the background. The Italian authorities do not approve of consultants working as kidnap negotiators as they view the work as immoral. While Seton or I worked quietly, advised the family to keep the police in the picture, and made no fuss, the Italian authorities, who must have known about us, were prepared to let us be, tacitly condoning the situation they attacked so strongly in public. However, if a family refused to co-operate with the police, they might in turn have acted against us or been compelled to do so by the investigating Judge. (We always took care that the family co-operated with the police as, apart from our own safety, we believed that co-operation on all fronts was the only real path to controlling kidnapping.) In this case, Seton had tremendous sympathy with the family's predicament, but he had to advise the Brunellis that, if they went ahead with the payment without telling the authorities of the new telephone number—which was unknown to the Carabinieri—he would have to withdraw from the case altogether. The Brunellis accepted his advice and asked him to stay on at their hotel for further advice.

The drop was carried out on 20 September, with instructions communicated via a message left in the Restaurant Commodore nearby, and calls to the Hotel Congresso. The drop team were to take the road to Aquila (in the hills east of Rome) and then double back just before the toll booth and head back into Rome. A further message would be found inside a cigarette packet in a wastepaper bin at a petrol station five hundred metres down the road (a similar place, behind a petrol pump, was used by the gang during the payment of the Martinelli ransom in Milan).

The period between passing the ransom money over to the gang and getting the victim back is naturally an agonizing one. In this case the Brunellis did not have long to wait for further news from the gang, but it was not the news they wanted to hear.

The next evening, a telephone caller to the house of Marcello's daughter said he was Alphonso. The message was not recorded but its gist was unmistakable. Alphonso said the ransom was dirty money, and because of that he wanted another 800 million.

* * * *

As the negotiations had proceeded Seton had become convinced that a double payment was less and less likely. Why was he wrong? Did this gang always intend to demand a double, as they had with the Palombini family, or was the strategy at fault? His strategy had been to get the offers reasonably quickly past about seventy-five per cent of the final amount, and then take a month or so to rub in the fact that the last twenty-five per cent was all there would be. So, he had got the family to 560 million in twenty-seven days and 630 million (seventy-eight per cent of 800) in thirty-seven days.

A comparison with other recent kidnaps showed that in many cases it had taken much longer to reach a figure of around 630 million. Seen in the context of Rome's 'going-rate' of 750 million at that time the figures were as follows:

Brunelli	630 (78% of total)	in 37 days, & last 170 in 27 to 800
Martinelli	630 (88% ")	in 51 days, & last 86 in 27 to 716
Antolini	640 (90% ")	in 69 days, & last 64 in 13 to 704
Oetiker	650 (87% ")	in 83 days, & last 100 in 43 to 750
Menasci	560 (70% ")	in 57 days, & last 240 in 29 to 800

Did the Brunellis get to 630 too quickly and thus lead the kidnappers to believe that there must be more money since the first lot had been so easily produced? Or were the gang always going to demand a second ransom? The Palobini family were buckling down to negotiating a third ransom demand which this gang (almost certainly the same group) had communicated after taking the second amount of money; it was reported that this unfortunate family had now paid 700 million.

Perhaps the double demand was becoming the norm. It had been demanded in the kidnaps of Renato Armellini (262 days in 1980 and 3,350 million [£1.675 million] paid), Barbara Piatelli (342 days in 1980 and 618 million [£309,000] paid), Valerio Ciocchetti (found dead, in February 1981, after 86 days and 800 million [£400,000] paid) and Ercole Bianchi (495 days in 1979 and an undisclosed amount paid). It prolonged the agony, increased the danger and could result in the death of the victim.

Now the Brunellis were faced with their second demand, did it mean they were back to square one? It must have felt like that. Seton had the task of reconstructing a strategy for the new negotiation which the Brunellis reluctantly accepted as inevitable. Renato and Maria were especially shattered and both they, and all the others, wanted to be sure next time. They wanted a guarantee for her return, or they would pay nothing.

If kidnap negotiations are like playing poker for high stakes, then the gang now held all the cards; they had the victim and now they had the family's money. The authorities were no nearer finding the kidnappers, except to say that they were pursuing the investigation. The gang were in no hurry and had probably killed once already that year (Valerio Ciocchetti).

Seton felt the gang could perhaps be made to feel vulnerable if they could be persuaded that they were endangering the whole of the lucrative Rome kidnap business by demanding double payments, the argument being that if ransom payments failed to produce the return of the victim, families would just stop paying ransoms. He thought that the negotiator, Alphonso, was certainly brutally amoral but also sounded an intelligent type who could see the risks. He wondered if the gang were part of a larger organization which might pressure them to settle for what they had got. If the gang could be convinced that the family did not now believe they would ever get Nicola back, it would undermine their position. The family's most powerful ally from now on would be the Press. He set about devising stories that could be run. The family had a number of friends in the Press and their help to place favourable articles could be enlisted.

He believed there was a real possibility of an agreement at between 100 and 130 million. The family would have to allow two months for the negotiations and insist on guarantees throughout. The alternative was to take a hard line, threatening to publish all the letters and tapes they had received to publicize Alphonso's voice, and do everything they could to show that they intended to prevent other families making the mistake of paying ransoms without guarantees of the victim's release. This would be coupled with extensive publicity about the Palombini case in which the same points would be made. If the gang called, they would be told the family had given up hope of ever getting Nicola back and were resigned to life without her. However, if the gang were prepared to be logical the family might just be able to raise some money from friends.

Whichever strategy was implemented, a major Press campaign should be mounted, linking the Brunelli and Palombini cases and advising other families on how to prevent such double payments.

Other tactics included an open letter from the Brunellis stating their belief that they would not see Nicola again, and the organization of a reward for information about kidnappers to which other victims, families and friends and the general public could contribute. Seton even mooted the fake suicide of Nicola's father with maximum publicity of the 'funeral'. This idea was dropped as it sounded a little close to the bone: Massimo, who was doing an admirable job of translation for Seton during the family meetings said his uncle Renato was in a highly nervous condition. Renato's wife, Maria, kept her feelings remarkably private though it was clear she was suffering too. The second demand had put tremendous extra pressure on the three brothers since, having pooled their resources for the first—and as they thought the only—ransom, they were faced with deciding what to do about the second. They had staked everything on the first ransom, but the gang was forcing them to find more and really face that thorniest of questions: how much value to put on the victim?

The Press campaign went ahead with articles inspired by Seton appearing in various newspapers over the next month. The most striking was an alleged interview with an 'Italian-American criminologist of Milanese family,' who had studied kidnaps for a decade. It appeared in *Paese Sera* on 30 September and was a learned analysis of the current kidnap scene with particular emphasis on the double payment syndrome. It was illustrated with photographs of Giovanni Palombini and Nicola Brunelli and a reproduction of a page of the academic's notes with a diagram linking various current and recent kidnaps. The public were not to know that the handwriting was Seton's. The academic did not exist: he was a creation of Seton's in order to get his own views over. Seton had been concerned that he should get final approval of the articles lest journalists put their own 'gloss' on them, and by doing so put across the wrong message. Other articles highlighted the reward being put up by previous victims and an appeal to release Nicola, from her classmates. Other articles were planted in *Il Messaggero*, *Il Tempo* and even the Communist *L'Unita*. The themes included further appeals by Nicola's classmates and an audience granted them by President Pertini in which he expressed his solidarity with them; an interview with her headmaster; and the foundation of OSA, an organization of former kidnap victims who said they had 12 billion (£6 million) at their disposal for rewards leading to the arrest of kidnappers and the recovery of their current victims. *L'Unita* did Seton proud, devoting a whole page to this last theme and a variety of other related articles. Indeed OSA caught the imagination of several newspapers and was given generous coverage.

The kidnappers on the other hand had resorted to a different tactic: a series of eight silent telephone calls, four to the home of Marcello's son-in-law, and four to the home of Alessandro Di Terracciano, the holiday complex manager, over a period of two weeks. When the recipient picked up the phone, there was no answer but there was clearly someone at the other end. Eight was more than a coincidence, whatever the vagaries of the Italian telephone system. Seton believed there were two reasons: the gang was applying pressure, and also reassuring the Brunellis that they were still out there somewhere. Interestingly, when the family started placing the 'Canary' ad in *Il Messaggero* again, each appearance was followed by a silent call; and at the usual time for the gang to ring, about 9 p.m.

After the Press campaign, Seton analysed what had been achieved. The main aim had been to identify publicly the gang that had kidnapped Nicola with the one that had taken Giovanni Palombini and Valerio Ciocchetti. That was done. A second aim had been to put across the notion that the family had to demand guarantees from now on and that they must get Nicola back after the next payment (the idea of refusing to make a second payment had understandably been rejected by Renato and Maria). The negotiations from now on would have two aims: firstly, to settle on a financial figure and, secondly, to secure a guarantee (to underline the nature of quid pro quo which Alphonso had taken little notice of).

How to go about this? The family could settle the money and then work out the guarantee, or vice versa. Eventually Seton decided on a combination of both strategies: make an offer of 110/120 million, then refer to the possibility of more to be obtained from friends but only if linked with guarantees.

What should the second total budget be? The three families had done some hard talking about this and Seton's first thoughts were to keep the amount low, at 150 million. But, after further consideration, he advised 350 million, because what was known of the character of the gang was not encouraging. He divided this into a 120 million first offer, and the rest to come 'from friends' but not at first revealed. However, after all this, the Brunellis needed more proof that Nicola was all right.

The Palombinis were co-operating closely with the Brunellis and revealed that analysis of taped calls in both cases confirmed that the caller was the same man. Details of the second drop made by the Palombinis were very similar to the Brunelli payment. The drop run was started from a hotel near E.U.R. around 9 p.m. from which the team were directed to a second message in an old Marlboro packet hidden beneath a stone, which in turn led to more orders found under a bridge. The release of Signor Palombini was twice promised but (of course) never materialized.

The Brunellis decided to have the kidnappers' voices analysed in case they turned up something useful. They approached Professor Trumper, a Welshman working at the University of Padua's Institute of Linguistics. It was a discouraging response: Professor Trumper was undoubtedly thorough but he needed two months for the job and it would cost 8–10 million (£4–5,000). Seton doubted its worth, so Massimo contacted another expert, Professor Gentile from Naples. He offered to come back with a report in four or five days and for no charge. (Why didn't the Italian police provide this service for the family? The American F.B.I. and German experts in the Bundeskriminalamt are researching voice characteristics to find a trademark for the voice as sure as the fingerprint is for someone's physical presence, but the research is very costly and has not been altogether successful.)

Fifteen days after they had demanded more money the gang broke their silence with two brief calls, which Maria took. A coded phrase similar to the old one was used: 'The sea is very calm'. The message contained the following two elements: Nicola's mother was not to put the ad in *Il Messaggero*; and Alphonso was no longer involved—the family would now deal with 'Giacomino', who said he would call later that evening—but never did.

The Brunellis could not wait. They ignored Giacomino's advice and put a series of increasingly harrowing ads in *Il Messaggero*, all headed with the familiar: 'Lost Canary, in Torvajanica, Green Eyes,

Big Reward', followed by, successively, the pleas: 'Anguished, we await news,' and 'We request news, we don't understand,' and 'We request news, confused'. (Never had there been so much fuss about a lost cage-bird.) The last most despairing appeal drew a response the same evening, a brief call to Renato. Three times the caller wanted to know if it was Renato Brunelli speaking.

'Listen a moment,' he went on when he was satisfied. 'We are those who have Nicola . . . In two or three days you are going to receive a message from Nicola. Everything you have to do is inside.' He refused to give the code-word, though Renato demanded it several times, and rang off saying, 'You will receive Nicola's thing tomorrow or the day after. Understand?'

It was 10 October, case-day eighty-six, and the family seemed no nearer to a solution. Nicola had disappeared in mid-July, and now the seasons were well advanced into autumn—indeed few of the Brunelli family remember much pleasure in that grey summer—and yet she was as hopelessly remote as ever. Five days later the promised letter had not arrived, nor any calls. What had gone wrong?

Seton went back to the last call. The speaker had refused to identify himself but Seton was sure that he was from the same gang holding Nicola and that he was sticking to a planned line, or even a form of script. Why the silence? The gang appeared anxious to keep the family placated. There might be several reasons: firstly, Nicola could be dead, and the gang wanted to postpone the resulting uproar as long as possible; secondly, there could be technical, negotiating reasons, like creating the impression that proof could not be provided, to pressure the family; or perhaps it was just that their boss was away for a while. Seton firmly believed that a letter would arrive eventually. He did not think an experienced gang would kill a young girl, however ruthless they might be. The position of the child within the Italian family tradition would count for something, even with this bunch of criminals.

He worked out a scale of responses to draw the gang out into the open again. The ads would be placed on three successive days, each worded more strongly than the last. If that didn't work, he would arrange a newspaper interview with Nicola's parents in which they would say they believed her to be dead (what depths must be reached before parents can pretend in public that their daughter is dead?). The article would be accompanied by a photograph of Renato at his front door as if the interview was spontaneous. That would, it was hoped, alarm the gang that no more money would be forthcoming. If, after all this, the gang still did not show, he wanted to stage an even more dramatic scenario: a suicide attempt by Renato (other members of the family thought the problem might be preventing the poor man from actually going the whole way). Alternatively, a burned-out car could be produced, with what would appear to be a body inside, and speculation set up that it was the remains of Nicola Brunelli.

Happily, such gruesome stunts were not needed. The three ads went in, with the usual line about the lost canary with green eyes followed by the absolutely clear statements: 'We don't understand what is happening'; 'We wait for the news that you promised'; 'We are worried because we haven't received the letter that you promised'.

This last specific announcement sparked an immediate response, in the form of a short call to Renato telling him there was a letter waiting to be collected from on top of a telephone box in front of San Eugenio's hospital (clearly becoming a popular place for kidnappers to leave messages: it was used in the Pagani case). In fact there were two letters in the envelope, the first from Nicola, the second from her kidnappers.

Nicola's letter explained that the letter promised days before by the gang must have gone astray in the post, possibly during a train strike the previous week. Strikes in Italy were continually interrupting negotiations, whether of newspapers so that ads could not be put in, or of banks so that ransoms could not be drawn out. So, the delay had had nothing to do with threats, subtle tactics, or anything else that Seton had thought up; the letter had simply got lost.

Nicola's letter read in full:

> It has come to my knowledge that you haven't received my previous letter. It must be because there was a strike on the railways and other things. I have been assured that the present letter will be delivered directly so I renew hope that you will conclude as soon as possible this endless imprisonment. Don't trust the forces of the state, i.e. for the reward and the other stupid things. The truth is: words don't resolve anything unfortunately. If you do not again give the payment requested it will be difficult to see me again. My custodians are severe but I believe in their word. They are not like the

others. I can't foresee the hour when I will come to embrace
you. I really miss you. A very dear greeting to you all from
your dear Nicola.

The other letter read:

> Respected Brunelli
> As your daughter has clearly illustrated, the fact that the letter
> has not been delivered previously is not our fault.
>   We repeat that the sea is warm to bathe in. It is substituted
> with A HARE RUNS FASTER THAN A DOG.
>   The advertisement in *Il Messaggero*—Female Canary etc.
> etc. has to be changed to the phrase: 'Lost dog—Poodle,
> White, Villa Pamphili. Big Reward.'
>   When you are sure that you can obtain our request, ONLY
> THEN, place your advertisement. We want 900 million, we
> don't give any importance to the blocking [*of assets*], or your
> health, or other things. If you want, it won't be difficult to
> conclude. To be fair to you I understand that the previous
> people didn't keep their word. We can't judge them. We
> guarantee our words with the highest honesty.
> Rosario.

It was clear to Seton that the gang was going out of their way to show
that they were not the same people as had abducted Palombini, and
who had successfully obtained two large ransoms without returning
the old man. Their proof of Nicola's well-being was acceptable but
not conclusive, because it did not prove that she was alive—as a new
proof question would have done. But the Brunellis should not push
too hard on this since it might delay things. The extra 100 million in
their demand Seton construed as being evidence that the kidnappers
were showing their complete contempt for all the recent publicity,
which had by now included a television interview with Aldo Palombini
and a documentary on kidnapping. The gang would either negotiate
hard for the full amount or be prepared for less, say between one
third and a half.

The problem was the guarantees. Seton devoted a lot of thought to
the thorny question of guarantees for Nicola's safe release, which the
gang had unwittingly referred to in their letter. All the family knew
that they would be asking for guarantees from men who could not be

trusted but, although they had been caught out once, they wanted to believe that they could get Nicola back, assuming she was still alive.

Eventually Seton concluded that another budget had to be agreed, then they would negotiate up to the budget and only then, once the money was 'on the table', insist on guarantees. Also, he thought that if they agreed on the money first, then, when discussing the guarantees, the kidnappers could not insist on the whole of their demand, saying, 'No guarantees unless you pay the whole 900 million.'

How much to play with? Seton settled on a maximum of 350 million (£175,000) which was as much as the three families could rake up together, having already paid the first ransom (there had been some hard talking among the families about the second ransom). There was no need to delay placing the poodle ad; they should get negotiations started at once. The Brunellis agreed to all of Seton's suggestions, and fixed on a starting offer of 100-120 million (£50–£60,000).

The day after the two letters arrived, I joined Seton in Rome to take over the case; he had to return to London. I was coming in late to this case although not ignorant of the situation. John had frequently telephoned me over the past weeks and we had discussed different tactics and the various ideas he had thought of. I picked up the files at the office in London and, by the time I arrived at the El Dorado Hotel in Rome, I was fully briefed on all the details of the family and the negotiation.

I was introduced to Massimo, who had been John's invaluable interpreter, in the restaurant which he was running now for his father, and I met the rest of the family at the next C.M.C. meeting. My first task was to produce a script for the next round of expected telephone calls with the gang. It was a complicated second negotiation and the family's insistence on guarantees was not going to make it any easier. I had my doubts about the wisdom of asking for these guarantees since I was aware that kidnappers will agree to any demands—provided they get what they want. 'Of course, of course. We guarantee to release her,' they would say, but they would take the money first and then the family would be back to square one—like the Palombinis.

I could not see this gang agreeing to a direct swop (most unusual in Italy) or any real guarantee. However, I knew from John that the three brothers had been definite about the guarantees; the implication was that if they paid this second demand, and she was not returned, then

they would pay no more. It was my job to convince the gang of the
Brunellis' tough, businesslike line, but it would be hard and
dangerous. Seton was correct: we had to get the kidnappers used to
the idea of guarantees early on.

I wanted the script to be clear and so started with the heading:

> AIM: to make an offer, conditional on proof; to express
> businesslike manner; to express distrust of promises; to state
> need for realistic guarantees of victim's safe return.

I then arranged the following order of thought for whoever took the
next couple of calls:

> I shall not waste your time with words or excuses.
> I have a proposal to make (a money proposal).
> But first we must be sure Nicola is alive and well (as of this
> moment).
> Please ask her this short question . . . (or send a tape of her
> quoting a paper of that day).
> And phone tomorrow with the answer.
> I will make a ransom offer.
> *Note*: if the gang say 'I promise she's OK.' reply, 'Such
> promises meant absolutely nothing before, nor did such
> promises help Palombini or Ciocchetti.'

The second call would go like this:

> Take and confirm proof.
> (If unsatisfactory, family must say so—refer again to gang's
> meaningless promises.)
> Then:
> I shall make an offer in a moment.
> First understand your demand is out of the question, as you
> well know.
> But more important:
> How can we accept your word to return Nicola?
> Such promises are worthless etc.
> We want some realistic guarantees.
> In the meantime my first offer is . . .
> Call back at . . . p.m. the day we put an ad.

This was agreed and the 'Poodle' ad appeared in *Il Giornale* on 19 October, the ninety-fifth day of Nicola's ordeal. That morning her father's hopes were raised. The Carabinieri took him on a raid which they hoped would turn up the gang. (Was this not extraordinarily casual? Distraught parents cannot be any possible use on such a delicate police operation.) They found nothing.

Renato did not want Maria to be the negotiator any more and was proposing Mario Trantini, an experienced politician and long-time family friend. While accepting the tactical usefulness of changing negotiators, I was not happy with the proposed change, but not for any reasons of criticism of Signor Trantini, a much respected political figure. I believed that all communications came best direct from the family. It showed they meant business.

The 'Poodle' ad produced immediate results. First a silent call to Alessandro di Terracciano, then the real thing later that evening to Nicola's parents. Maria took the call. The start was fraught with misunderstandings which look almost comical in transcript, but bear in mind Maria's highly nervous state.

'The hare runs faster than a dog,' shouted the caller three times in a thick Sicilian accent, getting increasingly angry, until Maria remembered the new code phrase. She recovered herself to handle the rest of the conversation masterfully.

'Mr Rosario . . . wants to know how much money you have got ready?' The kidnapper, like all his kind, was interested in only one thing. But Maria ignored him and demanded proof that her daughter was alive.

'We give you every guarantee,' came the response.

Maria ignored him again, and ploughed on, demanding that he ask Nicola what her Aunt Juliana gave her every Easter, and repeating the question twice to make sure the kidnapper understood. Finally, he agreed to call back again the following evening.

The call had gone well, and I made my first assessment, concluding that all depended on whether the proof answer was correct. If it was not, Maria or Trantini, whoever was to be the spokesman, should insist on another one, even saying bluntly in the next phone call, 'You'll get no money for dead goods.' If the answer was satisfactory, the negotiator should follow the second script I had outlined, stressing the impossibility of the demand, that all promises were so much hot air, and, in their turn, demand absolute guarantees for her return before making the first offer. He or she should maintain a cool, businesslike approach.

I felt that the nature of this gang was such that they did not care for histrionics and, now that the Brunellis had been double-crossed on the first payment, it was necessary to demonstrate a tougher, bitter line. Their money, after all, was short. Interestingly, this theme of mine coincided exactly with the mood of the family at that time. They were deeply upset that their first agreement had been broken. The earlier frenetic anxiety was gone, replaced by a grim determination to do their duty and see the matter through once more.

I also noted that the caller had not mentioned any specific demand, merely asking how much was available. Was this a hint of willingness to bargain? The Sicilian accent suggested the gang was backing up their claim of selling Nicola to another group. Or, it might presage hard bargaining ahead, as Sicilians were notoriously ruthless.

A compromise was arranged regarding the negotiator. Maria would take the next call, demand the answer to her proof question, and then hand over to Mario Trantini to negotiate the finance. Renato and Maria were psychologically exhausted, and Trantini, who had years of experience shouting at hecklers on the political hustings, would now be able to underline the family's tough commercial line more ably. Using Trantini fitted in well with the tactic that the gang had beaten all emotion out of the family (true anyway) because of their treachery over the first ransom, and that the negotiation was now purely mechanical.

To the delight of Nicola's parents, the man with the Sicilian accent rang back punctually the next evening with the correct answer: a chocolate rabbit. Then, Trantini took the phone from Maria.

'I'm the person who'll conduct the negotiation with you on behalf of the family and the group of people giving me the money,' he stated baldly. 'You've already got the Brunellis' money . . . I've seen what's happened to Ciocchetti and Palombini . . . and also to Brunelli . . . we want a realistic guarantee that Nicola will come back.'

'But you'll have all the guarantees you want,' came the smooth reply.

'*Ecco!* At the moment I can give you 120 million but you must behave with realism and come down from your demand, it is absurd.'

'It's not absurd,' protested the kidnapper, indignantly. 'OK, I'll report back to Dottore Rosario. Goodbye.'

Trantini put the phone down with genuine relief: 'I've made countless speeches in my time, and some of them important, but I've never felt so nervous as I did just then waiting to speak to this criminal.' He was sincerely astonished at the sudden strain: 'My throat dried utterly and I had to cough, like a novice.'

I reckoned the gang was pleasantly surprised by the family's first offer. The caller had been quiet, reasonable and unhurried, he had not reacted violently when Trantini called his demand 'absurd'. These latest two calls had lasted seventy-two and ninety-five seconds. The Brunellis should expect times to be similar in the next calls and we would tailor our scripts accordingly. Trantini seemed a sound negotiator but I would recommend him to avoid inflaming the other side with abuse in the future; he needed to be cool, distant and businesslike.

Another 'Poodle' ad should go in and Trantini should say, in the next call, that the gang must make a reduction before he could recommend that the family attempted to borrow more from friends who would not lend money to a useless cause. This would be the core of the next script and, so far, the gang's almost cordial tone suggested they were not dug in at 900 million and would talk about their demand.

As predicted, the kidnappers had promised all the guarantees the family wanted, but I had no doubt that these were empty words. The other matter which seriously bothered me was the evidence that this gang were not prepared to recognize the basis of negotiation at all; quid pro quo, or money for the victim. Their talk of 'selling' the girl to another gang was bluff, I was sure. (Why give away the goose that lays the golden eggs?) They had broken their word once and (as with the Palombinis) might do so again. Worse than broken promises was the growing certainty that this was the same group that had murdered Valerio Ciocchetti, who had been shot and dumped in the River Tiber.

These factors alone made it hard to advise the conduct of the negotiations without seriously increasing the danger to Nicola, but the Brunelli family was at breaking point too. I detected the beginnings of rows between the various factions of the family which could lead to a complete break-up as they argued about the actual value of Nicola's life. It is never easy for one family to put a definitive price on the victim's head, but for three families. . . ?

The plain fact was that, since the gang refused to recognize the quid pro quo of negotiations, the outlook was bleak indeed. However, short of help from the authorities, Renato had to continue the talks to release his daughter. What else could he do?

The advertisement went into *Il Giornale* again on the next two days
and the second time drew a brief call to the house of Signor Bini,
another family friend, whose phone was not monitored by the
Carabinieri. The 'hare' code phrase was used and a longer call
promised for later that evening when the C.M.C. could be gathered.
But this time, on 23 October and case-day ninety-nine, no second
call came through. The family were not to know it, but it was the last
time they were to hear from the gang.

The following day, on Saturday 24 October, I flew back to London
to confer with Seton. Hardly had we started talking in John's office
when the telephone rang. It was Massimo, on the line from Rome.
Nicola, he said, had been freed that morning after a shoot-out with
police at a villa in Lavinio, a seaside resort not far from Torvajanica.
Seton immediately caught a plane to Rome and was present at an
emotional meeting that evening when Nicola was reunited with her
family.

The story of her release reflects credit on the much-abused Italian
authorities. It was the culmination of a police operation that had
started ten days previously when a wanted criminal, on the run for
months after escaping from prison, was spotted at Magiona near
Pomezia just inland from Torvajanica and traced to a villa there.
Landovino De Sanctis, forty-two, was a highly dangerous member of
Rome's underworld with a long record for murder, theft and robbery.
He had escaped from prison three times.

De Sanctis had murdered twice: first a policeman who tried to stop
him robbing a post office in Rome in 1975, and later a nineteen-year-
old criminal who had offended him. He had been on the run since his
third jail-break, from Rome's Regina Coelis prison in June 1980,
when he scaled a wall and displayed remarkable acrobatic skill in
doing so. He had come under suspicion of involvement in the spate of
kidnaps in 1981.

Two members of the anti-kidnap squad set up a surveillance
operation with trigger observation points around the villa in Magiona.
They ordered their men to arrest him when he was seen leaving the
villa on 23/24 October. A road block was set up to catch him in his
Volkswagen Golf but, in a hail of fire from the officers manning the
road block, De Sanctis swung the car round and drove off at high
speed. While a massive manhunt was begun in the area, the
Carabinieri raided the villa. They found the owner, Alberto Signore,
forty-four, two women, Maria Cristina Lippi, thirty-three and

Loretta Lippi, twenty-five, and Alfredo Turani, forty-three, from Rome. They also found 50 million lire (£25,000) which they identified as part of the Brunellis' first ransom payment. All the arrested people were taken to Rome and their interrogation led to the capture of a family of three more, Angela Cottarelli, twenty-seven, and her brothers, Gianfranco, twenty-five, and Virgilio, twenty-three, at an address in Rome. Here, the police found a 100,000 lire (£50) banknote which had been part of the money paid for the release of Giovanni Palombini.

But, though they were so far on the right trail, they had not found the two missing kidnap victims and the manhunt for De Sanctis had been unsuccessful. The break-through came when Maria Cristina Lippi mentioned a villa 'near the Lido dei Pini' in Lavinio and the message was flashed to the searchers. They concentrated around the Lido and came across a block of four pre-fabricated villas called the Villa Claudia. The Polizia and Carabinieri surrounded it and spotted the Volkswagen Golf that De Sanctis had been driving. There was no sign of life, so they moved in. As they approached, the police officers heard a shot. They burst in and found De Sanctis holding Nicola to his chest as a shield and brandishing a pistol. But the criminal was wounded in the left arm—presumably from a police bullet fired when he escaped the road block—and he was easily overpowered. Nicola was weak but unharmed. She was freed after exactly one hundred days as a captive.

She was taken to police headquarters in Rome where she was reunited with her parents and, displaying remarkable composure, gave an impromptu Press conference before going home for her first proper bath and change of clothes in three months. She was filthy, her fingernails overgrown and, as one reporter wrote, 'her hair stuck together as if it was smeared with glue'.

* * * *

Of Giovanni Palombini, however, there was still no sign save for his driving licence, found in the hide-out from which Nicola was rescued. The police believed he had been kept in a cell like Nicola's, next to the girl in one of the gang's hide-outs, and they had recovered some of the money paid for him. Some police thought he was still alive, but they were the optimistic few; the large majority believed he was dead.

Five days later his body was discovered in a shallow grave in a remote field near Valmontone, south of Rome. The police said they had had a telephone tip-off but there was speculation that the information had emerged during the detailed interrogation of the De Sanctis gang, of which thirteen had now been caught.

His body had been found, but when did Giovanni Palombini die? As the police inquiry deepened it became clear that his death had not been as recent as forensic tests, performed after the discovery, at first suggested. The last proof that he was still alive had been sent in a letter to his family on 29 July—only twelve days after Nicola had been kidnapped—and after he had been imprisoned for 104 days, and two ransoms had been paid. The proof was in the form of a Polaroid photograph of the old man, in which he wore dark glasses and his face was bandaged around as though he had severe toothache. Since that day, all further requests for proof had been parried by the kidnappers: he was too ill, proof would be sent soon, etc. When they did send a message purporting to be in his handwriting, it was patently forged. And now it seemed that the photograph had been set up too; a macabre stunt. The police found that Palombini had been shot dead and his body stored in a deep freeze, with the legs broken to fit it inside. For the 'proof', it had been taken out, propped up, photographed and then returned to the freezer. De Sanctis persistently denied to Judge Imposimato, the investigating magistrate, that he had murdered the old man. He kept claiming that he had sold him to 'a band of Calabrians' because he was afraid the old man would die any moment.

De Sanctis had managed to extract a total of 1.5 billion (£750,000) from the two families of Palombini and Brunelli, of which little has been recovered, without returning either of his victims. A list found in his possession showed he had every intention of continuing this lucrative trade. It contained the names of six famous figures in industry or show business, including the film star Virna Lisi, wife of a wealthy Rome architect.

* * * *

We talked to Nicola in 1985 during the course of our researches and she told us of her ordeal and what she thought of it after the intervening passage of four years.

She bounced into the family's restaurant, now an ebullient seventeen-year-old, nearly as tall as her cousin Massimo, over six foot. Her hair was long and fashionably semi-permed. She would have looked older but for a brace on her teeth, but it was easy to see that when it is removed she will be an even more striking girl than she is now, full of teenage vivacity and giggles. She clearly has a good rapport with Massimo who brought her to our table and looked after her with amused concern. It was impossible to imagine that four years before she had spent one hundred days in the hands of one of the most brutal kidnap gangs Italy has ever known, which killed two victims and demanded payment after payment without release. She had dined already but asked Massimo for a plate of chocolate profiteroles and tucked into them with relish. Then she started her story, in fluent, if ungrammatical, English which she had studied the previous year in Canterbury:

> Last night I remembered in perfect detail the last day of my imprisonment. The young remember everything. I think they remember especially the brutal things and not the enjoyable ones. [*It was difficult to imagine there had been anything enjoyable about her captivity.*]
>
> At the moment I was captured in Torvajanica, I was going through the door of the chalet. We had forgotten the keys and I returned to the restaurant to get them. The kidnappers were waiting for me in an [*Alfa Romeo*] Guiletta. I was just closing the door of the chalet when someone shouted, 'She's the one!'
>
> I turned to face them and they grabbed me one by each arm and each leg. I'm very tall (even four years ago when I was thirteen) and I managed to escape. I knocked one down by kicking him but the other three caught me and carried me bodily to their car. I didn't understand what was happening. I was aware of events around me but I didn't understand. I suppose it was shock. [*The 'shock of capture' is a common phenomenon and soldiers are taught to expect it in themselves if they fall prisoner.*]
>
> They drove off with De Sanctis at the wheel, but after three minutes they changed cars. They put Scotch tape over my eyes and ears and pulled me roughly to another car. They put American handcuffs on me; the harder I struggled, the tighter they became. We drove for about twenty minutes to a house that was in the country—I heard a cricket—and the first night I stayed in the car. But I didn't sleep.
>
> I told them several times that my father was ill. Each time they replied, 'Don't worry, everything will be over soon.'

The next morning I was taken to a house with a cloth blindfold this time. I stayed there for only a day. I knew the Polizia were active around there because I could hear the sirens. I was in a state of shock for three days and understood nothing of what was going on. I was terrified for two or three weeks but for the first week I was also calm. I hoped the Polizia, the Carabinieri and my family would rescue me. But the gang told me the Polizia and the Carabinieri were useless so I lost hope in them and that left me only with my family.

I was moved into five different houses in the three months. First I was kept in a tent, inside a room, near a kitchen, but I didn't get any hot food. They gave me tinned food, tomatoes, ham, and the diet was occasionally varied over the whole period with pizza, biscuits, pastry, chocolate, or scrambled and boiled eggs. I got sick of tinned tuna fish and Philadelphia cream cheese which I was given a lot. But I didn't have much appetite anyway. I spoke only to one or two people although I know now that the gang were thirty to thirty-five strong [*thirty-three had been arrested at the time of this interview.*]

They kept Scotch tape over my eyes for three days. When they pulled it off I couldn't see at all. I used a portable toilet which they emptied every few days. My wrists were bruised from the handcuffs. There was no bed, just a mattress and my hands and feet were always chained to two heavy lumps of concrete. It was three weeks or a month before I was able to walk again properly after my release.

I was stuck in this tent measuring one by four metres but the second tent, in another house, was only one metre eighty centimetres high, which was my height, so I couldn't stand up straight. When the Carabinieri freed me, I couldn't walk. I had lost the use of my legs, temporarily, from lack of exercise and I had to be carried to the police car by three men.

In the first month I hoped to be freed every day. Every day they said, 'We have called your family and tomorrow you'll be going home.' After a month of that I didn't believe them any more.

For three months I didn't see any of them. I just heard voices and could talk to them through the walls of the tent. They gave me a newspaper from the north of Italy to read because it wouldn't have anything about me in it. So I didn't know what my family was saying about me.

I smoked my first cigarette in captivity: they became like a sister to me. Eventually, I asked for a Rome newspaper but they made sure before they gave it to me that there wasn't an article about me in it. They said my family didn't want to pay the ransom, so after two months, I began to think that my family didn't want me back home. They brainwashed me. It wasn't until I did get back home that I learned my family had paid a ransom on 1 September, but my captors said they didn't pay anything. One night they told me there would probably be a payment that evening but the next day they said, 'No, Nicola. Nothing happened.' Now I know there was a payment but the gang changed their mind. Three of them wanted to release me but the others said, 'No.' There was an argument and the next day they decided to keep me.

My mind was crazy towards the end. It became very important to see something outside the tent, anything. It was awful not to be able to see the sun, the daylight. All I could see was a little hole in the tent. But at the end they asked me if I wanted a miniature television. I said, 'Yes please.' And they gave me one. At last I saw my family again.

I had only two periods when I went into shock: when I was captured and the last day. I usually went to sleep about 11 p.m. and my guards slept nearby. But that night they were agitated, going from one room to another for hours. I was very tired so I went to sleep. The next morning there was only one man left (De Sanctis). I didn't understand. This was something new.

In that last house I was kept in a large wooden box. Through the wall, I heard the man who was left, the kidnappers' leader, say, 'Nicola, it's all over.'

I replied: 'What's over? Are you going to kill me?'

At that moment he switched on the lights and came into the box. For three months I hadn't seen any of their faces, as they were outside the box or either they or I was hooded. But now he came in wearing nothing over his head.

'I don't want to see you,' I shouted, and turned my back on him so he could not say I was able to recognize him and give himself an excuse to kill me.

But he just repeated, 'Nicola, it's all over.'

'What's over? My life?'

'No. It's finished for me. The police have arrived.'

For me the police did not exist. I had given up all hope of rescue over two months earlier. They couldn't exist.

'Don't worry,' he continued. 'They're here.'

He picked up the keys to unlock my chains but he couldn't find the right one. My hands were free but not my legs. He wanted me to stand up and stood behind me to protect himself. I was very scared.

'Look at me, look at me,' he ordered. I refused.

'If I see you, you'll kill me.'

'No. They'll kill me.'

He pushed me out of the box and into the dining room. The front door was there and a little window beside it, but I couldn't see much because my eyes were so unused to the light. I heard shots and four roughly-dressed men burst in through the windows and one through the door. I was convinced they were more of the gang. One took me in his arms and shouted, 'How many of them are there?'

'Only one,' I said.

'OK. Run!'

'I can't even walk!'

So three of them grabbed me up in their arms and ran out of the house with me, still wearing the chains. One said, 'Are you the girl we've been looking for? You can't be thirteen —you're too tall.'

I burst out laughing. I will remember that man all my life. They thought I was a girlfriend of De Sanctis.

'No,' I told them. 'Don't take me to another prison after this one.'

It had been three months and I was free.

We went into a bar and a lot of the customers came up and shook my hand. I didn't really understand why. People who didn't know what it was all about were asking each other who I was. I still had the chains on my legs. They asked me what I wanted to drink. A glass of wine, I said. We had champagne. Then the police drove me to Rome. Outside the police headquarters there were a lot of photographers and reporters. The police found some bolt cutters to get the chains off my feet. They noticed my hands. My nails were six centimetres long. I hadn't bitten them once, and I feel very proud of that.

I was taken into a room and there were my father and mother. We had more champagne. When I returned home at about 4 p.m. everybody I knew was standing outside in the road. I went to wash and then Massimo arrived with all the dishes he knew I most liked to eat. But I couldn't eat any of them. I wasn't used to eating at that time of the day and I didn't feel hungry.

Looking back on it all, I thought they wanted to kill me. I was sure of that. It didn't seem possible to me that my family could pay the money.

Every night when I went to sleep, I heard music downstairs. Sometimes I heard people playing tennis. I knew we were not far from Torvajanica because of the short distance we had travelled in the car. I guessed we were sixty kilometres from Torvajanica. In fact it was only twenty.

The kidnappers wanted to make me believe they were from Milan. They put on Milanese accents [*De Sanctis had been four years in prison in Milan; and escaped from it*]. The leader always used the Milanese expression *Tutto mi.*

They gave me newspapers, puzzles, games books and I drew a lot. They used to check what I was drawing. I had to write four letters which they dictated to me. I didn't want to write them but they told me to and they told me to say I was ill when I wasn't. I was just tired and sad. They threatened me with a pistol to make me do it.

The gang told me I was strong. They said they thought a girl would cry and they were surprised when they realized I had cried only when I was captured. That was probably my mistake. If I had let them see me cry maybe they might have released me. I did cry but I did not want to let them see me.

Has it changed my life? Nowadays, I do not see everyone I meet as a potential friend. I know now that there are people who are your friends and people who hate you and want to kill you. At thirteen you think everyone is your friend. After an experience like this you realize the world is bad. That reflection can bring you to think twice about things. Now I don't have many friends. I prefer to be with just one or two and not a lot of people I don't know.

For the future I would like to travel and study veterinary medicine. I had masses of letters from as far away as the U.S.A., offering me a place to stay. I even had one from Belfast; I replied, 'No thanks.' I prefer to remain in Rome rather than risk capture again.

* * * *

One further curious incident occurred during the case. After De Sanctis's arrest, the Brunellis suddenly remembered an evening during the negotiations when a man had come into the restaurant, in the Hotel El Dorado, alone and had deliberately chosen a table near the door. The head waiter and Massimo noted him particularly for he was not the usual sort of customer; he paid little attention to his food and coldly observed the scene around him. Later when the family saw pictures of the man who had masterminded Nicola's kidnap, they realized they had served him dinner in their restaurant.

PART II

SIX

The Lindbergh Legacy

Since the mid-Seventies there have been more kidnaps for ransom in the United States than in the notorious years of the gangsters in the Thirties. In the years spanning 1926 to 1936 there were 101 cases of classic kidnap for ransom. In the peak period of the Thirties, 1933 to 1936, there were forty-eight cases—an average of twelve a year—which provoked an outcry of public revulsion and demands for tougher laws. However, in the ten years 1974 to 1984, there were no fewer than 141 kidnaps and between 1980 and 1984, as far as records go, there was an annual average of fourteen cases. What is disturbing about the latest figures is that they are persistently increasing from year to year (eleven to twelve to eighteen over the years 1981, 1982 and 1983). While the annual historic peak was actually in the Thirties (twenty-six in 1934), there were in fact twenty-three kidnaps in 1974, the year Patty Hearst was abducted.

At the outset, kidnapping must be put in perspective within the overall crime trends in the U.S.A. The incidence of classic kidnap for ransom has always been low compared to murder, or non-negligent manslaughter, which has averaged over 7000 victims a year for the last fifty years. In the last five the toll has risen to over 18,000 annually. Kidnapping is but a small percentage of the total of all serious crime in the U.S.A.

The most infamous kidnap case in the history of the United States was that of Charles Augustus Lindbergh, the twenty-month-old son of the famous pilot who had achieved world-wide acclaim for the first solo flight over the Atlantic. Colonel Charles Lindbergh's baby son was found murdered, on 12 May 1932, six weeks after a ransom of $50,000 had been paid. This was the case that gave its name to the Lindbergh Statute (see page 154).

Kidnappers generally choose wealthy victims, like the Lindberghs, or stars or celebrities, like Frank Sinatra's son in 1963, and cases always attract tremendous media coverage. Violence, the public image of the victim, a huge ransom, police detective efforts, and a macabre curiosity over whether the victim survives are some of the reasons for the huge public interest.

* * * *

The effect of kidnap on the public conscience was never greater than in 1932 when the Lindbergh baby was taken from his bedroom shortly after his mother had kissed him goodnight; it was the last time she saw him alive.

The child disappeared from his second floor nursery between 8 and 10 p.m. on 1 March 1932. The Lindberghs and their staff immediately searched for him, desperately hoping there was a simple solution to his absence. They found an illiterate ransom note on the window sill. It demanded $50,000 for his return and gave a strange arrangement of circles and squares as the kidnappers' identification sign.

Lindbergh called the local police at once and within minutes the departments of three states had been alerted by teleprinter. Within hours newspapers across the world had the story over their front pages.

On case-day six, 6 March, a second note was received by the family, with the strange identity sign, in which the kidnappers expressed their dislike of the Press coverage and said that they would wait until the furore died down before taking the negotiation further. Meanwhile they upped the demand to $70,000: the kidnappers were punishing the family, and the authorities, for putting them under pressure. Kidnap is a very private affair; commercial kidnappers prefer to do a quiet deal for cash. They have quite opposite views about the media to their politically motivated counterparts, the terrorists.

Lindbergh had appointed various acquaintances—some of whom were professional criminals who offered their services—to act as negotiators with the kidnappers, and made appeals in the Press for the baby's return, and for the kidnappers to get in touch with the family.

But on case-day eight a third note said the Lindbergh's own negotiators, or intermediaries, were unacceptable.

On the same day an eccentric, retired school principal, Dr John Condon, volunteered through an article on the front page of the *Bronx Home News* to act as intermediary and offered an extra $1,000 from his own pocket. The kidnappers were obviously keen to be getting on with the negotiation without the glare of publicity: the next day Dr Condon received a fourth note from the gang accepting him as intermediary. The Lindberghs agreed.

Dr Condon continued the negotiations through the newspapers and four days later, after an anonymous telephone call, a fifth note was delivered by a taxi-driver. This note directed Dr Condon to an outlying subway station and a vacant stand where, under a stone, he found instructions to meet someone in the Woodlawn cemetery by 233rd Street and Jerome Avenue at 8.30 p.m. that same night.

Dr Condon met one of the kidnappers and did his best to negotiate for the Lindberghs, discussing the payment of the ransom. He asked the stranger to prove he really was the man who had the baby. On 16 March, day sixteen, a seventh note arrived with a sleeping suit, and the Lindberghs confirmed it was the one their baby son had been wearing the night he was snatched from his cot.

It is sad that this proof of ownership was construed as proof that Charlie Lindbergh was still alive. While the normal questions that prove adult victims are alive cannot be put to a baby, demanding the child's fingerprints on an up-to-date copy of a newspaper—a glossy magazine, say—would be satisfactory. (Dead people cannot leave fingerprints: when the brain is dead it can no longer instruct the body to exude the moisture which leaves the tell-tale print.) The baby's prints could have been compared to those on toys in his nursery. Proof questions do more than just satisfy the terrible worry of parents, and then only for a short time. They have a definitive effect on the negotiation. The kidnapper loses his power over the family if he has killed. Forcing a kidnapper to realize that he will only get his money for the safe return of his victim is the strongest card that a family can play. It obliges the kidnapper to think of the negotiation in terms of quid pro quo.

An eighth note, on 21 March, insisted that the family meet the demands in full. It also said the kidnap had been planned for a year, presumably to indicate a high level of sophistication, control over the situation, and underline the inability of the police to help. The ninth note was still stronger in tone, and the kidnappers, refusing to use a code in the newspapers—which would have relieved the pressure of the media coverage, upped the ransom to $100,000. The tenth note instructed the family to have the money ready for the drop the next day. Dr Condon acknowledged this in the Press.

On case-day thirty-three, 3 April, Dr Condon again followed the sequence started by a note given to a taxi-cab driver, through instructions he found under a stone in 3225 East Tremont Avenue, to another cemetery, Saint Raymond's in the Bronx, where he met the stranger he knew as 'John'. In the shadows of graves and headstones he persuaded the stranger to accept the original demand and handed over $50,000 in exchange for a receipt and the thirteenth note which explained where the baby could be found. The stranger then walked out of the cemetery, north into the park woods.

Following instructions in that thirteenth note, the police searched for the boat *Nelly* near Martha's Vineyard, Massachusetts, in which the kidnapper said he had concealed his victim. But they found no sign of the Lindbergh baby.

On 12 May, seventy-three days after the child was taken in the night from his nursery, his badly-decomposed body was accidentally discovered some metres from a road, four-and-a-half miles from his home, near Mount Rose, New Jersey. The infant's head was crushed, there was a hole in the small skull, and some of the body members were gone. The coroner's examination showed that he had been killed by a blow on the head and had been dead for about two months. It is likely the kidnapper had murdered the baby soon after the abduction, very probably the same night. He had then negotiated through thirty-three days knowing that he had nothing to give in return for the payment.

Extraordinary as it seems today, both the police forces of New Jersey and New York had promised not to interfere during the entire period of Dr Condon's involvement. This was at the request of Lindbergh. But why was a full surveillance operation not used? Even stupid kidnappers realize that their most dangerous moment is when they have to materialize from safe invisibility to pick up the money they have extorted. The police ignored the two opportunities they had to follow and 'house'—surveillance jargon for 'locate the home of'—the man known as 'John'. Perhaps their decision was influenced by the thought of what might happen to the victim if the kidnapper realized he was being followed. Perhaps, in the glare of publicity, the

ABOVE: Bruno Hauptmann, convicted kidnapper of the Lindbergh baby, executed 3 April 1936.

LEFT: Charles Augustus Lindbergh, the twenty-month-old son of Charles Lindbergh, at the family's home in New Jersey.

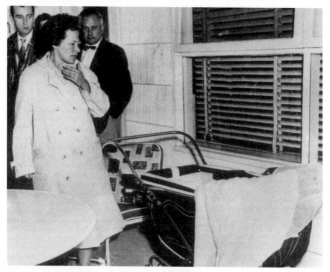

ABOVE: Mrs Beatrice Weinberger shuts her eyes in anguish as she looks at the empty pram from which her four-week-old baby was taken.

LEFT: Patty Hearst, kidnap victim turned terrorist. Armed with an automatic weapon, she is posing in front of the Symbionese Liberation Army insignia.

OPPOSITE PAGE, *above*: Looking drawn and tired after three nights without sleep, Frank Sinatra announces the safe release of his son to Hollywood pressmen.

OPPOSITE PAGE, *below*: Frank Sinatra Junior, aged nineteen, enters the house near Los Angeles where he was apparently held by kidnappers. He is accompanied by FBI men.

ABOVE: West German show jumping star Hendrik Snoek demonstrates to newsmen how he was put in chains by his kidnappers.
BELOW: The funeral of Hans Martin Schleyer, killed by terrorists on 19 October 1977. His wife, following the coffin, is flanked by her son and daughter-in-law.

ABOVE: The anxiety of the victim's family: Mrs Boni Beihl, wife of kidnapped West German consul in San Sebastian, Eugenio Beihl, and her daughter Lucia stare out of the window of their home as their wait for news continues.
BELOW: Following his release after nineteen days in captivity, Dr Julio Iglesias speaks before a press conference. At his side is his son, the well-known Spanish singer of the same name.

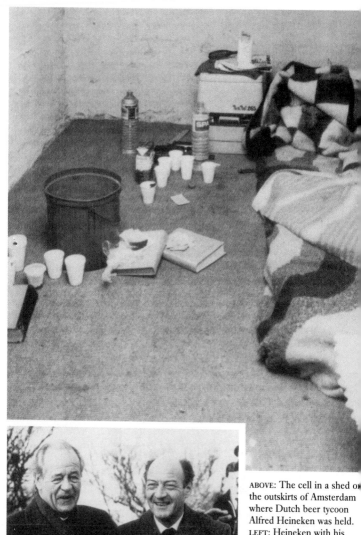

ABOVE: The cell in a shed on the outskirts of Amsterdam where Dutch beer tycoon Alfred Heineken was held. LEFT: Heineken with his chauffeur Ab Doderer during a short photo session following their rescue by police after three weeks in captivity.

TOP: This photograph of Mrs Muriel McKay was taken in 1968 and issued on a police poster following her disappearance.
CENTRE: Police, investigating the kidnap of Mrs McKay, search the fields surrounding Rooks Farm, Stocking Pelham, Hertfordshire.
RIGHT: A haunting photograph of Lesley Whittle whose tragic case ended in her murder at the hands of homicidal maniac Donald Neilson.

TOP: Happy to be alive, kidnap victims Emmanuel Xuereb and his wife Maria after their ordeal.

CENTRE: Jubilant, Don Tidey hugs his daughter Susan after his release following a police shoot-out in County Leitrim on 16 December 1983.

BELOW: Irish kidnap victim Jennifer Guinness, photographed at a Dublin press conference with her husband John, after her dramatic release in April 1986.

police were afraid that the all-too-easy failure of a surveillance attempt would have brought fierce criticism and accusations of risking the little boy's life. Also, the police had no idea how many were in the gang; their surveillance effort might have been countered by other kidnappers keeping look-out. Indeed, Dr Condon said he was sure other members of the gang were watching him. In any event, when 'John' walked away with the money into the darkened woods behind the cemetery, the tenuous leads that he had created during the negotiation faded into obscurity with him.

The investigation dragged on for twenty-eight months, until, on 19 September 1934, a German-born carpenter, Bruno Richard Hauptmann, who lived in the Bronx, New York, was taken into custody by representatives of the three police agencies interested in the case; the F.B.I., the New York city police and the New Jersey state police. It had taken a long time to find the kidnapper and part of the problem lay in this triplication of work.

The police were bound by laws that were deficient in a way that is hard to believe in retrospect. At the time of this kidnap felons could cross state lines and place themselves beyond local police jurisdiction. Nor did the F.B.I. have authority to investigate or take action against criminals flitting from state to state to avoid arrest and prosecution. The situation was entirely to the advantage of criminals. Public opinion grew, fired by the developments of the Lindberghs' misery, to have the law changed.

From the start of the case, the Attorney-General and the U.S. Department of Justice had begun to work for full co-operation between the police agencies. Governor Moore of the State of New Jersey had asked for the F.B.I. Director, J. Edgar Hoover, and F.B.I. agents, to attend various co-ordinating conferences as the case developed. However, during the crucial period of the negotiation and the payment, the F.B.I. were not involved; they were kept as much in the dark as any member of the public.

The lines of command must have been complex and cannot have improved the chances of conducting a smooth operation, either in gaining the confidence of the Lindberghs, and Dr Condon, during the negotiation, or in working towards the detection of the gang. Mounting a well co-ordinated surveillance operation must have been a nightmare with so many chiefs at the helm.

On 17 May, five days after the child's body had been found, the F.B.I. was put in the position of clearing house for a host of involved government agencies: the police forces, in particular the New Jersey state police, the Intelligence Unit of the Internal Revenue Bureau, the Treasury Department and the prosecuting authorities of New Jersey. The F.B.I. were to receive and pass on all information relating to the case to the New Jersey police via an F.B.I. liaison officer at Trenton, New Jersey. Now the case had overall co-ordination, but this had only been cobbled together to solve the Lindbergh kidnap. Public opinion still demanded that politicians give the police forces more permanent authority.

Finally, on 22 June 1932, the Federal Kidnapping Statute was enacted, over two years before the kidnapper of Charles Lindbergh was caught. It was popularly known as the 'Lindbergh Law' and is now to be found in Chapter 55 of Title 18, U.S. Code Sect 1201. This law gave the F.B.I. exclusive jurisdiction for the Federal Government over all violations of that Act. But it was not until 19 October 1933 that it was officially announced that the Bureau had exclusive jurisdiction in the Lindbergh case.

Without doubt, this lack of the necessary legal framework slowed the detective investigation into this and other cases. Once provided, the accumulation and analysis of all the facts could take place under one roof: that of the F.B.I.

A year later, still before the arrest of Hauptmann, several further Acts were passed, as a direct consequence of the continuing public reaction to the Lindbergh kidnap and the Kansas City massacre in which, on 17 June 1933 at the Union railway station, Kansas City, four policemen were murdered and two wounded by Charles 'Pretty Boy' Floyd and Adam Richetti. The public was fed up with the gangsters and the spate of kidnaps—twelve in 1933 peaking to twenty-six in 1934. The Lindbergh Statute was amended so that it became unnecessary for the crime to be for ransom or reward. A clutch of ten new Public Laws (Numbers 230 to 235, 246, 376, 402 and 474) in 1934 armed the Federal agency in their fight against serious crimes, most of which transcended state police jurisdiction.

In murder cases the police can at least be sure that the perpetrator is 55% likely to be a relative or acquaintance of the victim, and that gives them a start. In kidnap cases the police are faced with a mountain of meticulous tabulation and analysis to unearth—with luck—the one clue that will lead to those responsible. Unless quality surveillance locates the kidnappers, the police must be determined to commit themselves to a long struggle, to exhaustive research down every possible avenue of investigation. This effort is costly in both manpower and financial terms. It requires enormous commitment by the already overburdened police agencies and by the politicians supporting them. To solve the Lindbergh murder the F.B.I. demonstrated this commitment, recognizing that Herculean efforts should be made to prevent such a complex crime becoming popular.

Once they had complete jurisdiction, the F.B.I. set to work. Staff organized over 50,000 index cards, correlating these logically in sequence so the information could be used and cross-checked. Agents followed thousands of leads. They analysed the handwriting in the notes from the gang; they investigated anyone with local knowledge of the cemeteries, of the Lindberghs' house, of Martha's Vineyard; they examined all the things used by the kidnappers—the ladder, the box which contained the ransom money, the notepaper, the strange identification sign, the ransom money that was recovered at garages and shops. They investigated rumours that well-known gangsters were responsible; they researched registries of boats for the boat *Nelly*; they found former students of Dr Condon who had criminal records; they checked the cemetery employees; they cross-related the gangs in other kidnaps.

Forensic investigation continued in the Crime Detection Laboratory. Scientific tests were carried out on ransom money recovered from banks, on bank deposit slips, on stock transactions, and on paper comparisons. Searches were made for fingerprints, blood-stains, secret inks, or anything out of place that might give the police the single clue that eluded them.

Finally they went through hundreds of criminal records with the few eye-witnesses, showing photographs and data from the files holding at that time 4,800,000 fingerprint and 6,000,000 index cards. All by hand!

There are now nearly 180 million fingerprint records but they are computer-filed in the F.B.I.'s Identification Division. After the Lindbergh case the investigation was bound in no less than sixty-five volumes and a 600-page report prepared as an aid to future cases.

One of the features of this—and most other kidnaps—was the vast number of false leads. They came from all over the United States and all had to be exhausted by further investigation. In one, the police followed up 296 gold certificates, all ransom notes, that had been reported by the Federal Bank Reserve of New York. In another, through bank deposit notes, they came to check everybody with the name 'Faulkner' who had lived in New York City since 1895. Some people tried to extort money by fraudulently claiming to have information leading to the kidnappers and some of these were prosecuted.

Eventually, after two-and-a-half years of fruitless work, the police had a lucky break. Wearily they checked yet another report about ransom notes, but this time the bills had been recovered at a garage where the attendant had noted the licence plate of the car whose owner paid with ransom money. He was Richard Hauptmann and police put his apartment under surveillance. They watched all night and, when Hauptmann appeared at 9 a.m. on 19 September 1934, they arrested him as he sat in his car.

He was indicted in the Supreme Court, Bronx County, New York, on charges of extortion, and in Hunterdon County, New Jersey, on charges of murder. Then the Governor of the State of New York agreed to surrender the prisoner to the Governor of the State of New Jersey and Hauptmann was moved back to New Jersey, where the crime had been committed, to await trial.

The trial lasted five weeks. Finally, on 13 February 1935, the jury returned a verdict of guilty and Hauptmann was sentenced to death. Appeals to the Supreme Court of the State of New Jersey and to the Supreme Court of the United States were turned down at the end of 1935, and the Pardon Court denied his petition for clemency. Richard Hauptmann was electrocuted on 3 April 1936 at 8.47 p.m., four years and one month after the little baby was seized from his cot.

Much has been written about Hauptmann's trial, casting doubt on the evidence and the testimony that convicted him, and suggesting that his own defence was not pursued as vigorously as it ought to have been. Hauptmann was almost certainly an innocent victim of the law named after the very case of which he was unfairly held responsible. But as far as we are concerned it is the conduct of the case then, and its legacy since, that is interesting. If Hauptmann was innocent then it is to be hoped that the authorities will reopen the investigation to clear his name, for the sake of his wife Anna who is still alive and campaigning for his name to be cleared.

The Lindbergh case is interesting for it showed that Americans, with their special sensitivity to moral issues, could be outraged by kidnap. They called for laws to strengthen the police and judiciary to deal with kidnappers. After the case the various agencies of the United States were armed with the necessary tools to defeat kidnap, and they were backed by public opinion that abhorred the crime. Investigation teams were supported by helpful public response providing a mass of information, some of which was, admittedly, misleading.

Could the F.B.I. and state police live up to this public confidence? Or, once the spate of cases in the mid-thirties had been controlled, would future investigations falter under the pressure of long cases? This infrequent crime diverts resources badly needed to solve other more numerous crimes. The Lindbergh kidnap showed that there are certain aspects of kidnap that require a flexible approach from the police: the obscurity of the perpetrators places special demands on surveillance capabilities, on the investigators, and the police need to develop a sympathetic relationship with the family. Did the growing F.B.I., newly equipped with Federal powers, have the right attitude of mind in the delicate circumstances of kidnap?

The number of cases fell away towards the end of the Thirties and Forties and in the year after the Second World War there were few cases anywhere in the United States. The victims were often children and the public reaction was always strong; parental sympathy crosses the barriers of social division. One particularly gruesome case was that of six-year-old Robert Greenlease, who was kidnapped and murdered by a couple, Carl Austin Hall and Mrs Bonnie Heady, in 1953. The F.B.I. caught the pair who admitted digging the boy's grave before the kidnap, and buying quicklime to dispose of the body.

* * * *

A case three years later indicates that the F.B.I. were still prepared to commit tremendous resources to kidnap investigation.

After lunch on 4 July 1956, when everyone was celebrating the National Independence Day holiday, Beatrice Weinberger pushed her one-month-old baby, Peter, along the pavement in his carriage back to their home in Westbury, Long Island. She put the baby carriage on the patio and went into the house for a fresh nappy. When she came out the carriage was empty and a scribbled note lay on the still-warm linen where Peter had been moments before:

> Attention
> I'm sorry this had to happen, but I'm in bad need of money, and couldn't get it any other way.

Don't tell anyone or go to the police about this because I am watching you closely. I am scared stiff, and will kill the baby, at your first wrong move. Just put $2000 (two thousand) in small bills in a brown envelope, and place it next to the signpost at the corner of Albemarle Rd. and Park Ave. at *exactly* 10 o'clock tomorrow (Thursday) morning. If everything goes smooth, I will bring the baby back and leave him on the same corner 'Safe and Happy' at exactly 12 noon.

No excuse, I can't wait!

Your baby-sitter.

Mrs Weinberger's hysterical screams attracted the neighbours who, since her husband was away, were her nearest support. They searched hopelessly for the little child and then called the local police.

The letter, hastily scrawled by hand, showed the classic features of kidnap communications:

1. The family was warned not to tell the police. Some families obey, but, even in countries with poor police-public relations, this threat is seldom realistic: however badly the police are criticized, families in trouble turn to them. Also, it is often impossible to hide a disappearance. Most kidnappers recognize this but try it on to worry the family, throwing in the idea that they are watching all the while. This is unlikely for it's not easy to watch a place without some danger of being caught.

2. There was a threat to kill the one-month-old baby which must have terrified Mrs Weinberger. But threats to kill are quite normal. The unusual feature was that the kidnapper said he was scared. Was he trying to scare the family even more with worries of his ineptitude? This could have indicated an experienced gang trying a double-bluff. However, signals in kidnap communications are complex enough without double-bluff and most thinking gangs recognize this, keeping their demands and threats simple: generally of the sort, 'How much?', or 'Pay now or we will kill by Saturday.' The indication was that this kidnapper was new to the game.

3. What was most telling was the urgency of the letter. He wanted the drop within twenty-four hours, almost before the mother could get to an open bank for the money. And the ransom demand was tiny, $2000. Both these factors indicate inexperience. Executing a safe drop requires careful planning on the part of the gang. After all it is their pay-day.

4. Most importantly, the kidnapper gave precise instructions as to the drop location at the time of the kidnap, and where he would leave the baby. In retrospect, it does not seem feasible that the kidnapper expected to be able to avoid police cover at the drop, at 10 a.m., and two hours later leave the baby at the same spot; especially since he had told everyone what his plan was. Either it was bluff to cover a more intelligent plan—in which case the baby would *not* be left at midday—or it was a stupid idea. His plans sounded faulty, indicating a frightening degree of inexperience.

5. Finally, his signature—'Your baby-sitter,' showed an awful sense of humour, or, perhaps, inverted guilt that again suggested a chaotic mind and lack of experience.

Inexperience in the gang is always dangerous for the victim. The case would have to be handled very carefully.

According to the Federal Kidnapping Act the F.B.I. could not be involved until seven days after the crime, unless there was evidence that the felons had crossed state borders. After a week a rebuttable presumption arose that the victim had been carried out of the state. So, the local police carried on by themselves, closely assisting the family. Following the kidnappers' instructions, they left a parcel by the signpost on 5 July. This parcel was a dummy package, containing no money. It was the police intention that they would pick up the kidnapper as he came to the drop site. Men in plain clothes positioned themselves around Albemarle Road and Park Avenue and waited to see who would come to pick up the parcel. However, frightened by the unusual level of activity near the site, the kidnapper never appeared.

Perhaps the police had an efficient surveillance capability, but they certainly took a tremendous chance putting out a dummy ransom parcel. If kidnappers get away with what they think is the money and then open the package to find none, their victim will suffer the consequences of their anger. It is vital that both sides are 'honest' with each other to establish a coherent negotiation. If the authorities use tricks then they must be undetectable.

The Weinbergers remained in agonizing suspense until case-day seven when a man telephoned the house in the morning. Though Mr Weinberger had hurried home, his wife took the call.

'Listen carefully, go to Exit 26, turn right, follow the curve, on the right side you will see a mail box, William Shank 3109, there will be a blue bag. Take out the note and put the package in. Will meet in forty-five minutes.'

Morris Weinberger consulted with the police and they agreed he should leave a note for the kidnappers saying that no ransom would be paid unless further identification were provided. He found the mail box as described but no blue bag. After a fifteen-minute wait that must have felt like hours, he left the note and drove home.

At 2.29 p.m. the kidnapper called again. He was annoyed and wanted to know why no one had been to the mail box where he claimed to have waited for an hour. He gave new instructions. This time he told Mrs Weinberger to go to Exit 28 of the Northern State Parkway where she would find a blue bag near the curb. She was to place the money in the bag. Mrs Weinberger did not demand that the kidnapper gave proof that he had her little son, or that he was still alive.

Again the police decided that they would cover the area, putting policemen discreetly around the site of the blue bag, and the Weinbergers agreed not to go. After one hour in which nothing happened, the police searched the bag and found another note in the same handwriting as the first:

> If everything goes smooth, the baby will be wrapped in an army blanket and placed at the exit of the Parkway closest to your house in exactly one hour.
> Your baby-sitter.

The blue bag, made out of a car seat cover, was tied to a piece of string over twenty yards long leading to a clump of bushes. It was ludicrous: the kidnapper planned to lurk in those bushes, watch Mr Weinberger make the drop, and then pull in the blue bag, in the blithe assumption that the police would not make some attempt to cover the drop and see the blue bag moving on its own across the road verge. It must have been very worrying for the police and family to have realized they were dealing with kidnappers so inexperienced. They cannot have been sanguine about the baby's chances of survival.

They were right. There were no further contacts from the gang. The police were left with a fantastically wide base on which to begin their investigation. This time the kidnapper really could have been anyone. There were no witnesses and no clues apart from the telephone calls and the handwritten letters.

The F.B.I., which had been alerted at the start, assumed responsibility for the investigation after the seven-day period set down by the Lindbergh Statute. The Bureau set up a headquarters locally, open twenty-four hours a day, and all leads were followed with due regard 'that the safe return of the child was of absolute importance.'

The only clues offering any hope at all were the two letters. So, accepting the colossal task ahead, the F.B.I. set their handwriting analysts to work. It was a mighty task indeed. Having no idea in what section of society to look for the kidnapper, they began to compare his writing with that on all the cards and forms so beloved by bureaucracy: the New York State Motor Vehicle Bureau, Federal and state probation offices, schools, aircraft plants, municipal records and so on. It was an exhausting job.

Six weeks later, after checking over two million handwriting samples, the search ended with the discovery in the United States Probation Office that one Angelo John La Marca had a hand similar to that of the two kidnap notes. This similarity was confirmed by F.B.I. experts in their special investigation headquarters.

Now the police had something to work on. There was a chance that the child was still alive even though there had been no contact from the gang, so it was essential that the arrest was not bungled. Surveillance teams were deployed at La Marca's house in Plainview, Long Island, and at other places associated with him. Then, at just after two in the morning La Marca and his wife returned home and he was taken in by F.B.I. and local Nassau County police officers.

At first La Marca pretended he knew nothing of the kidnap, but when shown the results of the handwriting analysis he confessed. He had been arrested and put on probation for making illegal alcohol but by no means was he a hardened kidnapper. Simply, he had been under financial pressure and, seeing Mrs Weinberger push her baby home, decided to get rich quick. Kidnap, he thought, was the answer to his problems. He had scribbled the first note leaning on the steering wheel of his car and dashed across to exchange it for the baby on the patio.

His spur of the moment decision cost him his life. He was found guilty and, after all appeals were denied, executed in Sing Sing prison, New York, at 11 p.m. on 7 August 1958.

Following La Marca's instructions after his arrest, the police searched the Parkway where the kidnapper said he left the boy, still alive, on the second day, 5 July 1956. They found him. Near the baby's badly decomposed body lay a nappy safety pin, the very pin that his mother would have used for the fresh nappy she had gone to fetch when Peter was kidnapped.

How well did the authorities cope? Was police surveillance heavy-handed on the first attempted drop on the second day? La Marca said he was frightened by an unusual degree of activity at the scene (policemen in plain clothes trying to look casual?) and it was driving away from there that he dumped the little baby on the verge of the Parkway. It is easy to criticize in retrospect; good covert surveillance is hard to achieve; a team cannot be put together at a rush and surveillance requires specialized training.

From the negotiating point of view the kidnapper showed himself as very inexperienced and that is always bad news: for the family and the police, because they know the chances are high that the victim might be killed; and for the kidnappers themselves, because their own ignorance, or stupid arrogance, will almost inevitably lead to their arrest.

Kidnapping is too complicated a crime for the inexperienced to carry out successfully, unless the police forces are lazy in their investigation or unprepared to commit the resources necessary to solve the case. In this respect the American agencies come out with full marks. They had gone through two million cards before they struck lucky, and it only took six weeks.

* * * *

If we are now convinced that the F.B.I. are prepared to utilize their full resources to solve a crime after the negotiation has turned sour, or the victim has been murdered, then what is their approach during the negotiation? What priorities do the F.B.I. adopt in the negotiation? Is ransom payment illegal? Does the victim have paramount importance? And what assistance do they give the suffering family in coping with the negotiation itself? Before citing recent examples, let us take a look at a 1963 case, involving one of America's most famous personalities, which illustrates these points.

On Sunday 8 December, Frank Sinatra's son, Frankie, was taking time off from his own show in a motel near Los Angeles when he responded without thinking to a knock on his room door and the call, 'Room service!' The ruse worked. A gang rushed in, seized him and drove off with him, leaving his room-mate tied up.

The kidnappers phoned Frank Sinatra to tell him they had his son and said they would call again at nine the following morning. They were surprised to find that the singer sounded quite different on the phone to his records.

Sure enough, the same member of the gang called the next day and allowed Frank to speak to his son. Then the kidnapper ordered Frank to go to Ron's Garage at Carson City, thirty miles south of Reno. The kidnappers seemed calm and under control.

The singer drove to the garage where the attendant was amazed to find that the caller asking for the famous Frank Sinatra in his remote garage had not been joking. Sinatra had not long to wait. The same kidnapper rang and coolly instructed him to prepare a ransom of $250,000. The money should be in notes and not in serial sequence. Sinatra was ordered to wait for drop instructions at the home of his son's mother, Nancy Sinatra. The couple had been divorced some years before but the distress of the kidnapping brought them back together as they waited for news of their son.

The F.B.I. had been brought in from the first and Frank Sinatra had offered his complete co-operation. For their part, the F.B.I. response is best described with a quotation from J. Edgar Hoover: 'Just keep your mouth shut, Frank. Don't talk to anyone but law officers. And don't go discussing the kidnapping with your show-business friends. They can't keep a secret.' He went on with more forthright advice, 'My men will want to tap your phone and examine all your mail before you see it. If it's a ransom job, I won't tell you to pay the money or not to pay it. That's your decision. But when it's all over, if you've paid up, we'll do our best to get your money back.'

This clear statement of the F.B.I. policy is remarkable in that it did not constrict the family during the negotiation. If Frank Sinatra wanted to negotiate for his son, pay or not pay a ransom, or anything in between, it was to be his decision. Hoover did not want criminals to use extorted money to finance other illegalities but he recognized the immediate problem: to do their best to save the victim through careful negotiation.

He placed no pressure on the family not to pay. On the contrary he encouraged them to make up their own minds, to decide what value to put on their son's life. At the same time he offered advice and back-up. The full power of the F.B.I. would be committed to helping the victim's family. Then, afterwards, the agency would clear up the mess, however it panned out.

Frank Sinatra, understandably, accepted this generous co-operation and gave his own assurance that he would help them in their investigation. Like every father in his position he wanted to pay the ransom, but unlike fathers in some other countries, he had the full support of the police and the authorities.

The ransom was prepared with the assistance of Frank Sinatra's friend, Alfred Hart, President of the National City Bank of Beverley Hills. The F.B.I. recorded every serial number of every note with a Recordak camera. The list of numbers was forty-one pages long.

That evening the kidnapper called Nancy's home and instructed Frank to go to a call box in the Western Airlines Terminal at Los Angeles airport. He was to wait for a call from a man calling himself John Adams and then give the name Patrick Henry. He was to bring the money in an attaché case. It was a large, heavy case, weighing about forty-five pounds.

The drop run had started.

Sinatra left Nancy's home and went to the airline call box. There he was ordered to go to a service station eight miles away. Once there, he was told in another telephone call to drive to a garage two miles further on. It was past midnight when he found the third call box in a Texaco garage where he waited again. This movement from phone box to phone box—sometimes called the 'triple switch'—was an attempt to shake off the police, or reporters, who might be following Sinatra.

The kidnapper called, as promised, and told Sinatra to go to the Veterans Hospital on Wilshire Boulevard, close by, and leave the attaché case between two school buses parked outside. Sinatra found the buses as described and, at 12.30 a.m., he left $250,000 on the street between the buses.

No sooner had he driven off than a young man emerged from his hiding place and, under cover of darkness, walked quickly over to the buses. He picked up the attaché case and drove off in a car.

He was not the last on the scene. F.B.I. agents had followed Sinatra, from the time of the first call in Nancy's home to the buses by the Veteran's Hospital. The surveillance team had worked well, keeping out of sight. They had not even alarmed the kidnapper who was waiting in the shadows to pick up the ransom. He had clearly been carefully checking the area as Sinatra arrived, but, his concentration doubtless drawn irresistibly to the attaché case, he had not seen the surveillance team behind. Quietly, the agents had slipped into positions from which they could oversee the two school buses. From the moment the kidnapper came into view to the time he drove away he was filmed from one of the surveillance team cars. In the darkness, the F.B.I. used infra-red photography, illuminating their unsuspecting subject with a beam of light which is quite invisible to the human eye.

This was not the full extent of the surveillance operation. The attaché case contained a beacon-locating device. These devices can be very small, though the smaller the equipment—especially the battery —the less powerful the signal and the shorter time it will continue to emit. Their use depends on keeping close to the beacon, using a receiver which measures the strength of the signal. If the signal dies out all is not lost: helicopter searches can be mounted with the receiver, quartering the likely area until the signal is found again. The team continues on the ground, first in vehicles and then on foot, and all the while taking increasing care to remain covert as the search nears the beacon and the kidnappers.

In this case the F.B.I. team operated smoothly and had that element of luck that every successful operation needs. They followed the kidnappers' car and 'housed' them. The aim of their operation had been achieved. Agents staked out the house with officers in positions where they could trigger the waiting car teams if the gang moved again.

The gang telephoned Nancy's home and informed the couple that their son had been released on the overpass of the San Diego freeway. Sinatra left at once, with his headlights off and at speed to avoid the gathering of reporters. However, he returned soon, despondent and worried. There had been no sign of his son on the overpass. Had the kidnappers killed Frankie?

At 3.10 that morning an officer of the privately funded Bel Air police force was patrolling the area for his wealthy patrons when a dishevelled young man stopped his car and asked to be taken to 'Mrs Sinatra's house.' With a blindfold still round his neck, young Frankie was safe and well.

The F.B.I. moved quickly, raiding the gang's house where they arrested three people; Barry Keenan, Joseph Amster and John Irvin. All three were charged and convicted. Their motive was obvious, but why choose the Sinatra family out of all the other rich people in Los Angeles? The Sinatra family had come to the notice of the gang above all the other potential victims through personal contact. Keenan and Amster were petty thieves and had been classmates of Nancy Sinatra. This association was vague, but enough to give them the particular knowledge they needed, and they had mulled over the details of the kidnap for a long time.

* * * *

Perhaps as famous a kidnap victim as the Lindbergh baby is Patty Hearst, the daughter of multi-millionaire newspaper magnate Randolph Hearst (who incidentally reported on the Lindbergh kidnap all those years before). Her case is well-documented, but it is worth noting how social and political influences can complicate negotiations. She also demonstrated in a most dramatic way the kidnapping version of the so-called Stockholm Syndrome. (This term was coined after a bank seige in Sweden in 1974 during which the hostages established a peculiar rapport with the terrorists.)

She was engaged to a fellow student, Stephen Weed, and, on 4 February 1974, had just returned to their house with him when she was kidnapped by the Symbionese Liberation Army (S.L.A.) The S.L.A., like many anti-government groups, had confused political ambitions, and their negotiation for Patty's release was no mere commercial transaction. America was torn by social divisions and anti-Vietnam disaffection and the S.L.A., to enhance their political status, adopted a 'Robin Hood' image. They demanded that Hearst pay the $3,250,000 ransom to fund food programmes for the poor. If the money was spent by the Hearsts to release Patty, it was wasted.

On 2 April, the S.L.A. sent a bunch of red roses and a message saying they would release their victim. Patty dashed her parents' hopes the very next day by announcing her intention of joining her captors. She admits that she had always been spoiled by her wealth until her kidnap when, in captivity, she realized there was more to life than had been her fortunate experience. Carried along by the vigour of anti-establishment trends, the centre of attention of the nation's media, and in a degree of physical danger that must have been remarkable by comparison with her past, she became disenchanted with her own background and was converted to violent revolution with her guards. She made public statements rejecting her parents and all they stood for.

This sudden twist to the usual course of events in a kidnap admirably suited the publicity-seeking S.L.A., and the newsworthy confusion was fomented by the gang leader, Cinque. He directed that Patty, only 19 years old, take part in a bank robbery knowing that there were television cameras and recording apparatus inside the bank. It carried her message of revolt across America. She was a bright, all-American girl who gave two fingers to conservative society, and this struck chords of sympathy throughout the States.

At the end she was lucky. On 17 May hundreds of policemen and F.B.I. agents surrounded the S.L.A. hide-out and a fierce battle ensued. Thousands of rounds were fired and finally the house burst into flames. Six corpses were recovered but Patty Hearst was not among them. She had been out on another S.L.A. task and, returning to witness the conflagration from a distance, she survived the violent end of her adopted tormentors. At her trial she convinced the jury that she had been forced to join Cinque and the S.L.A., with dramatic revelations in the court of how she had been sexually abused and humiliated. She admitted her involvement in the bank raid and, in consideration of the extenuating circumstances of her gruelling kidnap, was given only a short sentence in jail.

* * * *

Kidnapping is complicated enough without adding the erratic and volatile ingredients of politics. The complexity is not appreciated; especially not by the criminals. Long gone are the days when swashbuckling villains carried off young girls beyond the reach of the impotent authorities—gone at least in countries with organized and efficient police. The Quinonez case, in 1983, shows some of the problems that gangs face and further illustrates the American authorities' attitude to kidnap.

Roberto and Clelia Quinonez were wealthy. He was a former Salvadorean ambassador to the United States and they had extensive business interests in El Salvador in car dealerships, coffee plantations, coconut farms, banks, land and a brewery. The family had been recognized as a target in El Salvador during the 1970s when Clelia

Quinonez's father, brother and another relative were all kidnapped by left-wing terrorists raising money for the revolution. The ransom in each case was over $500,000. Roberto and Clelia decided to move to safer regions. They chose Miami. At the same time they kept their businesses in El Salvador.

On the afternoon of 8 July 1983, Clelia Quinonez drove home from her work in their family estate brokerage firm. The driveway of their house in Coral Gables, Miami, is shielded from the road by hedges, and, when she got out of her Mercedes with her arms full of books, she was suddenly assaulted by three men who had leapt out of cover.

'Take her keys! Take her keys!' they shouted, and started to punch and kick her into submission. They shoved her roughly back into her own car and one of the men drove it several blocks away to a waiting station wagon, its rear windows sprayed an ominous black. She was bound tightly, her hands in front of her and the rope passed around her neck. Her eyes were covered by bandages and she spent several uncomfortable hours in the back of the station wagon which was driven through the night to her place of imprisonment.

At 4.55 p.m., five minutes after Clelia Quinonez was attacked, her husband received a call at his export company office.

'We have your wife,' the caller said. The voice was that of a middle-aged man with a Central American accent. He said he wanted $1.5 million in small denomination notes.

Roberto Quinonez said at once the sum was impossible. He was not that rich, he said. The kidnapper's response was classic, 'You have a rich uncle and a rich family. Besides, that's your problem.'

The kidnapper described the ransom as a 'war tax' and said it should be paid in El Salvador by Roberto's cousin. The term is frequently used in El Salvador in politically motivated kidnaps and made Quinonez think his family had been targeted yet again by the Left, this time reaching out to Miami where the Latin American population is enormous and Spanish is the chief language.

Along classic kidnap lines, the caller warned Quinonez not to alert the police and told him where he could find his wife's Mercedes. When Quinonez found the car, parked away from their house as described, he was forced to accept the chilling reality of his wife's kidnap. He did not hesitate to contact the F.B.I. who immediately tapped his telephones at home and in his offices. The same kidnapper called frequently over the first few days of the case and Roberto Quinonez was advised by the F.B.I. to ask a proof question to show that Mrs Quinonez was still alive. (Clearly the F.B.I. procedure now included this vital detail.) If the gang could not answer Quinonez's question then it meant Clelia had been murdered.

Quinonez's question was a refinement on the proof question. As a result of his family's extensive experience with kidnap he and Clelia had devised a code to be used between them if either were kidnapped. When the kidnapper called, he asked him to question his wife about a dog called Pancho, and how it had been carried for medical treatment recently. The key word was 'Pancho' which was to tell his wife to use the code.

The kidnapper called back and to Roberto's relief the answer could only have been Clelia's: 'The gentleman left on vacation to Mexico by plane.' The code-word was 'vacation' which meant she had been kidnapped, and the next words were supposed to indicate where she was being held: in Mexico.

However, the F.B.I. were not convinced she had been spirited out of the country and continued to check the telephone taps. They had noticed that the caller had obviously underestimated the speed with which the authorities could trace calls. During one call the F.B.I. traced the lines and found the kidnapper was speaking from a Miami callbox. The surveillance team that had been waiting for this was deployed immediately and agents raced across Miami in time to see a man leave the pay-phone and go to his car. They had been given instructions not to arrest the man then, but follow him and 'house' him. The safety of the victim was paramount and the arrest of one kidnapper might panic the others into killing Clelia Quinonez and going to ground. The agents managed to note the car number of the kidnappers' negotiator and traced the vehicle to a Miami rental firm. The car had been rented by Juan José Caceres, who had given his home address in Alexandria. The F.B.I. placed Caceres, his home and all the telephones he used under tight, twenty-four-hour surveillance. The major problem for kidnappers is the negotiation: they have to make contact so many times, risking detection each time. The gang had made their fatal mistake, and the F.B.I. had had their piece of luck.

Caceres continued to negotiate the demand with Quinonez and there was no clue to the whereabouts of the prison where Clelia was being held. Then came a call from Caceres, in Miami, to a pay-phone in Washington, outside a motel at 1451 Belmont Street NW. Caceres spoke to a variety of young people in several calls to the same pay-phone in Washington and the F.B.I. became convinced this group constituted the other half of the gang. Maybe Clelia Quinonez was being held there, well out of the way of the 'heat' in Miami.

A large surveillance team was deployed to cover the pay-phone at all hours: over twenty agents in two shifts of twelve hours each. They staked out the area, with agents in trigger observation positions and others waiting in foot and mobile surveillance teams, to follow whoever used the telephone at the time Caceres called from Miami. Vatter, the F.B.I. agent in charge of the team operations control at Buzzard Point, was in close communication with the F.B.I. in Miami. It was hot in mid-July and one woman lost ten pounds sweating out her twelve-hour shift enclosed in a static trigger van parked near the telephone. Concealed in the body of the van behind mock stacks of contents she had been left in position by the driver who had walked away leaving the van seemingly abandoned.

The team was triggered several times and followed young men to an apartment block close by, on 15th Street. There was still no confirmation that this Washington group had Mrs Quinonez but the negotiation was souring. Tension grew, not between Caceres and Roberto Quinonez, but between Caceres and one of the young men, a sixteen-year-old Puerto-Rican youth, Craig Blas.

'We did our job,' said Blas to Caceres on 12 July, case-day four. 'We expect you to do yours.'

'I'm doing mine, but you must be patient,' responded Caceres. 'We've been waiting for this for two years.'

But Caceres was losing heart. The phone tapping had revealed a conversation the day before between Caceres and his wife in which she told him, 'They're not going to control that thing. Understand me?'

Caceres had replied, 'It looks like I don't have the stomach for it.' 'Don't worry,' his wife said.

In spite of his wife's remarks Caceres called Roberto Quinonez on 12 July and said that another man, called 'Commander José', would speak to him.

Caceres spoke to Blas again on 13 July and the sixteen-year-old showed he had a command well beyond his years. He told Caceres that he would only 'hold on to this until Sunday (17 July),' and then if nothing had been settled, 'Yo tiro,'—'I shoot.'

It seemed the group in Washington were edgy and wanted a quick solution. The acrimony between Caceres and Blas increased and the

F.B.I. were worried for Clelia Quinonez's safety. Her chances of survival lessened, the more unstable the gang became. So, the F.B.I. planned a raid on the apartment on 15th Street.

When 'Commander José' rang Quinonez, from Washington on Thursday 14 July, Quinonez insisted on speaking to his wife before agreeing to a payment. The bait was out, but would the fish bite? The gang was clearly inexperienced and seeking a fast conclusion; they sounded volatile from the wiretaps and everyone was worried lest they killed their victim before the payment. Were they too late? Was Clelia Quinonez still alive?

A few hours later, that same evening at 10 p.m., F.B.I. agent Lenny Frieson was on covert surveillance duty in an ordinary car staking out the phone by the motel. He saw two black youths escorting a middle-aged lady out of the apartment block on 15th and around to the callbox on Belmont Street.

'It's her,' he spoke softly into his hidden microphone.

Vatter, in the operations room, asked a few questions to confirm the woman's identity. Then he waited to hear from the wiretaps that the call from that phone box was to Roberto Quinonez in Miami. He told the team on the ground around the callbox to stand by.

Roberto Quinonez lifted his telephone and heard a voice calling himself 'Commander José'. Then he heard confused shouting.

Frieson had driven up to the callbox and got out with his partner to ask the two men in the booth for help with a stalled car. The kidnappers' attention was diverted—torn between the call to Miami, controlling their victim and now the two men outside on the street. Frieson and his partner pulled out their guns and, shouting, 'Freeze, F.B.I.', ran over to the phone and stood between the dazed victim and the two kidnappers. At the same time other agents closed in fast.

Craig Blas and Robert Gerald were arrested and a .22 pistol was found on Blas. With the victim safe, the other members of the gang were arrested within a day: Juan José Caceres, forty-three, his wife Dora, and Salvador Lacayo, thirty-five, in Miami; Clifford Bibbs, twenty-three, Mack Carr, eighteen, and Jennifer Brown, twenty-seven, all in the Washington area.

It is interesting to note briefly the background of the gang and how they were brought together. Caceres and his wife were Guatemalans. He was an unemployed businessman while she was a third secretary in the Guatemalan Embassy and held diplomatic status. However, in spite of the Central American flavour, the original fears of political motives were misplaced. The motive was quite simple: money. Caceres and Lacayo, a Salvadorean, were short of funds. They knew of the Quinonez family and set up the idea of the kidnap using Craig Blas and a team of his choosing to carry out the attack and guard the victim.

Blas, whose family lived close to Caceres in Miami knew more of life than his sixteen years suggested. Alone, he went to Washington where he impressed Bibbs, Gerald and Carr with free drugs and recruited them into the kidnap gang. If Lacayo and Caceres were the leaders, with Blas as the go-between, then the three Washington youths were quite ignorant of the background to the trouble into which they were persuaded. Locals said of them, 'These boys have no education, and they have no idea what Salvador is,' and 'They probably don't even know how to spell Miami, much less find their way there.' Ignorant or not, the gang gave Roberto Quinonez and the F.B.I. a very worrying week.

Clelia Quinonez was in good health on her dramatic release. She said the sudden appearance of 'dozens' of F.B.I. agents was like being in an Elliot Ness movie. It was the first time she had been moved from the apartment on 15th Street since arriving there after the long drive from Miami on 8 July. She described her kidnap as very scaring. The three men attacked her from all sides as she stood by her car and started to hit her. When she screamed she was threatened with more beatings. Her hands were tied in front of her in the prayer position and she was kept tied like a 'Thanksgiving turkey' for twenty-four hours. In the apartment the kidnappers spoke to her in both English and Spanish, threatening to kill her if things went wrong. She said she thought constantly about her family who were kidnapped in El Salvador: 'My father was seventy-eight when he was kidnapped. That's all I could think of. If he could make it then I could.'

The leaders of the gang received long prison sentences: Lacayo got two life terms and Caceres seventeen years; his wife's diplomatic status was waived on the personal intervention of President Efrain Rios Montt and she got three years. The Washington recruits received lighter sentences: Bibbs and Gerald, eight years, and Carr, four years. Craig Blas, the intermediary, who was described by his school guidance director as 'fifteen going on forty', got only six years, perhaps because he was a juvenile at the time.

If the kidnappers had been planning to seize Clelia Quinonez for two years then they made an especially bad job of it. Caceres made over twenty calls to Quinonez and allowed the F.B.I. time to trace them. Then Blas and the guard team in Washington chose an apartment without a telephone so, having succumbed to the bluff of getting Mrs Quinonez to the telephone, they had to take their victim out on to the street to a public pay-phone. Dazzled by the money, perhaps, or just stupid? Certainly inexperienced kidnappers. It was fortunate that this inexperience gave the F.B.I. the opportunity to deploy their resources and find the victim. It was fortunate also that the F.B.I. were prepared to commit those resources.

Finally, since Quinonez called the police immediately, the F.B.I. were able to call for and obtain a complete Press and Media silence throughout the case. None of this appeared in the newspapers, or on radio and television, until after Clelia Quinonez was released. This crucial ploy has an immeasurable effect. How can one know whether the tensions between the kidnappers would have erupted into murder of the victim, fuelled by reports of how much progress the police were making? All that can be said is that the F.B.I. were able to control the situation as best they could. Most importantly, Clelia Quinonez survived.

* * * *

Public confidence in the authorities is obviously great but not total. Target families do not always report kidnaps to the police, sometimes hoping to negotiate a ransom and pay the gang quickly and quietly.

At 8 p.m. on Sunday 1 April 1984, Ernesto Castro left his restaurant, the Fontana di Roma in New York. He and his family had built up this and twenty other restaurants, through sheer hard work, from nothing. Later that night he rang his sister, Concepcion, and asked for his brother's telephone number. She recollected his voice sounding strained. He phoned his brother.

'They want ransom,' was all he said. Then another voice came on the line, 'We want thirty thousand.' The voice went on to give instructions about the drop in New York City. The kidnappers finished with the classic and terrifying words, 'The money and no cops, or your brother will be killed.'

At 10 a.m. that morning Benny Castro dropped $30,000 as instructed and waited for his brother to be released. He waited with this pathetic hope for five hours near a pay-phone for the call from the kidnappers. Nothing.

In the afternoon a friend called and, from the strangeness of Benny's voice, noticed something amiss. By chance he was a policeman and he came round at once. In tears, Benny told him everything and the police launched an investigation. But it was too late. Ernesto Castro was found by the Harlem River, on East River Drive in Manhattan. He had been shot twice in the head.

Why had the family not told the police? At the very least why had they not negotiated the ransom demand, establishing that essential ingredient of quid pro quo? It is also essential to demand proof of life. Kidnapping is a tough unpleasant business in which there is no room for weakness.

* * * *

Negotiation is an aspect of kidnapping—the crucial one—that seems better understood in the United States than elsewhere. The authorities do not object should the family of the victim choose to employ a negotiator, whether he be a lawyer, friend, or professional kidnap negotiator. The F.B.I. policy accords with that of the family: negotiate with the gang to release the victim whose safety is the first priority. The family will not have its financial assets frozen; on the contrary, the family decides whether to pay or not.

The F.B.I. admit that putting the safety of the victim first means bartering with the gang. The Bureau and every police department have their own guidelines on negotiating but they all accept that negotiating means giving something and getting something in return. This flexibility among the police may be surprising to some but the facts speak for themselves. In New York, in over 400 cases of hostage situations, the safety of the victim has been secured without death or injury. Kidnapping, where the location of the gang and victim are unknown, requires a more delicate negotiation; the police do not have the luxury of publicly surrounding the gang and victim with squads to underscore their side of the bargain.

Flexibility on the domestic scene is not to be confused with the United States policy on kidnaps abroad, which refuses any sort of negotiation for the release of hostages. Henry Kissinger pointed out that if terrorists or criminals thought they could hold the U.S. Government to ransom then thousands of U.S. citizens all over the world would be in jeopardy.

All negotiations have something of the theatre in them. They are a ritual where the rules are unwritten but should be followed by both parties for the convenience of each. District of Columbia Police Chief Cullinane noted this in March 1977 and said that it is important, for the credibility of each side with the other, to maintain their proper roles in the course of unfolding the ritual.

* * * *

Kidnappers continue to choose wealthy targets as a means of solving their financial crises. Another case in Washington in July 1984 shows a combination of classic kidnap for ransom motives, a 'perfect' target, the F.B.I.'s professionalism, and sheer stupidity on the part of the gang.

Edith Rosenkranz was the wife of the retired chairman of the Syntex Group which pioneered birth control pills in the 1960s. Millions of pills made millions of dollars and the Rosenkranz family were said to be fabulously wealthy. The firm received wide publicity when an infant formula causing loss of salt resulted in several babies suffering drastic fluid loss, a condition called metabolic alkalosis. Any publicity is an attraction for kidnappers on the look-out for potential targets.

Many families are wealthy enough to make good kidnap targets but there is often another reason that brings the attention of the kidnappers into focus on the eventual target. It may be personal contact, as in the Sinatra and Castro cases, or offered opportunity as with the 'on the spur of the moment' kidnap by La Marca. In the case of Edith Rosenkranz the kidnappers' boss shared the same enthusiasm: bridge. He met Edith and George Rosenkranz at bridge tournaments.

Glenn Wright, aged forty-two years, was a Houston businessman in financial trouble. He was also a law graduate of the University of Texas, a concert pianist, and a bridge player of some standing, an American Life Master who played at international level. He was an intelligent man but friends said he showed increasing nervousness. Wright himself said he had had to give up playing the piano at concert standard because he could not stand the pressure of playing in front of the audience. Wright had shared an apartment in Houston with Orland D. Tolden, twenty-five, for three-and-a-half years and enlisted his support in the planned kidnap for ransom. A third man, Dennis Moss, twenty-seven, completed Wright's team.

Norman A. Zigrossi, head of the F.B.I. Washington field office, said of Wright and his team, 'These men are not amateurs.'

Wright and his colleagues were certainly intelligent men, but were they really professional? It is true they had tremendous advantages over the ill-educated kidnappers of Clelia Quinonez (the three black youths from Washington). They knew exactly what they were setting out to do and they had no previous criminal records. So, were they amateur or professional?

Wright knew that the Rosenkranzes would be at an international bridge tournament which was being held at Washington's Sheraton Hotel in July. He arranged tickets for himself. Though he had not played seriously for two years, it is not unusual for players to come in and out of the game. He also paid the expenses for Tolden and Moss to come to Washington. He and Tolden flew to Dulles Airport on 13 July and, after hiring a black Thunderbird, checked into the Holiday Inn on 14th Street. Moss flew to Norfolk and drove to Washington in a 1982 black Chevrolet.

Then Wright took his team to the American Contract Bridge League summer championship in the Sheraton and pointed out Mrs Rosenkranz. Once the victim had been identified, Wednesday 18 July was chosen for the kidnap. However, Mrs Rosenkranz did not play on the Wednesday evening and they postponed their attack till the following night.

On Thursday evening, Moss saw Mrs Rosenkranz at the tables and had to bide his time, watching her, until past 11 p.m. when she left the bridge rooms with a younger woman. He followed them to the hotel garage where he suddenly appeared in front of them waving a pistol with a six-inch barrel. Threatening both women, and refusing to be bought off with the contents of their handbags, he abducted Edith Rosenkranz and left the other woman in a state of shock in the upper floor parking garage. Moss led his captive at gunpoint to his van in Calvert Street NW, where he handcuffed her and drove in the early hours back to Norfolk. Wright and Tolden returned to the Holiday Inn.

So far so good, for the kidnappers; but the actual attack is probably the easiest part in kidnapping. It occurs when least expected, on someone who has been deliberately chosen because he or she shows little or no regard for personal security. The complications begin after the victim is seized: communicating with the family to negotiate the ransom, avoiding the efforts of the police and, finally, giving instructions for the drop—lots of contacts, all risking the danger of leaving the single vital clue for the police.

The case lasted for less than forty-eight hours but in that time the kidnappers spoke to George Rosenkranz in nearly twenty calls. There was an element of farce: Wright left a ransom note behind a fire extinguisher in the Sheraton but no one found it and he had to retrieve it. Wright then spoke to Moss after which Moss called Rosenkranz to demand one million dollars.

Having got Rosenkranz to agree to pay, Moss was unable to co-ordinate the drop details with Wright and a first attempt to pick up the money failed. Moss became impatient and decided to act himself. He left Norfolk, with Edith Rosenkranz, and drove about northern Virginia looking for a drop site. He settled on the parking lot at Alexandria Hospital. (Considering that the most important aspect of the negotiation to any gang is bartering for the money and getting away safely with it from the drop, this group does not seem to have prepared very thoroughly.) The drop did not go well. Moss had told Rosenkranz to wait in the lobby of the Key Bridge Marriott. After his ad hoc choice of drop location, he called Rosenkranz there and ordered him to leave the ransom in the hospital car-park late on the second day.

It would have been interesting to have followed Rosenkranz from a helicopter. No fewer than fifty F.B.I. agents and one hundred Department police had been deployed on the case, and it would have caused Moss and Wright, who was with him in the van, heart failure to have seen the surveillance teams spread out behind and in the streets around Rosenkranz's car as he drove across Washington to make the drop. On the ground the two kidnappers never saw a thing out of place.

They waited a short time and then picked up the money. Their activities were closely observed by agents in the surveillance teams who then followed them for two hours. The ransom money had a beacon-locating device concealed in it and a helicopter team, which had a receiver monitoring the signal from the kidnappers' van, stood by ready to direct the ground team if they lost the target vehicle.

It is extraordinary that the kidnappers did not give more thought to the possibility of being followed. More extraordinary still is the fact that they picked up the ransom with Edith Rosenkranz in the back of the van. When they released her, agents in the surveillance team swooped and arrested both men. Mrs Rosenkranz was unharmed and the money recovered.

Edith Rosenkranz said her faith helped her survive the terrifying experience. She was able to rejoin her husband at the bridge tournament to the delight of the other players.

Wright's final act of stupidity was to have the key of his Holiday Inn room on him when he was arrested. The F.B.I. simply called round and arrested the third member of the gang, Tolden, as he sat in his hotel room.

So was Zigrossi correct in saying these men were not amateurs? He was not. The gang may have been intelligent, more so than the average perhaps, but they were thoroughly inexperienced kidnappers. They had no idea of the difficulties of kidnapping and, once they had their victim, made mistakes throughout. Given the resources the U.S. authorities are prepared to commit, their capture was inevitable.

The danger to Mrs Rosenkranz, however, should not be underestimated; she was threatened with death and drugged with tranquillizers. The inefficiencies of kidnappers must never be confused with softness. In the Quinonez case the F.B.I. rightly became worried when they detected signs of tension among the gang. Peter Weinberger's kidnapper was an amateur and the baby was abandoned, left to die at the side of the road. Amateurs, at kidnap, are dangerous.

*　*　*　*

The number of classic kidnap cases in the United States is steadily rising, but only in proportion to the overall serious crime rate, and in spite of the statistical evidence to deter potential kidnappers: in the thirty years to 1977 there were 647 kidnappings—of all kinds including child abduction by split families—and in only three cases were the culprits not caught.

The American authorities have the freshest and most pragmatic approach to kidnap. The safety of the victim is their highest priority. The family is not put under pressure, its assets are not sequestered, and its negotiators are not banned by actual law or moral pretext. The family can pay the ransom or not, as it chooses, and insure the ransom too. The F.B.I. devotes officers, surveillance teams and the latest equipment, time and money during the case and afterwards to catch the gang. And, most importantly, there is public confidence in the authorities, based presumably on their record.

SEVEN

A Strain of Violence

There is a flavour of savagery about kidnapping in Germany and kidnap does not suit the German image. Kidnap is not like crime against property. It is devious, cruel and indifferent treatment of the most fundamental human group, the family, which is revered in Germany. Kidnap is not a cut and dried affair, like bank robbery, but a long, often messy affair as the gang negotiate their pay-off with mendacious flexibility. What differentiates kidnapping in modern Germany is the high death rate of victims and the appalling cruelty meted out to some of the others.

The first case recorded in post war West Germany is typical and shocked police and public alike. Joachim Geohner was just seven years old, a schoolboy in Stuttgart, when, on 15 April 1958, a man approached him in the street and asked if the boy would like to see some deer he had spotted in the woods. The man was a gardener who worked near the Geohners' house and the child readily agreed. Having lured him away, the gardener murdered his victim at once and then demanded that the parents pay a ransom of 15,000 Deutschmarks (£1,280). The gardener's simple approach was quite inappropriate to the complexities of kidnapping and the subsequent negotiations. He was soon arrested and he committed suicide in pre-trial detention. What took the German police most by surprise was that such a crime was possible in Germany.

Once started, the trend continued. It is especially tragic that ignorance about the complexities of this crime leads men to kidnap, murder the victim and then demand a ransom. On 3 November 1980, eleven-year-old Cornelia Becker saw Gunter Adler, forty-seven years old, on her way to school. When he offered her a lift in his car, she agreed, unafraid because this man had talked to her several times before as she went back and forth between her home and school in Karlsruhe. But Adler took her directly to his own house, dragged her into the basement and beat her to death with a hammer. He stuffed the small corpse into a plastic bag and left it in the cellar while he took care of the ransom demand. The family received a letter the next day demanding 2 million Deutschmarks (£485,400) and containing Cornelia's school book and a monthly bus pass she had been carrying.

Adler, like so many inexperienced kidnappers, was in financial difficulties. His solution was kidnap and his approach to the crime was not much different to that of the gardener in the Geohner case, twenty-two years before. This, in spite of the fact that Adler was an educated man with a university degree in economics. Intelligent, but inexperienced in kidnap, he fondly hoped that the Becker family, who owned a factory in Karlsruhe, would accept the school book as proof. But they had informed the police and had no intention of paying without adequate proof that Cornelia was alive. They were not satisfied just to know who had seized her. Adler continued to write letters, six in all, and, during the negotiation, he took the grisly plastic bag from his cellar and buried it in a shallow grave in a forest. The police caught Adler on 21 December 1980 and he admitted planning to kidnap his victim, kill her and then demand a ransom by pretending she was still alive. It is easy to say that it was remarkably stupid of an educated man to have expected his victim's family to have paid without proof of life; but parents, willing to try anything, terrified of telling the police and unaware there is any other way, have ransomed their dead in the past.

Gunter Adler was brought to trial in August 1982, eighteen months after his arrest. The speed with which kidnappers are brought to court is an important part of the several influences that together deter criminals from trying their hand at kidnap. Other factors are the police investigation, the chances of being caught and the length of sentence. The German legal system is often slowed by the weight of legal procedure. The time between arrest, through pre-trial detention and indictment, to the trial itself depends on the seriousness of the crime and the complexity of the evidence so that, whereas some cases are brought in six months, delays of two to three years are common. Adler was found guilty under Article 239a in the *Strafgesetzbuch*, the German penal code. The minimum penalty is three years but if, as in Cornelia Becker's case, the victim is murdered, the sentence must be more than ten years, or life. Gunter Adler received life.

The police are conscious that individuals like Adler are difficult to apprehend since the list of suspects is as long as their motives are plain. They depend heavily on the support of the public, which, when it exists, is a powerful disincentive to kidnappers. The Abstellungpräsident (head of the German Criminal Investigation Department) of the Bundeskriminalamt (BKA), or federal police, in Wiesbaden states without reservation that public support is essential. It is perhaps fortunate that kidnap for ransom excites so much interest and people give the police more information in kidnap cases than any other crime.

Hendrik Snoek has reason to be grateful for this interest. On 3 November 1976 two masked men forced him from his own apartment in Munster. They took their victim to a bridge that spanned the motorway 125 miles south of Munster, and bound him with a heavy steel chain to the wall in an inspection chamber inside the massive concrete buttress of the bridge. They left him there, without food or water. The kidnap was widely reported, since Snoek was a well-known showjumper who had ridden for his country in the Olympic team, and the kidnappers demanded 5 million Deutschmarks (£1.11 million) which was paid immediately.

Doubtless the family regretted their hasty action in paying the ransom, for the victim was not immediately released. However, after only two days in his cell—'only' because two days is short by kidnap standards—in the icy cold of the November weather, Snoek noticed that he could reach a small opening. He found some paper, tore it up into small pieces and stuffed the shreds through the hole, hoping that someone would see them and investigate. He was lucky. By chance, a passing road worker stopped under the bridge and noticed what was happening. He released the showjumper, alive but shivering with cold. Whether Hendrik Snoek had been left to die, whether his family ought to have delayed payment, is speculation, but there are good reasons to extend a negotiation more than a few days; primarily, the family should insist on genuine proof of life before the payment which the police like to recommend, and secondly, by doing so they make the minimum impression on the gang—who may not be at all businesslike—that they expect them to honour the bargain.

The police investigation into the Snoek case settled on Peter Graef, thirty-eight years old, who was arrested after three months, and in May 1978 he was sentenced to thirteen years. He consistently denied the charges, but some of the ransom money was discovered in the home of a friend who, while held in pre-trial detention, committed suicide in May 1977. After two years in prison, Graef finally confessed and implicated another member of the gang, Norbert Wingerath, who fled abroad immediately with half the ransom. Later, however, he too contacted the police to give himself up. The belated sensations of guilt that were overwhelming for the gardener in the Geohner case in 1958 were repeated here in full measure.

Snoek was not the only one to suffer cold in a concrete cell. Gernot Egolf was thirty-two years old when two young men kidnapped him in Homburg, in Saarland, on 19 October 1976. The latter displayed a frightening degree of amorality. They held him in a World War Two bunker, sixty-five kilometres from Homburg near the French border, while his family, who owned a brewery, negotiated a 1 million Deutschmarks (£225,000) ransom demand. The ransom was never paid and the two kidnappers—a twenty-one-year-old forest worker and a twenty-two-year-old heating installation attendant—were arrested. Tragically their victim was not found until eight weeks after his kidnap, frozen to death in the bunker. His last hours must have been more than expectedly confusing and terrifying, for Egolf was mentally retarded.

More recently the public was more actively involved in saving another kidnap victim. On 27 July 1983, a nine-year-old girl, whose name cannot be disclosed, was grabbed from a bus stop. Her kidnappers pushed her into the boot of their car and kept her there for fourteen hours, while they drove about. On the way they stopped and made her speak into a telephone to her parents to prove she had been taken. Then they took her to a small apartment where they tied her up and bandaged her eyes with cloth. But the gang had not reckoned on public interest and the extra time that the unemployed have on their hands. A man had seen the men going in and out of the apartment building and considered their activities strangely out of place. He knew about the case from the news and, since he was unemployed, he spent his time watching the apartment. After a day, the self-appointed sleuth was satisfied that these were not honest men he was spying on and reported his suspicions to the police. The girl was released alive in a successful raid on the apartment after only two days of captivity. This degree of public co-operation could not be expected in a country where kidnap—and perhaps other lesser crimes—had become endemic and accepted, and where people had little regard for the police or authorities. The public is always interested, morbidly so, in kidnap cases, but the level of their practical support is a measure of the esteem in which they hold their police.

Do the German police deserve this support? What is their approach to kidnap in detail? The *Abstellungpräsident* explained that the country-wide policy is to give the first priority to the safe return of the victim. This is no boast of police humanity for propaganda reasons, but taken directly from the police manual, the *Polizeidienstvorschrift*, issue no. 131, which says that, where there is a conflict between catching offenders and the safety of the victim, the victim should have first priority. The police take the initial steps to help the family, start the investigation and guarantee the safety of the victim, while the eventual responsibility of catching the criminals belongs to the Public Prosecutor. The police are able to pursue their principle role of protecting the people; that is investigating and assisting the stricken family without, as is the case in Italy, being ordered by the magistrate to follow a course—for example refusing to allow payment —guaranteed to alienate the family. But, if the policies set the police in the right direction, what are the results in practice? Do they commit sufficient resources? If so, do they use them efficiently? The fact that most cases of kidnap in Germany are by individuals and not by organized crime networks suggests that experienced criminals look elsewhere to make a safer living. Police involvement at the end of Richard Oetker's case throws light on the police approach.

The Oetker family was exceptionally rich. They owned an enormous food and drink manufacturing empire and a shipping fleet. The head of the family, Richard August Oetker, was one of the richest industrialists in West Germany. His son, also Richard, then twenty-five years old, was kidnapped on 14 December 1976. The police were brought in from the start of the case and followed the brief negotiations that started a few hours after the kidnap with a telephone call to the victim's wife. The kidnappers demanded an enormous ransom reputed to be 21 million Deutschmarks (£5 million). The family agreed to the demand without negotiation. The gang thereupon called Oetker's brother and gave him orders that led him to various hotels in Munich, in the last of which he found a letter with drop instructions and a key. The gang ordered that the drop was to be made in a subway under the Munich *Hauptbahnhof* (main railway station). The letter explained that the key was to a safety deposit locker in the station where a suitcase would be found. The money had to be put in the suitcase and this should be placed next to a low iron door which was to be found in the wall in the middle of the subway.

The money was collected and crammed into the suitcase while the police deployed considerable numbers of surveillance officers and equipment inconspicuously around the station. At the appointed time, the man who had volunteered for the drop walked down the subway, sure in the knowledge that no one could escape; all the exits were covered. He placed the box near the small metal door and retired. Suddenly, the metal door swung open and hands pulled the suitcase inside a narrow service conduit. The door slammed shut again and the police were helpless; the door had no handle on the subway side and they had not covered the service tunnels that ran in a maze beneath the station. By the time the police had re-deployed in a rushed attempt to salvage the operation, the kidnappers had disappeared.

A few hours later the family was told to find Richard in a forest near Munich. He was alive but very badly hurt. The gang had kept their victim in a narrow wooden crate, one metre six centimetres (sixty-three inches) long in the back of a Volkswagen van. They had been worried lest he raise the alarm and had devised a novel technique to discourage Oetker from calling out for help. They connected electrical wire with crocodile clips to his hands and feet and incorporated a microphone in the circuit inside the wooden box. Whenever the microphone detected a noise inside the box the circuit delivered a powerful current through Richard Oetker's body. The spasms wrenched and jerked his limbs about, thrashing them against the wooden coffin in which he lay. The agony is impossible to imagine but it was exacerbated by the microphone switching on the current even when Oetker kept silent, in spite of his pain, because it was adjusted sensitively enough to pick up noises outside his box as well. Richard Oetker lived through forty-eight hours of this torture. When the police found him his legs had multiple fractures caused by the repeated spasms against the wooden box and his heart was permanently damaged.

The police investigation has so far only produced one offender, Dieter Zlof aged thirty-seven years, who was arrested on 30 January 1979 and brought to trial three years after the kidnapping. The wheels of justice turned slowly since Zlof denied the charges, and his trial took six months. However, the police found bank notes from the ransom payment in his possession and the court found him guilty. On 9 June 1980, Zlof was sentenced to fifteen years and ordered to repay 60,000 (about £14,000) Deutschmarks to Richard Oetker in token compensation.

Kidnappers, perhaps more than any other criminals, challenge the police to catch them. After a ransom is agreed the gang has to devise a novel way of snatching the money from under the very noses of the police who they must assume are covertly watching and waiting to catch them out. The Munich police, for all their commitment of surveillance, had in this case failed to consider the problem flexibly enough—lateral thinking one might say—and the money vanished down the tunnels beneath the station.

Something similar occurred in the case of another child of school age, Johannes Erlemann. Johannes was kidnapped on 6 March 1981 in Cologne and a ransom of 3 million Deutschmarks (£640,000) was agreed, though the victim's father was in prison for fraud at the time. The gang gave instructions that the money should be wrapped up and lowered through a manhole cover in the middle of a square. Accordingly the Cologne police organized their surveillance teams around the square and connecting streets in order to catch the gang later when they came to lift the money out of the sewer. Disguised agents loitered innocently about and watched as a member of the family let the money down on a length of rope through the manhole. Then they waited, until, when nothing more happened, they realized that they had been duped; the gang never planned to lift the ransom out of the manhole. The kidnappers had been quietly waiting under the manhole, sitting in a rubber dinghy, and when they took the money off the line, they paddled away along the sewers beneath the surveillance men on the streets above.

Doubtless, the kidnappers, who called themselves 'The Association of Poor Devils', must have enjoyed the police embarrassment, but their good humour did not last long. They were caught and the police found the kidnap had been a family affair. Ransom money was discovered in food tins in the Erlemann house and three brothers and a brother-in-law were found guilty. They received sentences of ten years, two of eight years and one of three years.

Most of the kidnaps in Germany are of short duration, as we have seen, and by individuals who are often quite inexperienced criminals and unaware of the difficulties involved. Is the high success rate of the police, which seems to put off the organized German criminal groups, due to the inexperience of the kidnappers themselves? How would the police cope against a gang which knew its business?

On 18 December 1981, eight-year-old Nina von Gallwitz was kidnapped, like Johannes Erlemann before her, on her way to school in a Cologne suburb. The kidnappers demanded a ransom of 1.5 million Deutschmarks (£320,000) from her father who was a banker. The parents were distraught about their daughter and, refusing to co-operate with the police whose handling of the case gave them considerable concern, they began negotiations that lasted over five months. It was Germany's longest case.

When the gang broke off communications with the Cologne police, von Gallwitz turned to a mediator, Franz Tartarotti, a TV journalist, for assistance. Tartarotti had been involved in negotiations for the release of three Germans who had been kidnapped in Tuscany, in 1980—two daughters and the nephew of another TV journalist, Dieter Kronzucker. That case had lasted sixty-eight days and all three had been released after a ransom of $2.3 million had been paid. Tartorotti succeeded in re-establishing contact with the von Gallwitz kidnappers but from that point von Gallwitz was loth to pass on much information to the authorities. The police, therefore, were not privy to many of the contacts between the gang and the family in Cologne, but they managed to decipher the communications code used by Tartarotti, and tried to keep in touch with the negotiation. After long months, the ransom was agreed—at the same figure as the original demand, 1.5 million Deutschmarks. Finally, the money was hurled out of the Dortmund to Basel express train on its route south of Bonn soon after midnight. Three earlier attempts to pay the money had failed, once by train and twice by helicopter, because the kidnappers did not turn up to collect as arranged. The victim was released unharmed. The kidnappers are still at large.

Tartarotti's role in the von Gallwitz case raises contentious issues. The German police do not rule out the usefulness of non-police negotiators. They put them in the same category as other advisers, such as psychiatrists, psychologists, and priests, whose advice is readily sought when circumstances demand. There are no objections to the family employing consultant negotiators, just as it does lawyers and accountants, should it wish to do so. The police leave the actual negotiating with the kidnappers to a member of the family or a family friend, except when the State is held to ransom, and provide background advice, like insisting that proof of life is demanded before payment. However, security consultants, especially those from firms who have links with kidnap insurance, may be treading on delicate ground since kidnap insurance is forbidden in Germany. There is no statute law against such insurance, usually underwritten by Lloyd's of London, but there exists a ruling by a supervisory board with Federal responsibility for commerce, the *Bundesaufsichtsamt für das Versicherungswesen*, that bans this particular insurance in Germany.

The BKA go further. The police view is that kidnap insurance commercializes the crime and that it is immoral to make money from kidnapping. This attitude echoes that of the Italian authorities, and the logic is hard to see. But, if insurance for theft of a man's property, his car for example, is allowed, then how much more reasonable is it to insure against the theft of himself, his wife and family? The difference is twofold. Firstly, kidnappers, unlike car thieves, steal and then demand you pay them value in exchange. Secondly, kidnapping, especially that of schoolchildren, is an emotional subject.

More reasonable, and within the bounds of its professional concern, is the BKA's argument that once a man is paying premiums for ransom insurance then he will take less care about his own security. The BKA is also afraid that, in the event of kidnap, the family will deal directly with those involved in paying the insured amount for the ransom and the police will be left out of it. There are even those in the BKA who suggest insurance encourages the idea of auto-kidnap (a person arranging his own kidnap) to avoid tax, or cash in on the money for which he pays premiums. In short, the police believe that insurance supports the crime of kidnap. This attitude is perhaps surprising in Germany, a country noted for logic, since it follows that all insurance, on houses, cars, luggage, jewellery and so on, encourages crime. Yet the thousands who claim for stolen possessions are presumably grateful for their insurance, and the police themselves would probably admit the impossibility of preventing all crime; only then would insurance become unnecessary.

In general, these arguments against insurance have provided, in some countries, a convenient scapegoat for an appalling record of the crime, and this highlights the unexpected German position. It is well-known that the level of insurance premiums depends on the level of risk that insuring underwriters are prepared to accept. In turn this becomes an independent measure of the capability of the police in a given area to control crime. For example, it is impossibly expensive to insure against theft of cars in Italy, and extortionate to insure against kidnapping in Guatemala; in these countries the car thieves and kidnappers are more powerful than the police. In Germany, there has been an average of only two classic kidnap-for-ransom cases per annum since 1958 (the year of the first case). The Germans, therefore, have little to excuse. Why they refuse to condone insurance remains a puzzle.

Another unusual feature of the German scene is that on two occasions kidnappers have made demands of local government. The first occurred on 17 October 1977, when Felix Wessel, only four years old, was kidnapped. The boy was released after one week when a ransom of 1 million Deutschmarks (about £220,000) was paid. Half the ransom was paid by the Hamburg city government. The police caught the gang of two—Hans-Juergen Wilsdorf was sentenced to ten years and Juergen Petersen to nine years—but they recovered only 20,000 Deutschmarks (about £4,500). It is interesting to note that the victim's uncle, Ulrich Wessel, had been murdered during the Rote Armee Faction's (R.A.F.) attack on the West German Embassy in Stockholm in 1975. Then, the Bonn Government had refused to deal with the terrorist R.A.F. or meet any of their demands, since it had discovered that by doing so earlier (releasing five convicted terrorists for the life of the kidnapped Major of Berlin, Peter Lorenz, in 1975) it had worsened the problems of political terrorism. It may be true that the duties of local government are different to those of central government, but the responsibilities are not entirely separate.

Sven Lehne, another schoolboy, was kidnapped in Munich, on 16 September 1982, and the gang demanded that the Munich city authorities pay the entire ransom of 1.8 million Deutschmarks (£425,000) or they would kill the boy. The ransom was agreed and the drop was arranged. Tragically, two policemen, who were trailing the car carrying the ransom money were killed when their surveillance helicopter crashed; they were on their way back to base when the drop was aborted after the kidnappers failed to show. Ironically, the boy turned up near the Austrian border unharmed and no ransom needed to be paid. As always the kidnap of children is emotive, and the readiness of local government to pay ransom demands in these circumstances is easily understood. But, while the central government has learned its lesson, local government still treads a dangerous path.

There have been other occasions when kidnappers have demanded money from government bodies. On 22 May 1979, two people were seized in Boblingen, near Stuttgart, and the kidnappers demanded 2 million Deutschmarks (£515,000) from the Federal government which was refused. In another case, a prison guard was kidnapped in Celle, on 21 May 1984, by a gang which demanded only 300,000 Deutschmarks (£79,000) from the state government of Lower Saxony. The ransom was paid but the police were on to the kidnappers who were arrested soon afterwards.

Though most kidnaps in Germany are non-political and purely for money, the kidnap that had the most impact on the minds of police and public alike was that of Hans Martin Schleyer in September 1977. Germans were familiar with the political demands made on central government by the Baader-Meinhof terrorists and the R.A.F., which seems now to be spawning a new generation of violence; but the face of Schleyer, their most famous victim, staring out of televised propaganda films of his captivity taken by his R.A.F. kidnappers, still haunts the BKA; they have never solved the case. The BKA admits that the investigation of the Schleyer kidnap was a flop.

The BKA were in overall command, as they always are in political cases and for those needing connections abroad through the Interpol bureau. The government, which had failed dismally in previous attempts to appease the R.A.F., were under considerable pressure to take a tough stand. Theirs was a black and white decision—rare in kidnap negotiations; capitulation by the State or by the terrorists were the only two options. The public were tired of seemingly endless terrorist violence, horrified by the calculated venom of the kidnap itself and deluged the police with information.

These kidnappers were thoroughly organized, and, unlike most, had been well trained, some in guerrilla camps in the Lebanon. They had kept Schleyer in their sights for at least a year, since November 1976 when his name was found on a hit list. Schleyer accepted three police bodyguards and an escort car to his own.

In the summer of 1977, at the memorial service for the chairman of the Dresdener Bank, Jurgen Ponto, who was shot dead in his home, Schleyer said, 'The next victim of terrorism is almost certainly standing in this room now.' On 5 September that same year, as his chauffeur turned off Friedrich Schmidt Strasse into a one-way circuit leading to Schleyer's home in a wealthy residential area of Cologne, the terrorists struck. His driver and all the police guards were shot dead, the gunmen firing hundreds of bullets, accurately and without compunction. Schleyer was bundled into a Volkswagen van and vanished. With extensive media coverage, the terrorists persisted in their demands for the release of colleagues, extending their deadlines twice, from 10 a.m. on 7 September to 12 a.m. on 9 September and to midnight on 12 September, until they realized the government would not co-operate. Then on 19 October, after the debacle at Mogadishu and the consequent suicides of Ennslin, Baader and Raspe in Stammheim prison, Schleyer's body was found stuffed in the boot of a car in Mulhouse, in France near the German border.

Among the mass of tip-offs to the police was information about strange activities in a block of flats in Cologne, on Wiener Weg 1, in apartment number 2065. By the time the police got around to processing that piece of information it was too late: the kidnappers had used the flat and gone.

The police now operate a very sophisticated computer in Wiesbaden, with terminals to all eleven Federal Landeskriminal (the equivalent of the British constabularies), to assist the collation and sorting of data during an investigation. The programme copes with descriptions of people, places, cars, fingerprint comparisons and so on. It helps the investigating team sift out information at various levels of relevance on particular sets of facts, or in making a search for particular sets of criteria. For example, checking the incidence of all of one type of car, or for all green trucks, or all references to an area which may be part of an address. The computer is not an end to the problems but it is a tool that mightily speeds the useful acquisition of facts.

Despite their occasional inflexibility on operations and moralizing about insurance, the police in Germany are formidable opponents for any kidnapper. They have the support of their government, which provides the funds for manpower and resources, for the Wiesbaden computer and for research, such as speech analysis in which the expensive search for a 'fingerprint' in the human voice continues. They have the support of the public and, in most cases, the confidence of individual families. In spite of popular belief arising from distorted impressions about the R.A.F. terrorists, there have been few kidnaps: from 1958 to the end of 1984 there were fifty-eight cases, or two a year. Most kidnappers have been individuals rather than organized criminal gangs. There is a strong strain of violence in these fifty-eight cases, sixty-one people were kidnapped and thirteen, or over twenty per cent, were killed. Some of the lucky ones survived horrifying treatment. For them it is of small comfort to know that investigations have solved eighty-six per cent of cases, and that ninety-five guilty men and women have been imprisoned.

EIGHT

The Basque Way of Business

Since 1970 kidnapping has been a regular and disturbing feature of Spanish life. There have been a number of abductions of a purely criminal nature, the most spectacular being that of Enrique Castro, known as 'Quini', one of the country's most famous and popular footballers, in 1981. However, the vast majority of the more than forty major kidnappings carried out in Spain over the past decade and a half have been carried out by terrorist groups, most of them by ETA, the separatist group fighting for an independent Basque homeland. Most of ETA's victims have been Basque businessmen and industrialists kidnapped for ransoms which have helped to finance ETA's war against the Spanish State. ETA has carried out its kidnaps efficiently and ruthlessly: five men whose families would not or could not come up with the ransom or other demands were murdered. But there has also been a string of kidnaps with political, rather than financial, objectives. The aims varied. They have included: the release of ETA prisoners; the extraction of political intelligence; propaganda; opposition to a nuclear power station; and the use of hostages as bargaining levers in industrial disputes.

ETA's first kidnap had a political motive. In 1970, they abducted the German Consul in Bilbao, Eugenio Beihl, to pressure the Franco Government over the trial of six ETA members in Burgos. He was soon released and the ETA terrorists' death sentence was commuted to life imprisonment, partly as a result. But kidnaps were relatively infrequent in the last years of the Franco regime. ETA was still building up its strength and the forces of law and order were oppressive but effective. In 1972, an industrialist, Lorenzo Zubala, was kidnapped and used as a bargaining counter in a labour dispute. In 1973, ETA planned to pull off the kidnapping of Franco's heir apparent, the Prime Minister Admiral Carrera Blanco. When his bodyguard was stepped up, they switched tactics and assassinated him instead, thus dealing a death blow to Franco's succession plans.

The floodgates opened after Franco's death in 1975 and the transition to democracy under the constitutional monarchy of King Juan Carlos. From 1976 the kidnappings came thick and fast, largely to finance ETA's rapid expansion but also for political purposes. Some of these posed a serious threat to the stability of the government of the day, as they were meant to. Assassinations and kidnappings of senior members of the Spanish Establishment were designed to provoke a backlash from the conservative-dominated armed forces, in which there were many elements only too keen to find excuses to seek a restoration of a right-wing dictatorship.

In 1976, during the difficult year after Franco's death, a shadowy left-wing terrorist outfit called GRAPO kidnapped two Establishment figures in an effort to destabilize the shakey government of the day. Antonio de Oriol y Urquijo, President of the Council of State, was kidnapped on 11 December 1976. While he was still being held, Lieutenant-General Emilio Villaescusa, the President of the Supreme Council of Military Justice, was abducted on 24 January 1977. Both were freed from different houses in Madrid during a police operation on 11 February.

In 1979, ETA had split into two factions (and was to continue dividing into offshoots of offshoots). They were ETA-militar (ETA-m, or the 'Milis'), and ETA-politico-militar (ETA-pm, or the 'Polis-milis'). The first was regarded as more hard-line and intransigent than the second which, as its name implies, was more inclined to take political considerations into account in the search for its objectives; although still a ruthless terrorist organization, it was willing to declare truces. One of these led eventually to half its members abandoning the armed struggle and returning to normal life in Spain while the other half resumed the violent way under the name ETA-pm-Eighth Assembly, commonly known therefore as the 'Octavos'. It carried out many kidnappings, as did yet another offshoot, the CAA—the Autonomous Anti-capitalist Commandos.

In 1979, ETA-pm reached into the top drawer of the political chest and kidnapped Javier Rupérez, a deputy in the *Cortes* (parliament) and a rising young star in the ruling party, the Union of the Democratic Centre. He was held for thirty-one days after being surprised in his Madrid flat and subjected to a steady interrogation which included Spanish foreign policy, particularly in the Sahara, and the private lives of his colleagues. Rupérez is a reserved and analytical man whose smooth but detached air may have been crucial to his survival. One tangible relic of his ordeal is that he took up smoking again, having successfully given up for several years before his kidnap. He even managed to survive the first few days of his capture without resuming the habit, a tribute to his self-control. He broke when his captors lost their tempers, shouted at him that his colleagues had abandoned and betrayed him and had therefore condemned him to death: at that he finally asked for a cigarette—and survived to be freed and tell the tale.

José María Ryan was not so lucky. He was the chief engineer at the controversial Lémoniz nuclear power station near Bilbao to which ETA was implacably opposed, and which it attacked and sabotaged many times. Ryan (whose name came from Irish ancestors) was a thirty-nine-year-old father of five, a modest and popular man. He was kidnapped in January 1981 by ETA-m who demanded nothing less than the demolition of Lémoniz, to be started immediately. A massive demonstration was held in his support in Bilbao and pleas for his life came from all over Europe. But the Spanish government stood firm and Ryan was murdered. The killing aroused intense disgust throughout the Basque country, Spain and Europe, and provoked a backlash against ETA.

A month after Ryan's death came the kidnap of the Barcelona footballer 'Quini'. Although it was a purely criminal affair and did not involve ETA, it gripped the Spanish public's attention for twenty-five days. Quini was a popular figure with the football public, a prolific goal-scorer for Barcelona and Spain and one of those figures with whom the sporting aficionado can identify. His kidnap on 2 March, from outside his apartment in Barcelona, came as a particular shock. For the football-crazy public of Barcelona it was a tragedy.

Although there was no trace of him for twenty-five days, it turned out in the end that his captors were a pretty inept bunch. One reason it took so long to find them was that they had no criminal record, but when they moved to pick up the ransom their naivety was very apparent.

The kidnap was planned and carried out by three unemployed electricians from Zaragoza who were desperate for money. They had no interest in football but picked on Quini because of his fame and obvious wealth. They drove to Barcelona and carried out a reconnaissance of Quini's flat at the end of January. They returned on 2 March and lay outside, reckoning he would emerge to go out for the evening. When he did they brandished a pistol at him as he got into his car and ordered him to drive to their van, parked a hundred yards away. They pushed him into the back, tied his hands and forced him into a wooden crate. They then drove him to Zaragoza and took him to a cellar beneath a workshop belonging to two of them where they kept him for the duration of his captivity.

The man who had thought up the kidnap, Martin Pellejero, went back to Barcelona over the next few days to telephone the footballer's wife from various public call boxes, telling her and then a family friend, acting as intermediary, that the ransom was to be 100 million pesetas (£500,000). He then made a big—and elementary—mistake. He said he would give them the number of a bank account in Geneva to which the money was to be transferred. He took a train to Geneva on 22 March, opened an account at Credit Suisse, and telephoned the family with the number. On 24 March, Nicolau Casaus, vice president of Barcelona Football Club, arrived in Geneva and deposited the full ransom demand of 100 million pesetas in the account. The next day Pellejero turned up and asked if the money had arrived. He withdrew a million pesetas, bought a plane ticket to Paris and returned to his hotel. A few minutes later he was arrested there. Casaus had been followed to Geneva, unknown to him, by the Spanish police and the Swiss had co-operated fully. Pellejero swiftly revealed where Quini was being held. That evening as Quini was trying to watch the grainy television picture of the Spain v. England football match at Wembley in which he should have been playing, the door of his prison burst open and a young armed man charged in, shouting at him and the one kidnapper who was guarding him not to move or he would shoot. Quini said, 'I thought my end had come'. It turned out to be the police, although the football star took some convincing of it.

He said afterwards that all he had to eat each day was two rolls and a yoghurt. He had had no idea where he was being held. Although his kidnappers later claimed they had frequently thought of freeing him,

Quini himself said he had feared he would die in their hands and had made a conscious effort to forget about his family's existence. He said he had even thought of trying to commit suicide. He turned out to be in good shape, though he had lost weight, and was back in training the day after his release.

By the time of the trio's trial ten months later Quini had mellowed and appeared to have developed something of the 'Stockholm syndrome'. When called to give evidence he said he forgave his kidnappers and wished them well. The Judges were less forgiving and sentenced all three to ten years' imprisonment, dismissing a defence submission that the kidnap had been less damaging than one performed by ETA, and adding that kidnapping was a crime that deprived the victim of his right which was almost as valuable as life itself. The other big loser was Barcelona F.C., Spain's wealthiest club, which claimed 25 million pesetas (£125,000) in compensation from the penniless kidnappers and also accused them of depriving it of winning the League Championship. The club got short shrift from the court.

One man's kidnap ordeal had started before José María Ryan's and ended after Quini's. He was Luis Suñer, a seventy-one-year-old magnate from Valencia who had made such a fortune from the poultry trade that he was known as 'the King of the chicken'. His wealth came to the attention of ETA-pm two years previously when it was revealed that he had made the largest single tax declaration in Spain. The only reward for this display of good citizenship was to be kidnapped on 13 January and held for three months. It was, and remains, Spain's longest kidnap and Suñer's freedom was only obtained with the payment of a ransom of 325 million pesetas (£1.6 million). On release, the old gentleman declared he was going to take it easier in future and dedicate less time to work.

At the end of 1981 came another headline-grabbing kidnap. The victim could hardly have been more sensational for the Press: Dr Julio Iglesias, father of singer Julio Iglesias, Spain's number one idol who had gone on to become one of the world's leading entertainers. Based in Miami, he was worth a fortune. The kidnap was the work of ETA-pm and with it they broke a ten-month truce. To kidnap Dr Iglesias they had gone further afield than usual, to Barcelona. Posing as German television journalists, they set up an 'interview' with Dr Iglesias and having gained access to his apartment seized him and took him away.

Dr Iglesias was taken to a hide-out in the remote village of Trasmoz, in the province of Zaragoza. The kidnappers concealed their presence there well. The house had been bought two-and-a-half years previously by an elderly couple. They were the only people associated with the house who were known to the villagers. All other visitors from ETA arrived at night hidden in the owners' car boot. The pretence was so effective that other villagers were entertained in the house while Dr Iglesias was held captive on the floor above.

However, as with the case of Quini, the kidnapping was to be a success for the Spanish authorities. A ransom of 10 million pesetas (£50,000) was demanded in a letter delivered to an office of CBS, Julio Iglesias's recording company, in Lebanon, giving an idea of the far-ranging links of ETA-pm. The ransom demand was well within the singer's resources but the family co-operated with the police from the start. Their first break came with the arrest of one of the gang in the Basque village of Axpe, as he tried to deliver a letter, dictated by Dr Iglesias. From him the police extracted Dr Iglesias's whereabouts and a detailed lay-out of the house. A massive operation was launched after a crisis meeting in which the Spanish Cabinet was brought up-to-date with the situation. The police, operating in the early hours of the morning, when the village was asleep, discovered the exact house in Trasmoz. A control centre was set up six miles away in a Civil Guard barracks with a direct line to the Ministry of the Interior in Madrid. The Cabinet authorized an assault: they reckoned they had the element of surprise and they emphatically did not want to get into a siege and hostage situation, the outcome of which would be impossible to predict, particularly as ETA-pm could be expected to complicate the case with political demands, and would, unlike ordinary criminals, have their political 'face' at stake.

All telephone links to the village were cut and before dawn the thirty-strong assault unit attacked, blowing in the front door with 1,500 grams of explosive and hurling in stun grenades. It was a complete success. The kidnapper nearest Dr Iglesias barely managed to reach his machine gun before he was overpowered. Four of the gang were in the house and all were arrested. Another was arrested later, making a total of six in all who received prison sentences ranging from eighteen months to eight years. It was a spectacular success for the authorities, especially as no ransom was paid, but it was somewhat tarnished by Dr Iglesias behaving rather like Quini at the trial of his captors, claiming he could not recognize any of them (and instantly contradicting himself in the case of one, Gloria Gutierrez, whom he fulsomely described as an 'adorable girl').

ETA's ability to strike at the top echelons of Spanish society was perhaps most graphically illustrated on 25 March 1983, when ETA-militar kidnapped Diego Prado y Colon de Carvajal, former president of the Banco de Descuento, a bank which had collapsed. More importantly, his brother Manuel, a former president of the State airline Iberia, was one of King Juan Carlos's closest advisers. Diego Prado was seized as he stepped out of his car in the garage beneath his house in an elegant Madrid street. He was anaesthetized, bundled into the boot of his own car and driven away. ETA appears to have miscalculated Diego Prado's wealth: they appear to have assumed that he had salted some of the money of the collapsed bank; in fact he was a ruined man and his brother, though quite wealthy and well-connected, was not one of the country's super-rich.

Nevertheless, as ETA declared the next day in a communiqué, he was a member of the Spanish oligarchy, and, as such, fair game. Within three days an emissary of the family was meeting ETA leaders over the border in Saint Jean de Luz to try to persuade them that they had vastly overestimated the family fortunes. It was useless: the ransom demanded was 1,200 million pesetas (£6 million), the biggest ever in Spain, and the message to the Prado family was: 'You have good connections. Find the money.' But it was not to be plain sailing for ETA. The Socialist government, and particularly the Minister of the Interior, José Barrionuevo, made it clear that they opposed any payment at all to ETA and announced they would do all they could to block one.

Ten days after Diego Prado's disappearance, the police began massive 'sweep' operations in several areas of Madrid in the hunt for the kidnappers' hide-out, presumed to be in the capital. The first day drew a blank but on 6 and 7 April an exhaustive search of the Pilar quarter, with 75,000 residents, turned up an ETA suspect, Pilar Nieva Fernández. The day after, the police got their breakthrough, with the discovery of no less than five ETA safe houses in Madrid and three more suspects, one of whom was linked to the Prado kidnap by a fingerprint. But, of the safe house where the former financier was being held there was no sign. However, the police operation had the effect of interrupting the kidnap commando's communications with their leaders in France. A long silence ensued with Prado's family growing increasingly concerned about his wellbeing. Although rumours about fresh ransom demands and negotiations surfaced occasionally in the Basque and Madrid Press, they were routinely denied by the family and it was not until 1 May that they received proof that Diego was still alive with the publication of four photographs and a letter to the pro-ETA Bilbao newspaper *Egin*.

The Spanish government was putting increasing pressure on the French to investigate the exile community in the South of France for possible leads to Prado's whereabouts, but they came up with nothing. Throughout May the family became more and more despondent. Manuel had managed to collect about 125 million (£625,000), far short of a figure likely to satisfy ETA. But ETA appeared to be feeling the heat from the authorities in both Spain and France. When the negotiations did get going again it was via the bizarre method of two priests: one acting for the family and one for the terrorists, but both bound by the secrecy of the confessional. Meanwhile Manuel was raising money by selling the family's sumptuous Madrid apartment. The demand was reduced to 150 million pesetas (£750,000) and the money handed over in France. Just after midnight on 6 June, Diego Prado, bearded, emaciated and heavily drugged with tranquillizers, was dumped on a road near Madrid and found by, ironically, an employee of Iberia, the airline once headed by the man who had collected the money for his release.

Diego Prado's captivity had lasted seventy-four days, Spain's second longest after that of Luis Suñer. During it he was endlessly interrogated, his captors displaying a particular interest in the Spanish royal family, although his brother could have told them far more. He had been held in a tiny room from which he had not once been moved. As the police suspected all along, the hideaway had been in Madrid, but was never discovered despite all the police's efforts (showing up, not for the first time, the doubtful worth of police 'sweep' operations). For all the pressure on ETA, kidnapping was still a proven way of raising large funds.

* * * *

Juan Felix Eriz is a stocky, dark-haired man with a square head and firm jaw who bears more than a passing resemblance to the late Jack Hawkins. Indeed, certain aspects of his life would have provided Hawkins with a worthy film script. He has the air of a man who has lived life to the full: although only in his early forties, he looks considerably older. The fingers of his left hand are missing, blown off by a faulty rifle that exploded when he was out shooting in the winter of 1982/3. He was born and bred in Spain's Basque country; he lives in the little village of Elorrio, north-east of Bilbao. The only interruption to his residence in the land to which he is devoted came in the last years of the reign of General Franco, when Eriz, a fervent opponent of the old General, was forced to spend some time in exile in southern France. Yet he is not an orthodox Basque nationalist. For most of his life he had been a Carlist, a follower of the descendants of Don Carlos of Borbon, who claim the throne of Spain. It was a claim that Franco ignored; he preferred the rather more substantial merits of Juan Carlos de Borbon as his heir when the monarchy was restored after his death. Eriz was twice imprisoned—in 1973 and 1975—for his anti-Franco activities. He was on the most radical, left-wing fringe of the Carlist party and in the late 1960s and early 1970s his political activities brought him into contact with many Basque nationalists living in exile in the South of France. These contacts were to come in very useful later. Eriz makes his living as a representative for several Basque iron and steel manufacturing companies. He is also the most celebrated kidnap negotiator in the Basque country.

There are many reasons why ETA has managed to operate so successfully for so long: a residue of sympathy among the Basque people for their aims, their own daring and courage, the frequent incompetence of the authorities, and the occasional brutality of the police and Civil Guard towards prisoners, which often served to turn the populace against them instead of against the terrorists. Their greatest advantage was that for many years they could operate more or less freely from their bases in southern France, living relatively open lives there, and going over the border clandestinely to carry out attacks, often on the Civil Guard and police: bombings, kidnappings and the other highly effective method of fund-raising which they had dreamed up—the 'revolutionary tax' as they termed it. Others simply call it extortion. It consists of demanding large sums from wealthy and prominent Basque individuals and businesses on pain of violent retribution if payment is not forthcoming. You might call it kidnapping without abduction. It is generally demanded in the form of a letter specifying the amount to be paid—and the services of a negotiator are frequently required to arrange payment by those who prefer the quiet life.

Just how much has been raised by ETA's various offshoots will never be known. Many brave people have refused to pay and occasionally suffered the consequences. Certainly, many of the best-known names in the Basque business community, including the big banks, arguing they could not afford to put their employees at risk, have capitulated to the extortion and have subsidized ETA over the years while publicly condemning its activities. Juan Felix Eriz says he has been involved in negotiating the payment of more than forty extortion demands for the 'revolutionary tax'; and he has also saved more than one potential victim from paying anything at all by spotting that the 'tax' demand was a patent forgery.

Eriz's first involvement came about by an accident of geography: José Luis Arrasate, the son of a neighbour from Elorrio, an industrialist, was kidnapped by ETA-pm in February 1976. Eriz offered whatever help he could and also decided there and then that he would try to organize José Luis's safe return. It took him a week to get in touch with the 'Polis-milis', but he found them. They wanted a 100 million pesetas ransom (£500,000). Eriz devized his own negotiating strategy as he went along but he had several factors in his favour: as a native Basque speaker and well-known local figure, he was trusted to some extent by the kidnappers; his anti-Franco views also stood him in good stead. As a successful businessman he understood all about negotiating—when to be tough and when to concede—and, coupled with his wide experience of life, could apply cool objectivity in his reading of the situation facing the victimized family. His tactics were successful over Arrasate: the young man was released for a ransom which Eriz had negotiated down to 30 million pesetas (£150,000). After that he was in frequent demand as a negotiator over kidnaps and 'revolutionary tax' demands. He has built up tremendous experience: up to 1985, he has acted as intermediary in five kidnaps and more than forty extortions.

He also acted as a go-between in 1977 and 1978 when the Spanish government of the day embarked on secret negotiations with ETA with the aim of engineering a peaceful solution to the Basque problem. The talks came to nothing and shortly afterwards both Eriz's fellow emissaries, a Basque journalist, and the ETA leader most responsive to the government's overtures, were murdered in mysterious circumstances, underlining the dangers inherent in dealing in the murky world inhabited by ETA.

In October 1980, Eriz found himself in the role of negotiator for the second time. For this, and all subsequent kidnaps in which he was involved, the initiative came from the family who invited Eriz to help secure the victim's release. This case was that of an industrialist from Bermea, in the Basque country, José Garavilla, who was a victim of ETA-m. Eriz managed to beat them down again from 100 million pesetas (£500,000) to 30 million (£150,000) and obtained Garavilla's release.

In January 1982, he was called in to help free a German-born industrialist from Bilbao, José Lipperheide, aged seventy-six, who was kidnapped by ETA-m for refusing to pay the 'revolutionary tax'. He was taken from his house, indeed from his bedroom where he was dressing, on the morning of 5 January. He was driven off in his chauffeur's car, transferred to a van and driven for between an hour and an hour and a half to the house where he was to spend the next thirty days. He was put in a small room about nine square feet in size with a wooden staircase leading up to a tiny space where he and his captors slept. He was treated coldly but correctly by his kidnappers, who talked little. They gave him newspapers to read, particularly *Egin*, the paper most closely identified with the independence movement.

'The hardest thing about the thirty days of my kidnap,' he recalled later, 'was the silence and the boredom.'

His family, naturally, did not know where to turn for help. For the first week they attempted to contact the kidnappers via a religious intermediary—priests, as we have seen in the case of Diego Prado, are often used as go-betweens because of the trust they enjoy—but without success. It was then that they turned to Eriz.

ETA-m had made known their first demand; an astronomical 800 million pesetas (£4 million). Arming themselves with bank statements showing the family's economic situation, Eriz and a member of the family met the kidnappers in the village of Iparralde, and made a counter-offer of 40 million (£200,000). The kidnappers, perhaps somewhat predictably, declared that sort of figure was not worth even talking about. There was a five-day delay after which ETA-m dropped their demand to 200 million (£1 million) and the family increased theirs to 80 million (£400,000). But this was still nowhere near acceptable to the gang. Some of the gang wanted to give the family only twelve more hours to come up with a further 120 million but the intermediaries managed to persuade them to extend that to seventy-two hours. The family, desperate to get the victim back, but faced with a tough deadline, reckoned they could raise 100 million and decided to sell their luxurious chalet, valued at 60 million, to raise

most of the balance. They put it on the market but, before it could be
sold, a group of friends came up with 50 million to make a total of 150
million (£750,000). The kidnappers accepted it. The money was
handed over in three stages (which is unusual in other countries and
suggests a powerful disregard of the law enforcement agencies) and,
at 10.20 p.m. on Friday 5 February, Lipperheide was set free on the
outskirts of Bilbao.

He had been guarded throughout his captivity by four men who
always wore Balaclavas to hide their faces. On the rare occasions they
had spoken it had been to question him about the Basque economy,
about which Lipperheide had replied that he was pessimistic.

His day had run like this. He would get up at about 11 a.m.; for
breakfast he would have a glass of milk and at about 1 p.m., a simple
lunch. There had never been wine for him or for his captors. At 3.30
he would shave, and at 9 p.m. would have supper. They had given
him less to eat and drink than they had had themselves so that he
would not have to use the lavatory often—it had been in the same
small room, ineffectually screened by a curtain and thoroughly
unpleasant. Lipperheide lost nine kilos (19.8 lbs) in his month of
captivity but made a good recovery—a tribute to his fitness and
mental toughness. He bore his ordeal philosophically. In an interview
a year afterwards he reflected on his capture:

> When I saw there was no alternative, that they were armed,
> that they had prepared it right down to the smallest detail,
> then I thought it was better that they should have captured me
> rather than one of my sons or grandsons. I am pretty old, I
> was about to be seventy-six and I don't have much life ahead
> of me. For a young man it might have been the end of the
> world but not for me. I thought: 'Well, I'm not going to live
> many more years so if they kill me, which was what I
> anticipated, then nothing much is lost,' because I have friends
> who are seriously ill, who have cancer, who are going to die in
> three weeks and they know it. That was the basis of my
> resignation, telling myself that one day it happens to us all,
> some day we have to die.

His remarks bring to mind the way in which Cesare Pagani—a young
man—reflected on his own mortality during his kidnapping. He said,
'The next worse thing that can happen to me now is that I die.'

Lipperheide, then a widower, actually had plenty of life left in him. In May 1984, he married a widow of forty-eight.

Eriz's next case was something of a curiosity: the kidnapping of a Bilbao dentist, Dr Luis Manuel Allende, who was held in a country shack for a week and released on payment of a 12 million pesetas (£60,000) ransom. The abduction appears to have been the work of the breakaway offshoot of ETA-pm, the 'Octavos', who took a harder line than ETA-pm. Although president of the dentists' association of Viscaya, one of the regions of Euskadi (the Basque name for their homeland), Allende was not a wealthy man—a fact which his kidnappers obviously realized: they demanded the relatively low sum of 25 million pesetas (£125,000) and settled for about half within a week, thanks to Eriz's persuasive powers. He was able to persuade them that the capture of Dr Allende was a mistake, that he was a popular man in the community and that to do him any harm or prolong the kidnap would be counter-productive for ETA and lose them support among the people. Such political arguments would be unlikely to wash with ordinary criminal kidnappers.

But this was a rare case of ETA taking a soft line. On several occasions they have not hesitated to carry out the ultimate threat to kill the kidnap victim. Some have been murdered because sufficient ransom money was not forthcoming quickly enough, as in the case of the businessman Angel Berazadi, kidnapped in March 1976 and found dead the following month. Others were killed for political motives, like José María Ryan.

ETA's brutal, intransigent side was to be amply demonstrated in Eriz's fifth case. It was to be his most dramatic case and teetered on the brink of tragedy. The victim was another industrialist, Saturnino Orbegozo, aged sixty-nine, and once again it was the Eighth Assembly of the ETA-pm which was responsible. They struck on 14 November 1982 as Orbegozo was leaving Sunday morning Mass in the town of Zumarraga in Guipúzcoa. He intended to drive to his steel lamination factory but instead was grabbed by two young men who hustled him into his own blue Mercedes and drove him off. Three quarters of an hour later he was switched to a Renault 5 at a rendezvous with the other two terrorists who made up the ETA-pm commando which had planned and executed the operation, one of them a twenty-two-year-old woman, Elena Barcena, nicknamed *La Tigresa*—The Tigress. Orbegozo was driven to a remote shepherd's cottage rented by the group near Donomaria in the neighbouring province of Navarre. For a week he was kept in a pit within the cottage, barely able to move and only taken out when, in the winter weather, it became too damp and cold for the elderly hostage.

For that week his family heard nothing from the kidnappers. Then the telephone rang in Juan Felix Eriz's house, while he was watching television. He was in great pain, having just suffered the shooting accident which had cost him the four fingers of his left hand; it was heavily bandaged. The callers were the Octavos, asking him to act as intermediary with the Orbegozo family. The family was only too pleased to hear from Eriz that the kidnappers wanted to do business: their own efforts to contact the gang responsible had failed miserably.

The telephone callers had fixed a first contact—in a square in Nice, over the border in the South of France. It was to be the start of an exhausting series of meetings in half the great cities of Europe. Eriz was instructed to display three large cigars sticking out of his breast pocket and to carry a copy of the Madrid newspaper *El Pais*: melodramatic stuff, but he complied. Ten minutes after he had arrived in the square at the appointed time, he was approached by a young man and a young blonde woman, both elegantly dressed. Their price for the release of Orbegozo was a cool 600 million pesetas (£3 million).

Eriz had learned for himself the elementary rules of the early stages of a negotiation. He demanded proof that Orbegozo was alive and that these were genuinely his kidnappers. A few days later, the Bilbao newspaper *Deia*, which is identified with the ruling middle-of-the-road Basque Nationalist Party, received a letter written by Orbegozo, his identity card and a photograph of the victim holding a recent magazine.

The next meeting was fixed for 5 December in Milan. But, the previous day, reports about Eriz appeared in two newspapers: *Egin*, which is associated with Heri Batasuna, ETA's political wing and openly allowed to operate in Euskadi (rather as Sinn Fein represents the Provisional I.R.A. openly in Ireland); and the Madrid newspaper *5 Dias*. The articles revealed that he was acting as intermediary in the Orbegozo case and *5 Dias* went further: it accused Eriz of pocketing 7 million pesetas (£35,000) from the Lipperheide case. (Eriz, enraged by the charge, sued for libel. He says he has never made a penny out of his involvement with any kidnap, claiming only legitimate expenses.) Not surprisingly, nobody from the Octavos turned up at the rendezvous in Milan, although Eriz made it. He returned home to Euskadi after his wasted journey, worried that the contact had been broken for good, now that his identity had been blown.

But, on 8 December, the telephone at his home rang again. It was the kidnapper called Joaquin. He arranged a third meeting for two days hence, this time in a square in Vienna. On 10 October, Eriz met the two from the Octavos in the Austrian capital. He explained that the family could not pay anything like 600 million, indeed the Orbegozo steel businesses were doing badly. The family wanted an accountant to be present at meetings to show the kidnappers that the sort of money being demanded was simply not available. The kidnappers refused (a gang generally could not care less about a family's financial problems; they just want the money and how the family gets it is their business) but they made a significant concession. They asked how much the family *could* afford. They would not accept less than 200 million (£1 million) and a deal had to be agreed by 22 December. (Saying 'we will not accept less than 200 million' would elsewhere, in Italy for example, be considered as a tacit reduction in the gang's demand to 200 million: effectively the kidnappers are admitting that their expectations of ransom are equal to 200 million or lower still.) But they kept up the pressure with a frightening deadline: the old gentleman would be 'executed' on Christmas Eve.

'He will be the Berazadi of 1982,' said one of the kidnappers to Eriz, in a chilling reference to the ETA hostage murdered in 1976.

The kidnappers may have brought their price down because their victim seemed in poor health. He celebrated—if that is the right description—his seventieth birthday in the Navarre hideaway and his captors opened a bottle of champagne for the occasion. By this time he had suffered two severe bronchial attacks and there was a strong possibility of a fatal heart attack being brought on by the poor conditions in which he was being kept—a cold cottage in the middle of winter, with rain leaking in from several points in the roof.

For the next meeting, on 16 December, the ETA-pm commando chose a fourth European city, this time Amsterdam, where Joaquin again showed up as arranged. Eriz had an offer by now: 80 million pesetas (£400,000) in two instalments—40 million immediately and the same again within two years (this delayed payment is an unthinkable concept with non-political kidnappers and presumably justified here as a sort of 'revolutionary tax'). The ETA reply did not come at once during Eriz's meeting with Joaquin. The terrorist took it back to his colleagues, but three days later, on 19 December, Eriz received their curt response. They wanted 250 million (£1.25 million) or the family would never see the victim again.

On 22 December, the day before the deadline they had laid down, ETA called Eriz to say their captive would be killed on Christmas Eve. The next day, ETA-pm released a communiqué announcing that negotiations had broken down, which was assessed as a last warning to the Orbegozo family. For them and for Eriz (and for the victim), it was a miserable Christmas. Eriz was still nursing the injuries to his hand and was taking Valium to calm the nerves badly frayed from the strange journeys and secret rendezvous with the terrorists. He called those days of waiting for word from the gang 'a torture which would be difficult to describe'.

There was a silence until 28 December, broken only by another communiqué from the kidnappers in which they accused the Orbegozos of contributing money to a secret 'anti-Basque' fund and of belonging to a 'reactionary and gangsterish' business. This was taken to be the final—and therefore real—threat of death to Saturnino Orbegozo, with the message designed to set public opinion against the old man in preparation for his murder.

It stimulated his distraught family to a last effort to collect more money. By selling cars (surely the last step to raise cash), mortgaging properties, and other means they raised a further 60 million (£300,000). On 29 December, their latest offer was put to the kidnappers via the pages of *Deia*: a total of 120 million pesetas (£600,000) was offered, made up of 60 million immediately, 20 million within 90 days, another 20 million by the end of the following year (1983), and the last 20 million in 1984. Not surprisingly, perhaps, ETA-pm swiftly turned down this complicated offer as an 'insult' and announced that Saturnino Orbegozo's 'execution' would be carried out forthwith.

It seemed like the end. Indeed, the end was closer than anyone expected. As the already massive police hunt intensified, the next morning, Thursday 30 December, the Civil Guard post at the little town of Santesteban received an anonymous tip-off: some odd looking people had been seen at weekends in the village of Donomaria. A group of six guards set off at once to check out the area.

As they approached a stone building on the slopes of Mount Otabro, they noticed the remains of food outside, though the door was shut. One of the patrol was sent back to the village five hundred metres away to fetch the keys from the owner. That done, the rest moved closer to the simple bothy, and, as they advanced, three figures emerged—the first, a white-bearded old man, followed by two young men with their hands on their heads. It was Saturnino Orbegozo and the two ETA-pm guards who had been with him for forty-six days. They were identified as Gregorio Manso, aged twenty-three, who had been arrested in France in 1979 for illegal possession of firearms, and Joseba Iñaki Odriozola, a twenty-one-year-old student. They had walked out of the hut in fear of their lives: all their revolutionary bravado evaporated before the reputation of the Civil Guard for shooting first and asking questions later.

Saturnino Orbegozo appears to owe his life, ironically, to the other branch of ETA: ETA-militar. On 29 December they shot dead two Civil Guards in San Sebastian. It is thought that ETA-pm postponed Orbegozo's murder because they were afraid of the bad publicity that three deaths would create. The public would not differentiate between the different terrorist groupings; it was all the work of ETA to them. But there is also a theory, from some of those close to the kidnap, that the man ETA designated to perform the killing could not bring himself to do it having seen and admired Orbegozo's bearing during the last tense days.

'My children won't pay any more,' Orbegozo is reported to have said. 'You will have to kill me.'

Also, who was it who tipped off the Civil Guard? They claimed it was a neighbour who, naturally, wished to remain anonymous for fear of reprisals. But to many it seemed an odd coincidence that the call should have been made just in time to save Orbegozo's life.

For Eriz the case was not yet over. As the authorities exulted over Orbegozo's providential release, Eriz himself was arrested and detained in custody on a charge of alleged collaboration with armed gangs, while a public debate raged about whether intermediaries should be allowed to negotiate the release of kidnap victims and whether ransoms should be paid at all. The government announced it would prosecute intermediaries and change the law to make it an offence to pay ransoms or the 'revolutionary tax'. These proposals were met with scepticism by former kidnap victims and Eriz, undaunted, declared that he would continue to act as an intermediary if requested. He was released by a judge on 3 January 1983 and all charges were dropped. Kidnaps—and ransoms—have continued.

'As long as there are kidnaps, there will be intermediaries,' said Eriz after his release, a sentiment he repeated when interviewed for this book.

Orbegozo's kidnappers were sentenced to varying terms of imprisonment when their cases finally came to court. Gregorio Manso received fourteen years two months, and Joseba Iñaki Odriozola got six years two months. A third member of the gang, José Antonio Ostolaza, was captured later and received four years two months.

To some extent the government's frustration at intermediaries was understandable. For a long time there had been suspicion in the Basque country that some negotiators were in the business for their own benefit and did it for a percentage of the ransom—the same accusation that was levelled at British negotiators working in Italy. In the Basque country this suspicion may have had some basis. But there were still people, like Eriz, who did it for humanitarian reasons, fulfilling a need the authorities could not.

Eriz's experiences have given him a wealth of insight into the operating methods of the different branches of ETA. The 'Milis' tended to stick to the Basque country for their operations with only two or three commando groups elsewhere. Their capture methods were crude: they would just march into their target's home and drag him off. They were tough negotiators but they would agree a deal quicker and would be open to political influence. If they could be persuaded that harming the victim or demanding too high a ransom would be counter-productive in political terms, they would respond and let him go for what his family could genuinely afford (the Octavos of the ETA-pm uncharacteristically did the same with Dr Allende). They also guaranteed that no other members of the same family or business would be touched again by them in future. Paying once thereby rated as a life-payment kidnap insurance premium.

According to Eriz, ETA-pm would seize their target after a more sophisticated approach, perhaps involving a commando of up to eight people, perhaps lying in wait for their victim at his home or office. ETA-pm were more widely spread throughout Spain although, as a result, they were also more infiltrated by informers. It was they who kidnapped Dr Iglesias from Barcelona and Javier Rupérez from Madrid. Their negotiating strategy was more advanced than that of ETA-m. They might play on the family's nerves with such devices as false telephone calls and emotional letters from the victim. But both branches of ETA interrogated their captives about the real state of the family fortunes and used the information they gathered in the kidnap negotiations. Lipperheide, for instance, took an active part in the negotiations to secure his own release from an early stage in the proceedings.

The importance of picking the right target cannot be underestimated. According to Eriz, if the son of a wealthy family was kidnapped a ransom would always be found; but there were cases where families had been reluctant to pay to retrieve an unloved parent. Conversely, the terrorists frequently went for a target whom their intelligence network had picked as unpopular in his local community and who would not be greatly mourned if he failed to return alive from his kidnap. Brutal thoughts, but Basque kidnappers—like others elsewhere—are a hard and realistic people.

What of Eriz's home-grown strategy? He always sought proof of life; picked members of the family for the negotiating committee who looked as though they might be calm in a crisis; urged the family to start collecting the necessary money immediately in order to lessen the damage that could be caused by the investigating magistrate freezing their bank accounts and also to have cash in hand in case of a quick deal being struck with the gang.

Where the Basque experience differs so vastly from other kidnaps in Europe, in Italy for example, is in the actual conduct of the negotiators. Because of the French government's policy in the 1970s and early 1980s of offering sanctuary to Spanish Basque exiles provided they did not commit crimes on French soil, ETA's leaders and members were able to live more or less openly in the South of France, chiefly in and around Bayonne, and plan their terrorism in Spain safe from the Spanish authorities. When targets, whether human or material, were fixed, commandos would slip across the border by a variety of means, mainly by the bewildering number of obscure mountain passes which cross the Pyrénées, but also by roads and round the coast by boat at night. Their operations complete, they could then retire back to their French bases and enjoy virtual immunity from Spain. (For years, the I.R.A. have enjoyed similar safe houses across the border in Eire from which they launch attacks as it suits them. Their addresses, and whether the terrorists are 'at home', in Eire are often well-known to the Royal Ulster Constabulary who remain helpless onlookers.) There were odd outbreaks in the 1970s of counter-attacks on ETA members by far-right groups operating from Spain, probably with tacit blessing of the Spanish government and even, perhaps, material aid. But it was not until 1984 that the French government cracked down on the terrorists it had harboured for so long. At the urging of its fellow-Socialist government in Madrid, the Mitterand administration arrested and exiled many ETA leaders either to South or Central America or to other regions of France (this latter course was inevitably less effective) and it also started extraditing to Spain ETA men wanted for alleged crimes of violence in Madrid.

However, while their French sanctuary existed, ETA, as we have seen, could carry out negotiations with kidnappers quickly, face-to-face and not by the often tortuous process of telephone calls and letters left discreetly in caches. Contacts could be made by either party. In his first case Eriz had to find the kidnappers and it took him only a week. 'Everybody in the Basque country has telephone numbers to call,' he says. Or, as in some of his late cases, ETA contacted him, knowing him by then and trusting him as a bona fide negotiator; in later cases he had to persuade the family that he was acting disinterestedly and was not an emissary of the terrorists. (He had little trouble with this; his reputation was high and remains so.)

A meeting was swiftly arranged, generally in France but further afield too, in cities such as Amsterdam, Brussels, Milan, Paris and Vienna. Those meetings were frequently long bargaining sessions rather like an industrial negotiation over a wage claim, with Eriz trying to reduce the kidnappers' demands. Eriz recalls one session, lasting from 10 a.m. to 6 p.m. in a Bayonne bar, which was punctuated by shouting matches between him and the ETA leader who was conducting the terrorists' negotiations, while various ETA guards stood around with machine guns—not an encouraging environment to press the family's case, especially when you have a damaged hand. In the Arrasate case, his first, the ETA negotiator was a well-known leader nicknamed 'Pertur'. In the Garavilla and Lipperheide cases, the terrorist leader was the notorious 'Txomin', Domingo Iturbe, leader of ETA-m. Txomin once demonstrated a curious sense of 'honesty' (for a terrorist and murderer) in returning 10 million pesetas (£50,000) to Eriz which had been paid to ETA-m as a 'revolutionary tax' by a family who claimed, and were able to prove, that they had already paid the same amount to ETA-pm. This was done to underline publicly the boast that payment was protection against further demands.

Eriz's tactics in his actual face-to-face negotiations are disarmingly simple and at his request we are not revealing them here, but meetings with such men can be a wearing job. 'You don't eat, you lose weight, you smoke incessantly, you don't sleep properly. All the responsibilities for a man's life rest on your shoulders and the risks are tremendous. The police are tapping your phone and trying to follow you to these meetings, while the kidnappers are always suspicious that you might betray them by leading the police to their hide-outs.'

The outcome of the face-to-face style of negotiations is that deals can be wrapped up more quickly. The average length of kidnap by ETA was about one month, whereas many in Italy last more than two months. One factor which helped resolve negotiations in a reasonably speedy way was the realization by the terrorists that the sooner they could be rid of a captive for a good price, the sooner the commando group involved could prepare another operation.

On the other hand, there was very little pressure on them to agree a deal before the authorities caught up with them; there was little fear their 'safe house' where the victim was held would be discovered by the Civil Guard or the police. This rarely happened for a variety of reasons. Firstly, the rugged nature of the country, with harsh mountains and thousands of remote villages and cottages, makes blanket area-searches almost entirely fruitless and searches done from, even specific, source information difficult to execute. Secondly, the Basque people's innate distrust of the authorities and their clannish feeling towards ETA means the police work in an atmosphere of little or no public co-operation. However the public might abhor crimes of violence, many Basques had, and still have, mixed feelings towards ETA, regarding them with a certain sympathy as well-intentioned fellow-Basques with a cause. In any event the public hesitate to provide the police with the necessary clues and information. The parallels with Sardinia in this respect are obvious.

The impotence of the authorities was demonstrated after the kidnapping of Civil Guard captain Alberto Martín Barrios by ETA-pm on 5 October 1983 in Bilbao. He was only a chemist with no inside knowledge of police strategy at all, but ETA-pm declared in a communiqué that, under interrogation, he was revealing important secrets about the workings of the security services in Euskadi. This was transparent nonsense but the terrorists demanded that a lengthy statement concerning a trial of ETA members currently going on be read on Spanish television, or Martín Barrios would die. Held to ransom by the seizure of a public servant, the government turned down the demand, despite the understandably impassioned and distraught appeals of the captain's family. Martín Barrios was found dead beside a country road on 19 October, two weeks after his kidnap. His murder sent shock waves through Spain and the whole incident was clearly designed to de-stabilize the country by provoking the armed forces to react. A massive hunt was launched throughout the Basque region during that fortnight but no trace of him was uncovered; proof, if any was needed, that, though its political base was eroding, ETA-pm could still carry out active operations with relative impunity.

Two of the commando which seized and murdered Martín Barrios were Elena Barcena, the 'Tigress', who was still being sought for her part in the Orbegozo kidnap, and Armando Velez Cendoya, known as 'José María', who had taken part in the kidnapping of Dr Allende.

For ETA, any member of the Civil Guard is beyond the pale, however Basque he may be (Martín Barrios was a supporter and season ticket-holder of the football club Athletic de Bilbao, which selects only Basque players). Franco brought in Civil Guards from other parts of Spain to subdue the Basques as ruthlessly as they could. This left a legacy of hatred that persists to this day, despite all the reforms of the democratic era and the autonomy now enjoyed by the Basque region.

In spite of such horrors, the impression remains that a certain code of honour has regulated most kidnappings in the Basque area. If you obeyed the rules and your family paid up, you were freed, frequently mouthing generous praise of your captors. The mediators were Basques and intervention from outside rarely worked. A London firm of security consultants was once called in to advise on a kidnap and its representative made a poor showing: his participation ended after he suggested that the ransom be delivered by parachute somewhere in France. (This optimistic plan, fraught with practical problems, was straight from James Bond.) Most ransoms are handed to professional smugglers to get across the Pyrénées, for a cut of about three per cent. There is no history of double payments or the murder of a victim once his family has paid.

For all that, the strains of kidnap are as appalling in Spain as anywhere. The tensions generated by worry about the victim and finance have nearly destroyed families, reduced individuals to nervous wrecks, and, in some cases, forced people to leave for ever the Basque country they love as much as their kidnappers do.

NINE

... Where Other Police Forces Cannot Reach

What can the Netherlands offer to a study of kidnap when the first kidnap in the country's history was as late as 1974 and there have been only three cases since? What makes Holland interesting is the way in which the authorities there dealt with these well-planned kidnappings. There are lessons to be learnt both for other police forces—and their governments—and for budding kidnappers.

* * * *

The first kidnap for ransom was that of Caroline Pessers, aged five, in 1974. The little girl was playing outside her home in Dan Bosch when she was seized and carried off by Eddie van Laar, a twenty-year-old metal worker. Shortly afterwards, Caroline's father, a cigar manufacturer, received a ransom demand for 100,000 guilders (£17,000), but it was never paid. Van Laar panicked after he made the demand and, returning to the barn where she was captive, he murdered his young victim before burying her in a field. He was soon arrested and sentenced in May 1975 to a twenty-year term for illegal imprisonment and murder.

Two years later, on 2 November 1977, Jewish millionaire Maurits Caransa was kidnapped outside his bridge club in Amsterdam. Four hooded and gloved men shoved the sixty-one-year-old property speculator into a car and drove him about an hour from the city to a house in the country. Caransa was handcuffed to a central heating pipe in a darkened room but he was relatively well treated; his kidnappers did not beat him up, allowed him to listen to Press reports about his case on two radios and permitted him to sleep fully clothed on a bed. The gang were evidently well-organized; they had done their homework and had known where to seize Caransa, they saw no reason to maltreat their prisoner, and they had picked a rich prize. Caransa was reputed to be one of the wealthiest men in Holland and the ransom demand recognized this fact. The gang were paid 10 million guilders (£2.3 million) and released Caransa after only five days, at 2.30 a.m. in a square back in Amsterdam. He was in good health and said he never felt in any danger of being killed.

This was a different type of kidnapping altogether. The police quickly established that the kidnappers were a mixture of Dutch criminals, who had done the local groundwork, like stealing cars and arranging safe houses, and an imported gang of experts who had carried out the kidnap itself. It is a measure of the international co-operation that is now possible between police that the only members of the entire group to be caught were the foreigners (though the Dutch police say they have identified the native section of the gang, but have insufficient evidence to secure a conviction). Two Italians were arrested on the Italian–Swiss border and opted for a four-year sentence in Italy rather than returning to face trial in Holland, while an Argentinian, Luis Alvarez, was pursued to California where he was arrested in Los Angeles, and Dutch authorities have since been unsuccessful in extraditing him. Alvarez had bought dollars in Los Angeles with 1000 guilder notes—unusually large denominations for a gang to demand—and these registered notes had been recognized as part of the Caransa ransom. Swiss police confiscated $200,000 in a Lugano bank in Alvarez's name.

The Italian connection was understandable. In the 1970s kidnapping was endemic in Italy—1977 was a record year with seventy-five officially recorded cases—and criminals there had built up considerable expertise. When banks, then supermarkets and then post offices became more difficult to rob in the Netherlands, one group of Dutch criminals tried kidnapping, and turned to the Italians for help. The South American connection was less obvious, although Argentina suffered innumerable kidnaps in the early part of the decade and it still holds the world record for the largest ransom. Brutal repression by the right-wing government there stamped out left-wing kidnappers (and replaced them with state-sponsored abductions of anyone deemed to be a political opponent, causing the disappearance of over ten thousand people). Left-wing and criminal kidnappers took their trade elsewhere; north to Colombia and Central America, and to Europe. Shortly before Caransa's kidnap in November, the head of the French Fiat group, M. Revelli-Beaumont, was kidnapped in July 1977 by seven Argentinians and two other South Americans. Revelli-Beaumont was released after seventy days and a ransom of $2 million had been paid.

Holland's geography obliges her to seek international co-operation and establishing contacts abroad has been a feature of her destiny. This willingness to co-operate with neighbours has been developed by the Dutch police in their battle against drug trafficking through Amsterdam's docks; it was apparently ignored by kidnappers, in the Caransa case in 1977, and later in 1982 when Antonia van der Valk was seized.

Mrs van der Valk and her husband ran a chain of motels and restaurants in Holland and Belgium. The family's private house was near one hotel and they gave no thought to their own security as they moved back and forth to the hotel during working hours. In the early hours on Saturday morning 27 November 1982, Mrs van der Valk was in the basement of her home, her husband still at work, when strangers came in through the open doors and asked her who she was. Surprised, she told them and they dragged her from the house into a waiting car. The plan had been to take her husband but they decided she would do as well.

This gang was highly organized and sought to confuse the Dutch police with a truly international plan. They drove Mrs van der Valk over the border to Brussels where she was held, but not mistreated, in a tent inside a house. The ransom, of 12.5 million guilders (£2.7 million), was paid after a drop run which spread over hundreds of kilometres and led through four countries—Holland, Belgium, Luxemburg and Germany—and in three different currencies—Swiss francs, German marks and Dutch guilders. A relative was finally instructed to leave the money in Trier, West Germany. Then, twenty days after her kidnap, on Friday 17 December, Mrs van der Valk was brought back into Holland and released in Eindhoven by two men who escaped.

The gang underestimated the Dutch police, and those of four other countries who were brought in to follow the case as it developed from one country to the next. By careful surveillance, police identified the suspects before the ransom was paid and followed them from country to country. They dared not act for fear of endangering the life of the victim which had been agreed by everyone to be of paramount importance; but, on 18 December, the day after she was released, the police moved in. Suspects were arrested in Brussels, six people were arrested in Konstanz, a town in West Germany near the Swiss border, and three others were picked up in Zurich. Four of these nine kidnappers were women and two Italians were arrested later. Swiss police were able to recover over £1 million of the ransom which had been deposited in a bank in Zurich by Giancarlo Tomei, a resident of Konstanz, where he was arrested.

Again Italian expertise had been involved. Mrs van der Valk said the gang spoke German with northern Italian accents, and it is likely this gang learned their skill in Turin and Milan, two cities which have seen a lot of kidnappings. The investigation was remarkable for its complexity: the victim, who was taken in Holland, was carried across the border to Belgium; the gang phoned from abroad during the negotiations; the police, with Interpol, co-ordinated not just administrative assistance but delicate surveillance operations through five countries; the drop was made in West Germany and arrests were made the day after the release of the victim in three countries abroad. Nothing like this had been seen before, but the police commitment it represented was essential to defeat experienced kidnappers who had prepared and planned carefully. The results speak for themselves.

* * * *

The fourth case is the best known because the name of the victim had already reached into households that other celebrities could not: on cans of Heineken lager-beer. On Wednesday 9 November 1983 at 7 p.m., the chief of the enormous beer company, Alfred Heineken, aged sixty, was kidnapped with his chauffeur, Ab Doderer, in Amsterdam, as they were leaving the company's offices. Three armed men held them at gunpoint and forced them into a stolen van. A taxi driver bravely gave chase but lost the kidnappers in the streets of the city.

This news spread instantly around Holland, where the name of Heineken is everywhere—on bill-boards, hoardings, bars, neon signs, beer trucks, and on crumpled green cans in the gutter. The victim was a leading figure in Dutch life and his kidnap affected everyone, including Queen Beatrice and the Dutch royal family with whom he had been friendly for years. The kidnappers had certainly picked a rich prize—Heineken was rumoured to spend huge sums on gems every year—but they had stirred up unimaginable trouble for themselves. The Dutch police immediately went into top gear. The importance of the victim, nationally and through his royal and political connections, put tremendous pressure on them. This, and their decision early on that they would not let kidnapping take hold in the Netherlands as it had done elsewhere in Europe, led them to realize that they could not allow this most important case to slip from their grasp, or the public would have little confidence in their ability to protect the lesser members of Dutch society. Their approach to the myriad problems suddenly thrust upon them was therefore one hundred per cent effort. They could not afford to lose.

By seizing such a man, the kidnappers had compounded the complexities and risks of obtaining a ransom—usually underestimated—but they were confident in their planning and this was a most carefully premeditated kidnap. It was a kidnap on a grand scale. At the scene of the abduction the gang took care to leave a ransom note demanding no less than 35 million guilders (over £8 million), in four different currencies—Dutch guilders, U.S. dollars, French francs and German marks, 50,000 notes of each.

The Dutch police started at base, setting up the groups they would need to pursue the investigation, and linking them to interested parties in every area of Dutch officialdom. At the top of the tree was the Policy Centre (P.C.) under the responsibility of the Director of Criminal Prosecutions. This committee had to keep the Dutch government constantly up-to-date and was the link to the royal family. The other members were the Attorney General for the area—there are five areas or *Resort* in Holland—who was responsible not for the solution of the case but for political aspects and had to report to the Minister of Justice, the Director of the Criminal Investigation Department and his Deputy, and the Public Prosecutor in charge of the case itself.

At the centre of the hub of committees and groups was the Operations Command Centre (O.C.C.) which was more than seventy strong. This team was commanded by a police commander, Chief Inspector Kees Sietstma, whose job it was to conduct the actual investigation. He controlled the development of various initiatives, ideas and all the tactical effort. Strategic matters, such as surveillance policy, the psychological approach, the decision whether or not to pay the ransom or to raid houses, were set out by the O.C.C. and put to the P.C. for their approval, while tactical matters, such as the number of teams to employ in a follow, were left to the discretion of the O.C.C. commander so that the maximum operational flexibility was preserved. Sietstma had spent years combatting the drug traffic through Amsterdam, and still has a map of Hong Kong on his office wall marked with lists of Chinese Triads. Covert surveillance, rather than the sudden raid with guns blazing of popular fiction, is the hallmark of successful operations against drug smugglers, and the commander of the O.C.C. was to rely heavily on his experience and his officers' expertise in the grey and difficult world of surveillance.

Around these two groups were a host of other units and establishments linked to the O.C.C. The list is long, but some examples show how widespread was the commitment to this investigation into kidnap. Close to the O.C.C. were the tactical police group, the technical team which dealt with specialist equipment, the Pro-active Criminal Investigation Department observation groups, the Dutch Special Branch, and uniformed and plain clothed police departments throughout the country. There were links, through the Dutch Interpol Bureau, with other police forces, such as the Bundeskriminalamt in Wiesbaden, Germany, the Sûreté in France, and police headquarters in Belgium. Expert opinions of every sort were sought to assist in analysing the kidnappers' actions and demands; for example, from psychologists, psychiatrists, priests, weapons specialists, and science advisers. Liaison with Dutch media was channelled to the O.C.C. for issuing official reports. The Dutch Post Office and telecommunications offices were involved, to facilitate surveillance—tracing telephone calls and to investigate the source of letters. Investigating the case, the police developed contacts with other, more diverse organizations such as employment agencies, banks, schools, the motor vehicle licensing centre, import control offices, commercial licensing offices and so on. Lastly, and most importantly, the O.C.C. was linked to the Heineken family and the board of directors of the victim's company, who had set up their own Crisis Management Team (C.M.T.) to consider their situation, their options and their courses of action.

A special team of computer technicians was grouped to programme a data management system that would be a useful tool to store and retrieve all the information gathered. The problem was with the volume of information and how to keep the analysts in the O.C.C. abreast of the game. The solution was to programme the computer to perform simple analytical functions. For example, if the input of a new piece of information concerned a red Mercedes, the computer searched for all other red cars previously reported, compared the list with another search for all Mercedes cars and gave the operator the result, thus keeping him up to date with other possibilities. Of course, if other information was available, such as a registration number or even part of one, then the computer could search all these and give the descriptions of all the cars fitting the new specification. The speed of the computer search and comparison functions enabled the O.C.C. to make consistent use of the welter of information that flooded in. Police analysts were able to check new data constantly as they tested each line of the investigation, without being overcome by the sheer volume of facts that quickly built up.

Once the structure of the authorities' resources commitment was defined and initiated, the O.C.C. had to establish priorities. One member of the Heineken C.M.T. had the task of liaising with the O.C.C. and met the police commander several times a day at the start of the case and at least twice a day later on. The family's main concern was whether the police would place the safety of Alfred Heineken before the authorities' desire to catch the criminals. Considerable discussion took place separately in the Heineken C.M.T. and in the O.C.C., and then together, before the priorities were agreed. These were that the victims' safety and release were of paramount importance, followed by the arrest of the gang, and lastly, the police would do their best to recover any money that might be paid in ransom. This order of priorities, which was approved by the P.C., accorded with generally humanitarian approach of the Dutch authorities over a wide spectrum of affairs, and had been adopted previously in the other kidnap cases.

What concerned the family and the C.M.T. was how the police would conduct the investigation within the agreed context. The kidnappers had their victims but they had to make various contacts and finally explain the arrangements for picking up the money. Each contact would give the police the opportunity to develop their investigation but might jeopardize the lives of Heineken and Doderer. The C.M.T. was particularly worried about police abilities on surveillance operations; while they could see the police wanted to collect what evidence they could to arrest and convict after the release of the victims, they were deeply worried that the gang would spot the observation teams. On his side, the O.C.C. commander knew it was absolutely vital that the C.M.T. passed everything on to the O.C.C. so that the police lacked nothing to assist the investigation. He knew the gang would contact the family soon. It was finally agreed that the family's C.M.T. and the police O.C.C. would co-operate on everything, keeping each other completely informed of the latest developments, but, when their aims started to diverge, they agreed to say so and then pursue their own courses as each best saw fit. Flexibility and genuine communications between the police and the family would prove essential.

The first obstacle to good relations between the family and the police was the question of whether to pay the ransom. Thirty-five million guilders was an enormous ransom by any standards. In Europe the amounts demanded of families have been astronomical, in Italy 20 miliardi (£10 million) is common, but the actual amounts paid may vary only between £50,000 to little over £1 million. In Central America international corporations have paid sums over $10 million dollars. The Dutch police were obviously not keen to release over £8 million on to the criminal world to finance other crimes. They believed that the consequences for society in a small country would be disastrous. The Heineken C.M.T. on the other hand were understandably interested only in the safety of the two victims, and, if they decided that the threat to Heineken and Doderer was great enough, they were prepared to pay the entire demand.

The gang had specified that the payment was to be made in four different currencies, made up in five sacks, and delivered by a police officer who should drive a van on which huge red crosses were to be painted. The start point for the drop would be Alfred Heineken's own spacious villa, *De Ark*, in Noordwijk, a rich residential town on the coast north of The Hague. The gang further ordered that the policeman should be unarmed, carry no listening equipment on his person nor tracking devices in the van. New instructions would be issued once the family had indicated that they had the money ready, by an advertisement which was to be placed in the congratulation columns of the newspaper *De Telegraaf*: 'All green for the hare'. The family was warned to recognize the kidnappers by the code-word 'Eagle' and reply with 'Hare' which signified the policeman who was to drive the van. The kidnappers had thought of everything. The policeman was even to carry his passport and some ready money; 250 guilders and 250 marks.

There were only two inconsistencies in the gang's instructions. Firstly, they demanded that the police should be kept out, which was plainly absurd since they also wanted a policeman to drive the van, and secondly, they wanted no publicity, which was also absurd since no one could expect the kidnap of Heineken to pass unreported; indeed, his villa was swiftly surrounded by journalists from all over the world. However, these two demands are classic inclusions in any kidnappers' first messages, and underline their preferred conditions of operation. In this case the gang were clearly well organized and could not fail to have seen the inconsistencies. The police view was that the boss was vastly confident and revelled in it. The choice of the code-words reinforced this view. It seemed the gang wanted to press home their psychological advantage by associating themselves with the eagle which dominates his prey, the hare, from on high.

In any event, the form of the initial instructions from the gang left no room for doubt that they were highly organized. It is possible, though quite counter-productive, for a gang to pretend they are inexperienced in order to frighten the family, but it is impossible for incompetent criminals to pass themselves off as efficient. But if they were clever, might they not also be ruthless? This part of their character had yet to be established, and its consequences were uppermost in the minds of the C.M.T.

The C.M.T. came to the conclusion that they must pay the whole demand. Fearful that the kidnappers' evident pre-meditation tokened equally efficient ruthlessness, and risking the possibility that the gang would actually increase their demand on receiving so favourable a response so quickly, the C.M.T. decided to pay everything without demur. Perhaps they hoped that the sheer size of the sum would satisfy. Understandably they hoped that early payment would lead to an early release, and in this, too, they took a risk. Negotiations, therefore, simply became communications to settle the details of the drop.

The O.C.C., unhappy with this decision, responded by suggesting that the C.M.T., who were expected to receive calls from the gang, should begin negotiations to reduce the amount of the demand. The kidnappers had the advantage of surprise and the police needed to buy time to put their operation in full swing. It would have been a disaster, from the point of view of the police, if the payment had taken place before the police were ready to reap the crop of evidence that every gang leaves when it materializes to take the money. The O.C.C. also suggested that the C.M.T. negotiate an interim payment of say, 10 million guilders (£2.3 million), to show faith with the gang, and even offer to find more later. But none of these ideas appealed to the C.M.T. who insisted that they wanted to pay the whole amount at once, for the safety of the two victims. The O.C.C. eventually agreed and the money was prepared.

The police had put their new organization to rapid use in finding the van and cars that had been used in the kidnap. Descriptions had been circulated to all units and soon the van turned up. Inside the police found two Israeli-made Uzi sub-machine guns, with plenty of ammunition, packed in two suitcases with a pair of spectacles and a quantity of German marks. Before reaching any conclusions about the kidnappers' use of such weapons the police took immediate steps to investigate the origin of these items. The van had been stolen as long ago as July. They found that the guns had been stolen from the Dutch army in Holland, and the suitcases were made in Germany. They traced the spectacles to the optician who had made them and he gave the name and address of his patient. Excitement in the O.C.C. grew as it seemed they had struck a lucky break to identify one kidnapper so early. Police made a raid and arrested the owner of the spectacles only to discover that he was the owner of the stolen van itself and blameless of kidnap.

The spectacles incident, though disappointing, provided an important clue to the character of the gang, who had clearly deliberately placed the glasses, which they had found in the stolen van, inside the suitcase, with the gun. It had been done to mislead. So, perhaps, all the other evidence left behind was there to mislead. It all pointed to an international gang, probably based in Germany. Indeed, police teams had also traced the paper on which the demand note was written and the sort of typewriter that printed the instructions; both were German. However, it was still not clear whether the gang were really from outside Holland, as had been the case in the previous two kidnaps. One possible conclusion was that the evidence, guns and ammunition, was left to mislead, and therefore reflected instead to a Dutch home team. In either case, the kidnappers were clever, and their actions utterly premeditated. Whether they had left them deliberately or not, the Uzi sub-machine guns suggested ruthlessness.

The family published the announcement in *De Telegraaf*: 'All green for the hare', but one journalist, who realized that there might be secret messages passed between the family and the kidnappers, was scanning the papers daily. He spotted the Heineken advertisement to the gang and traced it back to the family by discovering who had placed the notice. This setback, and the resulting swarms of reporters around the villa and company headquarters, was annoying but fortunately did not jeopardize the negotiations in this case. The gang phoned three days after the kidnap, to De Ark at 7 p.m. on 12 November.

The C.M.T. had been warned, with a brief call earlier, to be ready for a message and Heineken's secretary was waiting by the telephone. After agreeing the ransom the O.C.C. and C.M.T. had further concluded that there were aspects of the kidnappers' instructions that could not be accepted at face value. They had accordingly decided to ask three questions at the earliest moment. When the telephone shrilled in the victim's home, his secretary had a piece of paper ready with three points written out on it. The first was to open a dialogue with the kidnappers about the details of the drop: such as the choice of the van with its two red crosses; the mass of reporters who would attempt to follow anything so conspicuous, and it was impossible to keep the police away when the driver had to be a policeman. The second was to ask for positive proof that the two men were alive, and to stress that proof was required on the day of payment. Some of the victims' possessions had been received by the police in The Hague—a letter had arrived containing Doderer's passport and Heineken's wrist-watch—but these were not proof of life. The third point was to ask the kidnappers to show more confidence in the family and allow the driver to have a mate who could be there to help him follow instructions carefully in order not to foul up the payment. This was, after all, important to both the family and the gang.

The secretary was good at her job. She had a lifetime of dealing with people on the telephone and had done some successful telephone negotiating during two food extortion cases that the Heineken company had suffered. But she got no chance to make her points. The voice at the other end of the line was her employer's, and she listened with some shock as he listed more instructions. Nor could she make him talk to her: his voice was taped; the gang had forced him to read out their new orders and simply played the message over the open line. It was a short call. The family were told to go to Utrecht central railway station where, in safety deposit box number 2150, they found two photographs of Heineken and Doderer, each holding a copy of De Telegraaf clearly dated 12 November. This was the proof everyone required, but the outstanding three points had still to be made. It was assessed that it was essential to put these to the gang before paying any money.

Four days later, on Wednesday 16 November, the gang called again. Once more the C.M.T. had the eerie sensation of listening to Alfred Heineken's voice on the telephone without being able to converse with him; it must have been particularly hard on the family and highlighted the strangeness of their predicament. This time the instructions were for the policeman. He was to start the drop and drive to a motel at Schiphol, Amsterdam's international airport. The disembodied voice of the victim went on to say that the driver would find a coloured flagpole in front of the motel, and at the bottom, buried in the ground, would be a small plastic cup. In this cup would be more instructions.

This development put the C.M.T. in a quandary. They did not wish to aggravate the kidnappers by refusing to obey their instructions, but they had not been able to communicate the three points which they felt had to be put before they paid over any money. They decided to stick to their earlier decision not to pay until they had established their conditions with the gang. It was now four days since the photographs had been picked up in Utrecht station and the principle worry was to be certain that the victims were alive on the day of the drop, as near the time of the payment as possible.

The O.C.C., which had been privy to the telephone call, gave the order to pick up the trail that the policeman, driving his van with its garish red crosses, would have taken. Teams of police, dressed in plain clothes in order not to attract attention in case the gang were looking from some vantage point, went to the motel. Sure enough, in the ground at the bottom of the coloured pole was a plastic cup, with a screw-on top, of the sort that children take to school in their lunchboxes. The police opened the cup and found new orders from the gang—and a small torch thoughtfully left for them to read the paper in the dark.

The new orders told them to take the road, north, through Haarlem towards Alkmaar, leaving Amsterdam on the right. On the road before Alkmaar there is another motel at a small village called Akersloot, and here they would find another cup. The police continued the 'dummy' drop run with the intention of picking up what evidence they could and handing over the sites where they discovered cups to the Scene of Crime squads who would dissect the area for further clues and evidence for forensic analysis. At the second site, outside the motel at Akersloot, they duly found the second cup. Inside were instructions to keep going north, to a car park at t'Zand, on the finger of flat land that curves protectively around the polder lakes of Holland.

In the meantime, the C.M.T. had discussed the frustration of not being able to speak to the kidnappers, and put their three points. Such points are quite normal conditions in most other kidnap negotiations, and certainly in cases where the gang are an organized group. It was decided that, since the negotiation—or 'communications' because there was no longer any question of haggling over the money—had not been established, the relationship between the family and the gang was still volatile and nothing should be done that might panic the gang into harming the victims. Accordingly, the C.M.T. firmly requested the O.C.C. to call off the police teams who were following the trail of plastic cups, in case the kidnappers spotted the police presence and resolved to put the pressure on by committing some atrocity against Heineken or Doderer. The imaginations of families suffering during a kidnap conjure every sort of devilish possibility; and each one has a precedent.

Reluctantly, the O.C.C. agreed. Everyone realized that the gang would have to make some allowances for dialogue with the family if they wanted their money. Equally, it would be wrong to frighten them off with police following the drop trail. The commander of the O.C.C. waited four days, but his men were not idle. They were busy on a check of all the country's criminal groups to establish whether any had the slightest connection with the Heineken case. Uniformed and plain clothed police were ordered to question all the sources, or touts, they knew for information. Meetings took place on street corners, in cars and bars—some of them probably owned by Heineken—throughout Holland. Every scrap of data was analysed but all proved negative. Gradually one after the other, criminals known to the Dutch police were eliminated of complicity in the kidnap. Then, on Sunday 20 November, the C.M.T. agreed that it would be safe to allow police teams to follow the trail again. By now, the Heineken C.M.T. accepted that the drop run was cold. It was most unlikely that any member of the gang would be watching the places they had chosen en route, and therefore the risk that the kidnappers might see policemen was slight.

A third cup was found in the car-park at t'Zand which sent the police further north out on to the road along the immense dyke which keeps the sea from flooding the vast area of land-locked waters and low ground that is being reclaimed from the heart of the Netherlands. Over the thirty-kilometre long dyke, they turned south-west to the small town of Joure where the fourth cup, in another car-park, told them to look for a Citroën GS nearby. It was nowhere to be found. All they were left with was the fourth set of instructions that would have ordered the policeman making the payment to transfer the sacks of money from his van to the Citroën and then take the road to

Amsterdam. He was also to have found a two-way radio set hidden under a towel in the car and more orders would have been given him over the air, using the call-signs, Eagle for the gang and Hare for him. Having completed the huge circular journey round the dykes and land-locked seas back to Amsterdam, he was to have driven to Arnhem, via Utrecht, to the Motel Postallion. There, his final orders told him to wait in the lobby for more instructions but that, if nothing had happened after two hours, to book into a room.

Disappointed not to find the Citroën, the police reported back to the O.C.C. They had learned a great deal about the kidnappers' ideas for the payment, and much about their attitude to planning. As a matter of routine the police units with responsibility in areas the trail had passed through were contacted and the computer checked with the information that had been gathered. Then the advantage swung back in their favour. It transpired that the Joure police had noticed the Citroën GS on 17 November, a day after the gang had ordered the drop to commence, and discovered that it was on the list of stolen cars. They had impounded it. Police were sent from the O.C.C. to examine the car. It had been stolen in Amsterdam in June that year, showing once again how the gang had premeditated their project for many months. The state of the car was interesting: the Joure police had found it with a wheelbarrow strapped on to its roof and both headlights were covered with yellow filters, which is unusual in Holland. Evidently the kidnappers wanted the vehicle to be highly visible amongst other traffic. They found the radio on the front seat, under the towel, as the instructions had described and follow-up analysis showed that it was of Japanese make but that the frequency crystals had been set in Germany. Once more the evidence pointed to Germany.

The Heineken C.M.T. digested these facts and decided to make another announcement in the newspaper, but this time changing the wording to show the kidnappers that they wanted a dialogue, not merely to listen to a one-sided stream of orders. It was hoped that the gang would appreciate that the family were still keen to make the payment but, because they had not obeyed orders to follow the rally trail, would not fall helplessly in line with the kidnappers' every demand. The notice 'The meadow is green for the hare but urgent contact is necessary' was placed in *De Telegraaf*. The initiative was back with the gang and, while the family waited in trepidation for news, Chief Inspector Sietstma ordered his teams to increase the tempo of already hectic policework to try to identify the criminals responsible.

On Tuesday 22 November, nearly two weeks after the kidnap, the gang telephoned Heineken's villa. The first call warned the family to expect a full communication later in the day. When it came the line was appalling and it was not until the third call that the secretary heard the familiar tones of her employer, oddly distorted through another tape-recorded message. He told her she had only twenty seconds to make her point after he had finished. She spoke urgently but clearly and explained the three issues that worried the C.M.T.

The next day a typed reply was picked up on a road. The gang accepted two of the three points. They agreed to provide proof on the day of payment, and to change the start of the run from De Ark to the house of the vice-president of Heineken, in Wassenaar, another rich residential area nearby. The 'red cross' van was written off and had to be substituted with an orange Renault van, but the gang would not allow a second driver; the policeman was on his own. Both Noordwijk and Wassenaar are small towns north of The Hague which are popular in the summer for their attractive beaches, but this was late November and the weather was awful, with cold winds and rain sweeping over the flat countryside—the orange van would stand out well against the grey landscape.

All this was good news. Though the policeman had to go alone (it is unusual for kidnap gangs to agree to an extra person if asked—why should they?), the condition did not alter the fundamental rules for paying the ransom that the C.M.T. had set themselves—principally proof of life. It must also have been satisfying that the gang had responded so quickly; they gave every impression of being prepared to negotiate on the details when pressed. However, the kidnappers were keen not to give the family the idea that they were a pushover. Inside the letter were two more photographs of Heineken and Doderer. But this time the pictures gave no consolation of proof of life. Each man had a rope around his neck and they had their right arms in slings. Bluntly, the kidnappers explained in the letter that they had already amputated fingers from the victims' right hands and, should the family fail to deliver, they would both be sent back dead, for burial. This threat of death shook the family and the C.M.T., although on reflection it could be seen that the gang were deliberately applying pressure. Even the likelihood that they had not cut off any fingers—since they would have been well advised to give the threat real meat by sending the pieces as grisly proof—was small comfort. The threat remained. The O.C.C., though more able to take an objective view, realized that the temperature of the case had been raised another few degrees, while their political overseers on the P.C., being out of the real action, showed their concern by increased attention to the O.C.C.'s plans.

The gang also gave a new code for future contacts: Eagle and Hare was altered to Owl and Mouse. Clearly events had not diminished the kidnappers' sense of superiority. To show the letter had been received, the family was to advertise a Citroën 2CV for sale, giving the year, price and telephone number to call. The C.M.T. placed this new announcement on Friday 25 November, in the newspaper *Het Parool*, as instructed.

For the C.M.T., the men on the P.C., for the frantically busy O.C.C., for friends of the victims including the royal family, but most of all for the Heineken family it was a long, miserable weekend of waiting and hoping. The money was packed in five sacks and everything else was ready to go: all they needed was proof of life and the gang's instructions.

At 6 p.m. on Saturday, the gang made a brief call to the house in Wassenaar to check that the family was ready for the drop.

At 2.30 a.m., on Monday 28 November, the vice president of the Heineken empire was woken by a call to his home in Wassenaar. It was from the kidnappers. The orders were brief and to the point. The policeman was to leave the house in the orange Renault van within ten minutes, and drive to a petrol station near Schiphol airport where he would find a plastic cup behind the office. After a quick discussion the C.M.T. decided to follow these first instructions and see what developed. The gang had used the plastic cups to pass information before and if proof that the victims were alive was not forthcoming they could always call off the payment.

The policeman found the cup as instructed and inside were two photographs of the victims. They were good quality instant Polaroid pictures and both men had their eyes wide open. In each was Sunday's copy of the glossy magazine *Sport am Sonntag*, the date, 27 November, clearly visible. This was the proof the C.M.T. required. The payment run was on.

In the misery of kidnap there is a tendency to imagine that the kidnappers, brutalized by what they are doing, have no sense of humour. This is not so, though any joke may seem sick enough to the family. Also in the cup, the gang had left a one guilder coin—for the policeman to treat himself to coffee once he arrived at his new destination, another petrol station. It was a long drive, this time south of Rotterdam to Zevenbergschen-Hoek more than eighty kilometres away. Shortly after the policeman arrived, the gang called and issued new orders which sent him to a milestone a few kilometres further south, towards the town of Breda. In the ground beside the milestone he unearthed another cup which turned the trail sixty kilometres northwards again to Utrecht, where he was told to look for the inevitable cup, this time behind a restaurant called De Hammel.

It was past six o'clock in the morning and the traffic was thickening in the Monday morning rush-hour when the policeman found the cup behind De Hammel. He was tired after long hours of night driving but his excitement grew as he read the scrap of paper from the cup. He was to shift the sacks of money into a Ford Combi van parked nearby and drive it to a motel at Maarsbergen, where he would find another set of instructions buried at the bottom of a flagpole. The policeman recognized this was the same change of vehicles that had been prepared for the first abortive drop, using the Citroën GS; and, like the Citroën, the Ford was conspicuously fitted up, with a lady's bicycle tied to its roof and a yellow filter over one headlight. As he started the Ford Combi he knew he was on the last leg and wondered how the gang would actually take the money. He no longer felt tired.

He switched on the radio which he found on the front seat of the van and listened for the gang as he made his way out of the city of Utrecht towards Maarsbergen on the Arnhem road, the lady's bicycle standing up prominently above the traffic. Starting the week's work, the drivers of the cars swirling round him on the dual carriageways and slip-roads were unaware that they passed a van carrying 35 million guilders (over £8 million) in five sacks, or of the sinister significance of the bicycle. Suddenly the radio crackled and a man's voice identified himself as the Owl. The policeman acknowledged with his call-sign, the Mouse, and heard instructions for him to take the highway out of Utrecht. Then he was ordered to stop on a vast bridge where the eight-lane motorway soared over a small secondary road. He would find a hole specially cut in the metal grating that edged the viaduct and he should drop the five sacks through without hesitation. Minutes later, the policeman saw the last sack fall away beneath him, straight into the back of a waiting Mercedes Hanemag pick-up truck. The Hanemag drove off at once down the little road, and the policeman realized pursuit was impossible—even if it had been advisable—for there was no exit from the motorway for twenty kilometres. Leaning over the bridge, he watched the kidnappers and 35 million guilders disappear round a bend in the road as dawn lightened the grey sky.

The C.M.T. received the news from the O.C.C. and were satisfied—as far as anyone could be, having just handed over more than £8 million to criminals—that, within the context of kidnap negotiations, matters had gone well. Proof of life had been given immediately before the drop run and, after a long route delineated by a complex set of instructions, the money had been paid over. The Heineken family had completed its part of the bargain. Now they had to wait to see if the gang would complete the contract and return their two victims.

This is the hardest part of every case. The family has nothing left in its hand while the kidnappers hold both the vital cards: the victims and now the money. This is the time when all the assessments about the character of the gang that have been made during the negotiation become important, not because they will have the slightest effect, but because they will hopefully give the family confidence in thinking that the gang will return the victim. The tenor and style of the gang's negotiation should lead the family's C.M.T. to a hopeful conclusion about the nature of the kidnappers; otherwise there is little point paying more than a nominal amount to assuage future guilt should the victims be murdered. Sadly, however well such assessments have been made, waiting helplessly and not knowing whether loved ones will ever be seen again is utterly debilitating, as anyone with relations away on dangerous missions and jobs will agree.

The pace of life in the O.C.C. was different. Collation of a staggering mass of information about all the known criminals in Holland had been made by Friday 25 November, three days before the drop. Information was collected and cross-checked from abroad, too, particularly from Germany where so much of the gang's equipment had been bought. As facts were sifted and analysed, the commander of the O.C.C. had ticked off names and groups of criminals who had been listed as possible suspects. By that Friday he had dealt with them all and he turned the attention of his teams to sorting the hundreds of calls and letters from members of the public.

The public had responded to publicity about the case with a steady flow of tips. Some of these tips were specific, some were vague, some were complicated and long, while others were so vague as to be quite useless; some were quickly investigated while others would take up much time and many resources; but they all had to be exhaustively checked. The commander of the O.C.C. kept the pressure up on his men, knowing that once the drop had taken place the gang would be very hard to identify. During the case, he knew the kidnappers had to work to get their money, and they might still make mistakes which his men might pick up. Without a thought to the foul November weather, he ordered observation teams to stake out various locations that had emerged from the host of tips. One such team, following information in tip-off number 547, crawled miserably into position through wet tufted marram grass near the docks on the outskirts of Amsterdam harbour.

There were altogether over 1500 tips from the public; number 547 was a letter dated Wednesday 16 November. It was sent anonymously to the Heineken company, arriving on Thursday, and was in the hands of the O.C.C. by Friday. There it was put through initial processing to ensure it was not another piece of rubbish from the inevitable crop of people who are amused to mislead and upset police and families alike. The writer of number 547 apologized that his comments were based on suspicion and intuition: he said he had been used to seeing a group of five men together before the kidnap but now he never saw them together. He named three men and gave good descriptions of two. One, he said, owned a factory in an isolated part of Amsterdam called De Heining near the harbour area. The Jadu factory was a woodyard, in the corner of a remote and shabby industrial estate bounded on two sides by open rough grass and surrounded on the other sides by piles of wrecked cars. The buildings were a main block of offices with a flat roof, standing on one side of a corrugated iron Nissen hut, with a new wood building, recently constructed, on the other. The road to the factory ran between the estate and the rough ground.

The observation team found a satisfactory place from which they could watch the offices of the woodyard: satisfactory only in the sense of achieving the aim of the police operation, for the weather made it extremely uncomfortable. Theirs was not an enviable task. However keen to catch the gang, they cannot have looked forward to watching a place of work through a cold and stormy weekend. It must have crossed their minds that while they were stuck watching a desolate spot, other colleagues were waiting for the final word to start the drop run from Wassenaar. However, at 11 a.m. on Saturday, the owner and his wife drove up to the factory in a Mercedes, with the brother of one of the men named in the letter number 547. They went inside and, surprisingly, stayed there all day.

At 10.15 a.m. the following day, Sunday, the secret watchers noted two more men drive up to the factory. Both were men named in the tip-off letter. They stayed all day. At 4.30 p.m. the brother left the woodyard and was followed to a Chinese restaurant nearby. There he ordered two take-away meals and returned with them to the factory.

By this time the commander of the O.C.C. had been informed of the progress of the various observation teams out on the ground that critical weekend and had identified the team at the woodyard as being of interest. Two Chinese meals into four do not go satisfactorily. Perhaps, he mused optimistically, the two meals were for the two victims. He was not a man to allow himself to be deluded by wishful thinking, nor to commit heavily overworked resources to stampede after wild suppositions (his experience fighting drug smugglers had rid him of such luxury), but there was a pattern emerging from this woodyard—and nothing could be overlooked.

The pro-active surveillance team covering the woodyard observed the owner leaving at 16.45 hours that Sunday. The mobile team was alerted by the static 'trigger' observation group watching the offices, and began the 'follow'. The owner drove the Mercedes to Utrecht—to the De Hammel restaurant. He went around to the back of the restaurant and the surveillance officers were not able to report what he did; they dared not get close for fear of raising their quarry's suspicions. From Utrecht, the owner of the woodyard drove to a hospital car-park in Amersfoort. There he parked and waited.

The Dutch observation group commander allowed his team to catch up with the lead and, over the radio, routinely re-organized them around the area in positions where he judged they would be ready to react to whatever happened next.

The brother arrived, driving a Ford Combi van, and picked up the owner of the woodyard. The observation team swung into action again, and this time the 'follow' led them to an area of woods not far away in Zeist, a township just north of the main road from Utrecht to Arnhem. The Ford Combi parked and the police officers reported that the two men sat inside. They appeared to be waiting. Several minutes later, two other men walked out of the trees, taking the surveillance team by surprise, and joined the two in the van. Fortunately, the suspicions of the four were not aroused: they clearly had no idea that they were being observed closely and that all around, at likely routes out of the woods, on track and road junctions, other police, men and women, waited in civilian clothes, loitering as naturally as they could but ready to move at the signal from those near the centre of the web who had the targets in their sight. When the Ford Combi started and drove off towards Arnhem, the entire observation team moved with the van, invisibly ebbing and flowing about the unwitting target, the team's vehicles—of all types—constantly shifting positions, sometimes ahead, sometimes behind, and then racing round parallel roads to anticipate the Ford Combi's next change of direction.

The van was driven to a motel at Maarsbergen, on the road to Arnhem, and stopped in the car-park. The officers who had the target at this stage drove past, reporting that the four men had left the vehicle and were doing something by the middle flag-pole outside the motel. Other members of the team were able to get into positions from which, this time, they could see clearly what was happening. The commander of the O.C.C., who had observation teams following tip-offs everywhere, was taking an increasing interest in the group who had the men in the Ford Combi. When he heard his men report that the four men had buried something beneath the flag-pole, he decided to seize this opportunity for confirmation. As soon as the targets left in the Ford Combi, silently pursued by the observation team like unseen guardian angels, the O.C.C. commander ordered that whatever had been buried should be examined and returned without sign of disturbance. After tense moments of waiting, the O.C.C. heard that the police had discovered a plastic cup: and inside was a note, from the Owl to the Mouse, with orders to go into the motel and wait for a call, but, if nothing happened in two hours, to book into a room. It was confirmation that the men in the Ford Combi were part of the kidnap gang. It was midnight on Sunday 27 November.

The observation team continued their demanding task, tracking the van to Schiphol airport where the men parked and disappeared behind a petrol station. As at the De Hammel restaurant, the police dared not get closer to their targets and could not see what they were doing, but now that the men had been positively identified as part of the kidnap gang, there was no need to take risks in the surveillance operation. It was 01.00 hours on Monday and the team had been following the kidnappers for over seven hours, since 17.45 hours on Sunday afternoon. That is a long time to maintain the concentration required of first class surveillance officers, and it would have been tragic to lose everything now for the sake of a detail. The commander of the O.C.C. therefore decided to call off his pro-active observation teams, and instead he covered all the locations that had been identified during the chase with static groups. These were moving covertly into position shortly before the kidnappers called the vice president at his home in Wassenaar, at 02.30 hours, to order the start of the payment run.

The O.C.C. had directed a frenzy of police work since the day of the kidnap, on 9 November, checking and cross-checking criminals, leads, evidence, and tip-offs, working through a host of agencies in Holland and abroad, and the hard work had paid dividends. When the policeman set out on his lonely drive with 35 million guilders in the back of the orange Renault van he was not abandoned. The O.C.C. was able to monitor his progress along the route, hanging well back so as not to be spotted by the kidnappers who were expected to be watching at least part of the drop run. The police had been able to guess the form of the payment route but extra surveillance coverage was needed when the gang gave orders over the telephone, changing direction in a way that could not be predicted.

The kidnappers' adrenalin must have flowed as they waited near the motorway fly-over for a glimpse of the bicycle on top of the Ford Combi van, moving slowly amongst the thickening Monday morning traffic round Utrecht. As they accelerated away in the Hanemag pick-up with five bags of money in the back, they would not have been so happy to have known that they were being watched by the police. But minutes later, at 07.20 a.m., the Hanemag, making its way to Utrecht, suddenly turned on to an uncompleted section of motorway. The police could not follow because there was no cover for cars or men on the open, unfinished expanse of road and the surveillance team lost its target.

Fifteen minutes later, at 07.35 a.m., the static observation position at the hospital car-park in Amersfoort reported that the Hanemag had arrived, driven by the owner of the woodyard. He left the pick-up, now empty of sacks, and drove off in his Mercedes. The Mercedes was tracked again and followed through a circuitous route until, at 09.00 hours, the owner was 'housed' in an apartment in Amsterdam, at 348 Staalmeesterslaan. This apartment was new to the O.C.C. The money had been paid and all that remained was for the gang to release the victims, which they had said they would do within twelve

hours. The O.C.C. had to make contingency plans in case it materialized, from continuing surveillance reports, that the gang had decided
not to release their victims, ignore them altogether, or simply kill them.

Meanwhile, the man who had bought the Chinese meals on
Saturday drove off to a supermarket where he met two of the gang.
They were dressed in sporting tracksuits and had left two racing
bicycles, one with a flat tyre, behind an electricity sub-station. The
three drove back to the apartment and, judging by the noise, drunkenly
celebrated their success for the rest of the day. No one went near the
woodyard.

The problem facing the O.C.C. was to decide which of the two
locations, the woodyard and the apartment, was the kidnappers' crisis
centre and which was the cell-block. Or, was there a third location that
had not yet been identified? It would be disastrous to order raids on the
two places only to find that there was no sign of Heineken or Doderer
in either. A further complication to consider was the possibility that the
two men were held in separate places. None of the considerable
quantity of evidence pointed categorically to any one answer, but the
indications were that the woodyard concealed the two victims. Jadu was
remote, out of view of neighbours—but not entirely—and the two
Chinese meals between four was an inconsistency that niggled the
police analysts in the O.C.C. It was decided to postpone decisions until
at least the twelve hours had passed when the gang had promised to
release their victims.

On Tuesday, the owner of Jadu returned to the woodyard and was
observed to be busy around the yard. Columns of smoke soon belched
out of the chimney stacks and there were fears he was burning
evidence—or worse. It was time to take hard decisions. At stake were
the lives of Freddy Heineken and Ab Doderer. The Policy Centre, the
Heineken Crisis Management Team, and the Operations Command
Centre jointly agreed that plans to close in on the kidnap gang should
be put into effect. They agreed that the police should raid the
woodyard in the early hours of Wednesday morning. This raid would
be followed by a series of dawn swoops on all the other locations that
had been identified as having connections with the men in the gang,
including the homes of wives, girlfriends and families.

The small hours are always colder than any other time of the night,
and the early morning of the last day of November was no exception.
Concentration at its peak, in spite of the cold, policemen moved quietly
into positions around the woodyard sometime before 5 a.m., covering

likely routes of escape, ready with ambulances which everyone hoped would not be used, and waiting to close in and cordon the woodyard while selected officers entered the buildings to search for the victims. At 05.00 hours the raid started.

Chief Inspector Sietstma waited anxiously for reports, resisting the temptation to pester his men on the ground for information. At 05.30 a.m. his chief at the woodyard reported that they had searched the place from top to bottom and found nothing. It was too late now to go back; Sietstma ordered that the search be done all over again. The police started through the buildings once more, and one officer noticed a crack in the wood walls of the new building. It was a hidden door. Swiftly the police forced it open and found two separate cells behind, in a concealed space. They contained Freddy Heineken and Ab Doderer, chained and lying on mattresses, one in each cell—and alive.

It was 6 a.m. and at once the commander of the O.C.C. ordered other raids to begin. Thirty-three people were arrested in more than twenty locations around Amsterdam and in the west of Holland. The owner of Jadu, Jan Boellard, aged thirty-five, was picked up in the apartment on Staalmeesterslaan, with 3 million guilders (about £680,000) of the ransom money; and the man who fetched the Chinese meals, Martin Erkamps aged twenty, was caught near his father's house with another 3 million. But the three other members of the gang escaped.

Heineken and Doderer were happily in good health, considering their ordeal, but hungry. The gang, who had provided only one meal a day—and the Chinese meals on the victims' last Saturday—on paper plates and with plastic spoons and forks, had simply forgotten to feed them once the ransom had been paid. The gang provided no heat and Heineken had suffered from the icy winter weather more intensely than his chauffeur, who had devised exercises around the tight chains that held each of them by one hand close to the wall, restricting movement to their mattresses and chamber pots. They had not been allowed to speak to each other for four days, until they discovered they were next door to each other, separated by a wall of hardboard. Doctors and psychologists examined them after their release and found them healthy. They were soon back with their families.

The police had more work to do. Some of the gang had been caught and the evidence had to be collated to ensure these men were brought to trial. Those who had escaped had to be pursued. The man who had planned the whole affair was Frans Meijer and he had got away. The police visited his relatives and put the word out that he should give himself up. He was only thirty-four years old and within Dutch law the maximum sentence he might expect was twelve years. So, he could still look forward to another life as a free man after he had served his time; or he could stay on the run. He began to write letters to the newspaper *Het Parool* in which he said he was sorry for his actions and wanted to commit suicide in desperation at the rotten life he had led. He declared that he would take his life on Christmas Day. The police responded by using the newspaper to suggest he give himself up, and at the end of December Meijer surrendered, claiming he was suffering from mental disorders. If this was another piece of cunning then it was misplaced. In Holland, as elsewhere, a plea of insanity means detention without limit, whereas the others in the gang, having received sentences of twelve years, might be out with a one-third remission for good behaviour after only eight years. Meijer was sent to a psychiatric clinic for examination but towards the end of 1984, after his colleagues were tried, he escaped. At the time of writing, he is still on the run.

There is little delay through the Dutch courts, compared with other countries, and the two arrested men were brought to trial in September and October 1984. They were convicted: Jan Boellard received a sentence of twelve years, while Erkamps got ten years. In Dutch law, the charges that can be brought against kidnappers are borrowed from other crimes: one is 'the extortion of money', which carries a maximum sentence of twelve years, and the other is 'illegal imprisonment', which carries a sentence of four years. Both together give a theoretical maximum for kidnap of sixteen years, but the courts found that the offences were committed separately and that the second was dependent on the first, so the maximum could only be twelve years. However, the Public Prosecutor, who had asked for the maximum of sixteen years for the offenders, has continued to press in appeal for the sentence to be reviewed. His argument has been that whereas the gang said they would release the victims within twelve hours, dependent on getting the ransom money, they did not. Therefore, the charge of illegal imprisonment, which continued for more than twelve hours after the payment, should be treated separately. The Dutch are fortunate in having had little experience of kidnap but the law suffers from not specifying the offence on the statute book.

But what of the money? Some 6 million guilders (about £1.4 million) had been found during the arrests of Boellard and Erkamps, but that left 29 million guilders (£6.7 million) unaccounted for. The police knew that the money had been taken out of the Hanemag pick-up truck between the time that the surveillance team had to pull off as the Hanemag drove on to the unfinished motorway west of Zeist, at 7.20 a.m. that Monday, and the time that the static surveillance team had reported it appearing in the hospital car-park at Amersfoort, fifteen minutes later. Considerable efforts were made to investigate what had occurred to the five sacks of loot in those fifteen minutes. Then, perhaps as a lucky reward for a well-conducted operation, or perhaps because success encourages more attention and support from the public, on 5 December a couple of honest citizens handed in two small packets of notes. They had been walking in the woods near Zeist when they had noticed two bundles totalling two hundred $100 dollar bills. The commander of the O.C.C. remembered that observation teams had followed two kidnappers in the Ford Combi to the same woods near Zeist on the day before the drop. They had waited for some minutes before being joined by the two others who had walked out of the woods. The inescapable conclusion was that the money had been hidden somewhere in the woods. To search the woods would need a large workforce, so the O.C.C. arranged for all Amsterdam's riot police to join the 'finger-tip' hunt for clues to the ransom in the wood. After some hours, they turned up four barrels buried in the ground. They contained nearly 20 million guilders (£4.6 million). It seems the two men who had been dressed as cyclists had been waiting in the wood to cache the money which had been delivered by Beollard in the Hanemag.

The police continued their investigations to catch the other kidnappers, and officers throughout the country pressed their sources for anything they might hear on the criminal grapevine. At the start of 1984, the girlfriend of one of the men who had escaped talked to a man who, unknown to her, was a police source. She said her friend was in France, and, using the offices of Interpol, the Dutch police pursued the lead to discover two more alleged kidnappers in Paris, where the French police arrested them in February. Extradition proceedings have been instituted by the Dutch authorities and the two men are contesting the orders through the French courts. At the time of their arrest, another million guilders worth of the ransom money was found with the two men. To date, some 27 million guilders (£6.2 million) of the original 35 million have been recovered and 8 million (about £1.8 million) is unaccounted for.

The case had been a success, when events are compared to the list of priorities that the O.C.C., the P.C. and the C.M.T. agreed immediately after the kidnap. The kidnap was straightforward criminal commercialism, unblemished by political influence, and the authorities had agreed to place the safety of the victims as top priority. Furthermore their subsequent actions justified their adherence to this important principle. Secondly, two of the gang had been swiftly brought to trial, convicted and sentenced within the year, while the other members of the gang had been identified and two of them arrested by the French police. Lastly, more than three-quarters of the vast ransom had been recovered. From the start, when the whole web of police units, supporting groups and other agencies were set up, through the three weeks of the victims' captivity and the payment, to the identification of the kidnappers, the case is a model of police effort. The Dutch police have bound the report in a large volume and recognize the value of learning lessons from their experience. They have held seminars at their own Netherlands Detective School, the first in June 1984, and internationally, such as at the German Bundeskriminalamt in Wiesbaden later in the summer of 1984.

From the many lessons of the Heineken and Doderer kidnap, and the others, the police learned many lessons—on organizational structure; on chains of command and reporting; on investigative routine and methods; on speeding international communications and smoothing the paths to co-operation, through Interpol, with bordering police forces; on improving surveillance methods; on use of technical equipment in the field; on tactics; resource employment; and many others.

Having decided to prevent kidnap ever getting a grip in Holland, the Dutch threw everything they had against the kidnappers, resolving that they would not get away. The police committed men and material, money and resources. In the Heineken and Doderer case more than seventy men were at the core, in the O.C.C., with hundreds more involved in everything from the vital pro-active observation teams to uniformed police in every unit in the country following routine, but essential, detective work connected with the case. Associated with this activity was a colossal employment of machines and equipment. They created new teams and command structures, drew on past experiences—for example surveillance skills learned in the battle against drug traffic—and used the latest technical and scientific expertise. They used the increasingly swift methods of communications available for international co-operation between police forces, with the good offices of Interpol. In short, the police were totally committed, in public statement and, more telling, in deed.

The police were also backed by the government and the judiciary. The Policy Centre in the Heineken case is evidence that the politicians and members of the judiciary were concerned to discuss decisions of the O.C.C., in the manner of a father worrying for his daughter, but they were ready to approve, not to hamper. Moreover, in agreeing to operations on such a scale the government was committing that other most important resource: money. In the battle of police against crime there is a constant fight to keep on top, each working to better the other's techniques and, in the modern world with exotic equipment, money is the bottom line. Criminals finance themselves, with crimes like kidnap; the police need finance by government vote.

The Dutch police are fortunate in having a society which supports the general concepts of law and order. Over 1500 tip-offs came from members of the public, one of which was instrumental in locating the kidnappers and ultimately freeing the two victims. The Dutch police also had a very good relationship with the families of the kidnapped people. Alfred Heineken's family were concerned that the surveillance could be effectively carried out without compromising the police presence, but, with good professional advice and aware of police motivation and record, the C.M.T. agreed to co-operate wholeheartedly.

This final point completes a picture that should be the envy of police in other countries faced by more grievous kidnap statistics: a police force committing tremendous resources, backed by government with policy and finance, enjoying the co-operation of the public and working closely with the family. The separate elements depend on each other for success, as a table needs four legs. The Dutch examples show how.

TEN

The British Blueprint

Kidnapping has never been particularly popular among criminals in the United Kingdom. Almost all the major kidnaps for ransom in Britain since the first in 1969 were carried out either by foreigners or by loners who were outside the criminal mainstream.

The kidnap of Mrs Muriel McKay in 1969 was the work of two brothers born in Trinidad who came to Britain as young men. Greek Cypriots were involved in the abductions of Aloi Kologhiro in 1975 and of Mr and Mrs Emmanuel Xuereb in 1983. The kidnap and murder of Lesley Whittle in 1975 was, however, carried out by a Briton—Donald Nielson, who became known as the 'Black Panther' during the period in which he robbed several post offices and murdered three sub-post masters. One of the reasons it took so long to catch him was that he had no previous record; the one fingerprint found near Lesley Whittle's body had no match in police records. Nielson turned out to be a psychopathic loner, albeit a deadly and resourceful one, with a grudge against society.

A major factor militating against kidnap in Britain may be the existence of a well-trained and efficient police force. At least, that is the common image of the British police. However, the infrequency of kidnap for ransom in the United Kingdom has in the past had its drawbacks. The police had built up little experience in dealing with this complex crime. The result was that the two major kidnaps in the

early 1970s were widely publicized cases that turned out to be
disasters for both the police and the victims, even though no ransoms
were paid, largely, it must be said, because of inefficient and
inexperienced handling by the police. To their great credit, the police
recognized this and moved to put their house in order for the future,
as we will show.

* * * *

Mrs Muriel McKay was kidnapped from her Wimbledon home on 30
December 1969. She was the wife of Mr (later Sir) Alick McKay,
deputy chairman of the *News of the World*, owned by the Press tycoon
Rupert Murdoch who is an Australian, like McKay. The case was to
last forty-one days until the police moved in on Rooks Farm at
Stocking Pelham, Hertfordshire, (some thirty-five miles north of
London) and arrested the owner, Arthur Hosein, and his younger
brother, Nizamodeen. They never found any trace of Mrs McKay.
The Hosein brothers were tried and found guilty of her kidnap and
murder. With no sign of the body, the success of the murder charge
created a precedent in the British Courts. The two men were
sentenced to life imprisonment, forty-nine years for Arthur and
thirty-nine for Nizamodeen.

It was the first kidnap for ransom in modern British history and the
police investigation was praised by the trial judge, Mr Justice Shaw, as
a model of its kind. True, the ransom money was denied to the
criminal world, but what of the wretched victim? What sort of 'model'
was that? In practical and human terms it was a terrible catalogue of
naive blunders, due, likely enough, to the novelty of the case. For the
same reason the Press performed an equally disastrous role, blowing
up the whole series of dud leads, fed to them by the family and the
police, into sensational and totally untrue stories which misled the
public, encouraged the attentions of a number of mediums, and
attracted a mass of hoaxers whose false alarms seriously disrupted the
police investigation, certainly upset the plans of the kidnappers and
might well have helped precipitate the death of the victim. Mrs
McKay was probably murdered within three days of her abduction.
The likeliest theory for the non-recovery of her body is that it was fed
to the farm pigs. The Hoseins never revealed what they did with her.

The kidnap had all the hallmarks of deadly amateurism. The idea
was planted in Arthur Hosein's mind by a David Frost television
interview with Rupert Murdoch, then a newcomer to the Fleet Street

scene. It was clear from the programme that Murdoch was a very wealthy man, and Hosein, watching, was a braggart with dreams of being a millionaire. He had come to Britain from Trinidad in 1955 as a skilled tailor's cutter. He set up shop in Hackney, in London's East End, and his neighbours soon became familiar with his boasts of future fortune. Conscripted into the Army as a national serviceman, he deserted, was court martialled, and served six months detention. He was described by an officer as 'immeasurably the worst soldier it has been my misfortune to have under me . . . that is when he wasn't absent or in detention.' Hosein started up the social scale by moving out of Hackney to a house in Ongar, and, after marrying his German-born wife Elsa, to the dilapidated Rooks Farm at Stocking Pelham. There he played the country squire to his amused neighbours, but fooled no one except himself. He found it hard to finance his grandiose dreams but when he saw the Frost interview he suddenly saw the answer: kidnap Murdoch's wife and demand enough money to end all his troubles for life.

Tragically for Mrs McKay, Murdoch left England on a business trip to Australia, handing the reins of the *News of the World* and the keys of his Rolls Royce to Mr McKay. The Hosein brothers, who had checked the ownership of the car in the County Hall's taxation office, waited outside the *News of the World* offices and followed the Rolls Royce to the McKay house, believing it to be the home of Rupert Murdoch. There, in Wimbledon, they seized Muriel McKay.

They left plenty of evidence: pages of *The People* newspaper, printed for the Hertfordshire area and with Arthur Hosein's fingerprints on it; a billhook identified as typical in the Bishops Stortford region (which included Stocking Pelham); a yard of Elastoplast and a ball of baling twine commonly used by farmers. A Volvo driven by an 'Arab type' was spotted near Arthur Road, where the McKays lived. The Hoseins owned a blue Volvo, a later sighting of which near a ransom drop place was crucial to his arrest.

The day after the kidnap, a letter was received by Alick McKay from his wife; this had Hosein's fingerprints on it too. But the police were not convinced at first that it was a genuine kidnap; there were suspicions that it was a stunt to publicize Murdoch's *Sun*, recently bought and relaunched as a popular tabloid. Other theories were that she had run off with another man or had left home in a menopausal daze. It was doubly unfortunate that the McKays were a Press family: they constantly released all sorts of material to the Press which should have been filtered through the police, and the police had no one experienced enough to advise the family on such tactics as using the Press during a negotiation. The kidnappers made swift contact by telephone but, because the family had already informed the Press of the kidnap, it was thought the call was a hoax. (It seems, too, that the police had not understood the reasons for asking—and if necessary insisting on—the correct answer to a proof of life question.) In fact the call was genuine. Later, the kidnappers could not get through on the telephone for an astonishing nine days because the line to the McKays' house was jammed with every sort of inquiry from the Press and the public.

The police had enough good leads to have found the Hoseins a lot quicker than they did. They simply fouled them up by inexperience and over-enthusiasm. Some of the gaffes would be hilarious to look back on and worthy of an Ealing Studios film comedy, were it not such a ghastly case. They happened during attempts to make a ransom drop. A police officer took the place of Ian McKay, the victim's son who had been ordered by the kidnappers to make the drop, while another dressed as the chauffeur. A vast squad of police was drafted to shadow the McKay Rolls Royce on the drop run to a rendezvous in a country lane near Ware, Hertfordshire. Many of these were police motor cyclists disguised as Hells Angels, but their disguise was spoiled by years of police training: in complete contrast to the anarchic style of the Angels, they obeyed all the road traffic regulations and sat ramrod stiff on their bikes. A 'convoy' of forty-eight police surveillance vehicles cruised slowly round the area and past the drop site. Local police in a Panda car, unaware of the operation in progress, stopped one of the surveillance cars because its occupants were acting so suspiciously (surveillance is the art of remaining unnoticed). During another attempt at a drop run, a burly male police detective sergeant impersonated the McKays' daughter who had been ordered by the Hoseins to carry £250,000 on the number 47 bus from Catford, leaving at 5.45 a.m. for Stamford Hill. Two other officers, disguised as workers, sat near their 'lady' colleague on the bus, but a woman passenger became suspicious of the inadequately disguised 'lady' policeman. Worried, she left the bus and reported seeing a transvestite to a policeman on the beat who, doubtless wondering what anyone was doing in drag at that hour of the morning in Catford, called for support. Officers boarded the bus from a local police car and questioned the embarrassed detective sergeant. He managed to convince them of his bona fide employment and, absurdly, after this fracas with uniformed police and in ignorance of the general rule that kidnappers follow the drop run to spot the surveillance, the operation was allowed to continue. This lack of basic training, planning, preparation and co-ordination seems staggering by today's high standards of police surveillance.

The final attempt to pay a ransom also misfired because of lack of co-ordination between police forces. The Hoseins laid a complicated trail from the McKays' house in Wimbledon via telephone boxes in Edmonton in North London, Bethnal Green in the East End and Epping in Essex to a spot opposite a used car garage in Bishops Stortford, Herfordshire. Again police officers took the places of the McKay family but this time at least, a woman officer played the part of the Mackays' daughter. The last stage of the journey from Epping to Bishops Stortford was travelled in a genuine hire car whose driver became increasingly bemused by the unusual antics of his passengers and then terrified when one eventually threw himself out of the car opposite the garage with the two suitcases containing the ransom money. While a large number of officers in various disguises loitered around the area, the suitcases lay in the hedge, as per instructions for three hours until a passing couple who had left the pub nearby fell over them in the dark. The wife stood guard over them while her husband went off to the local police. These officers knew nothing of the operation and arrived to find the suitcases full of money (actually the bundles of notes were false with a few genuine £5 notes on the top of each). Finally the operation was called off.

Fortunately the Hoseins were as amateurish as the police. During this buzz of surveillance activity a blue Volvo was seen driving slowly past the suitcases with two men inside. The number was taken and traced (in those days a policeman had to be sent over Westminster Bridge from Scotland Yard to County Hall to check records for ownership) to a Mrs Elsa Hosein of Rooks Farm at Stocking Pelham. The police abandoned the surveillance operation, left two officers to watch the farm and went to bed.

With hindsight it would appear astonishing that in spite of the number of clues which accumulated from day one, on 29 December, it took the police so long to find the Hoseins. Arthur Hosein had left his prints on the newspaper left at the McKay house during the kidnapping and on other evidence throughout the case: on a second letter received by the family on 27 January and on a cigarette packet in an Edmonton telephone box used as a contact point in the first drop run. It was agreed that the kidnapper's voice had an Indian or West Indian timbre, the blue Volvo was seen several times during the case and much of the activity took place in Hertfordshire. But it still took forty-one days to track down the Hoseins. It is invidious to suggest that the police might have saved Mrs McKay, but the operational shortcomings in surveillance, in negotiating and in the co-ordination of police effort were there for all to see. Unfortunately, the lessons were not learned. In the next big kidnap things were just as bad.

*   *   *   *

'It was a total bloody disaster,' a senior Scotland Yard officer said years after the dust of the 1975 Lesley Whittle case had settled—and the target of his bitter criticism was the police's own handling of the operation. As in the McKay case in 1970, a series of elementary blunders, particularly in the surveillance, and above all in the utter lack of co-ordination between the three county police forces involved, meant that a string of clues was missed, and the ransom drop was fouled up. The victim lost her life. The kidnapper, Donald Neilson, escaped from the drop site and was not arrested until nearly a year later, in another part of the country, as a result of a random spot check by two constables in a patrol car.

Lesley Whittle was a seventeen-year-old college student, whose family owned and ran a successful coach business from the Shropshire village of Highley. Again, it was by chance that her name came to the attention of her kidnapper. Neilson came from a different part of the country, Bradford, in Yorkshire, where he was a jobbing builder who had gradually turned to crime. He happened to read an article in the *Daily Express* in 1973 about Lesley's father's will. It was enough to plant the idea of kidnap in his mind. He may also have read in an issue of *Readers Digest* at about that time an account of an American kidnap, that of Barbara Mackle, in 1969. There were several grim similarities in the two cases.

Neilson had mapped out the kidnap with the precision of a former soldier. At his trial he claimed that he planned to kidnap Lesley's elder brother, Ronald, aged thirty-two, who ran the business, but the first person he came across when he had broken into the Whittle's home in the middle of the night of 14 January 1975 was Lesley. He ordered her to get out of bed and get dressed and hustled her out to his car. He had an enormous disadvantage compared to experienced kidnappers: he was working alone. He worked alone on other criminal jobs and had already murdered three times during small-time robberies from sub-post offices around the country. This was to be his biggest operation, the one that he planned would set him up for life. He wanted a mere £50,000.

Without support, he needed a site where he could leave Lesley tied up and in no danger of being discovered while he organized the ransom payment. He found what he wanted at Bathpool Park, near Kidsgrove in Staffordshire, which he originally reconnoitred because a railway line ran beside it and he wanted the ransom to be thrown from a train. Walking around the park, he heard the sound of water beneath his feet and discovered an extensive underground network of tunnels making up a drainage system. This would be where he would hide his victim.

On the night of the kidnap he drove Lesley, trussed up in the back of his car, smothered and hidden from view beneath a mattress, to Bathpool Park and forced her down into the tunnels. He installed her in the dank underground prison wrapped up in sleeping bags against the appalling January cold, while he prepared his instructions for the drop on Dymo tapes, and made her record his messages to her family, to be played back on the telephone.

Neilson planned three alternative payment runs. The first was via the Swan shopping centre in Kidderminster. By telephone he ordered Ronald Whittle to go to the three phone kiosks in the centre and wait for a call between 6 p.m. and 1 a.m. the evening after Lesley was kidnapped. Detective Chief Superintendent Bob Booth, then head of West Mercia C.I.D., was in charge of the case, and, according to his account (made public nine years later) this was to be the first police blunder. Whittle was accompanied by an armed detective, posing as a friend. This man was a senior officer of the Regional Crime Squad who had been asked by Booth to oversee the operation. Neilson rang the boxes at a minute past midnight and got no reply. (Booth only knew the kidnapper had called because his people were tapping the lines.) According to Booth, the Regional Crime Squad had called off the operation after six hours of waiting at the phone box. At his trial, Neilson said he dialled each box several times and eventually heard an engaged or discontinued signal followed by a man's voice saying, 'Who's this?' He rang off, rightly suspecting a trap. Booth was furious, and said he regarded this as a major error, making the kidnapper feel uneasy and suspicious from the outset. He also said that many of the police officers on the case did not believe they were dealing with a kidnap negotiation at all, echoing the start of the McKay case five years before. There was also a great deal of ill-informed speculation about the case in the Press, as there had been in the earlier case. The news of Lesley's disappearance had soon got out, hit the headlines and gripped the nation's interest for weeks.

Neilson's second attempt to take the ransom came the next evening. He had picked the car-park at Dudley Zoo as the site for the drop, at the end of a trail of messages left in Black Country call boxes, starting in Walsall. But he was spotted acting suspiciously by an overseer at the Dudley Freightliner Terminal opposite. Challenged, Neilson shot the man several times, wounding him so seriously that he never recovered and died a year later. Neilson fled, leaving his stolen Morris 1100 car, containing a mass of vital evidence, parked only three hundred metres away. Amazingly, it was not discovered by police for eight days. Booth said later that he thought prompt discovery of the car, in which Neilson had left a tape recording and cassettes of Lesley's voice, could have saved her life. But it was Neilson's third and final attempt, the next night, that witnessed the worst mistakes during the surveillance operation and may have triggered Lesley's death.

The night Lesley was abducted, Commander Ernest Bond of Scotland Yard called Booth to offer him a specialist surveillance unit with sophisticated technical back-up. The next day they were in action. On the night of 16/17 January they were placed in ground control of the surveillance operation covering the payment.

Neilson had picked Bathpool Park itself for his last attempt to get the £50,000. He played a message taped by Lesley over the telephone to the home of Ronald Whittle's depot manager—presumably hoping to avoid the inevitable police taps on the Whittle home—and instructed Ronald to go to yet another telephone box, this time at Kidsgrove post office, in Staffordshire. The West Mercian police informed their Staffordshire neighbours that the Lesley Whittle inquiry had moved across the boundary between the constabularies, saying they wanted no help and a free hand.

Ronald Whittle arrived at the rendezvous late, because he did not know the area. Proper police planning should have put him right. He was carrying £50,000 in notes, all of which had been micro-filmed by the police—though he never knew it—and the suitcase containing them had been bugged with a beacon-locating device. Whittle was also issued with a radio transmitter which he used to keep in touch with the police who were tailing him. When he did finally arrive at the telephone box it took him half an hour to find Neilson's message (another tape) because it had been stuffed right down behind a panel. It was Booth's theory that the Staffordshire police had ignored his requests to leave the West Mercians to get on with the case, and sent an officer to examine the phone box where he had found the tape and replaced it too well hidden behind the panel. He said it made no sense for Neilson to make it difficult for Ronald Whittle to find the drop instructions. The tape told Whittle to go to a place in Bathpool Park and there to flash his headlights. This would be answered by a torch which he should then approach. Unfortunately a courting couple happened to drive into the park by the route Whittle had been ordered to take and they saw the torch. They also witnessed a police Panda car drive through the same area, with its police sign clearly illuminated on the roof. Whittle, delayed by the business at the phone box, followed after all this activity. It is no wonder that Neilson never showed his torch again.

The kidnapper had been watching from a concealed position and became increasingly worried that he was being trapped. In something of a panic and probably angry that the ransom had slipped from his grasp again, he returned to the grim prison in the tunnel where Lesley was tied up with wire round her neck, standing on a small platform in a deep shaft. He claimed later that she 'went over the side' while trying to make room for him on the narrow platform, but, in view of his previous ruthless behaviour, it is more likely that he callously pushed her off in a fury. She died instantly by hanging. Realizing he could make no more taped instructions and, misreading the chaos of the drop run for a tightening police net, he fled, successfully avoiding the Scotland Yard team which was trying to keep tabs on Whittle and Bathpool Park.

At Neilson's trial, Booth confirmed that a fully marked police car, which was nothing to do with the surveillance and must have been from the Staffordshire force, had driven right through the operational area, despite his request to the local police to stay away. Later Booth claimed that it was a Staffordshire car sent to pick up Neilson, but this was denied by Staffordshire Chief Constable Arthur Rees who insisted his force had stayed away. The fact remains that there was no co-ordination, so vital to any surveillance operation.

The morning after the abortive drop run in Bathpool Park, Booth agreed to a request from the twelve-man Scotland Yard team to let them search the park. They found nothing. Incredibly, even a van left by Neilson was overlooked, yet it was being watched by Staffordshire police who were suspicious since it contained equipment typical of a burglar and they were waiting for the owner to return.

Equally, it is astonishing in retrospect that no one thought to search the drainage system beneath the park. Booth was as ignorant of the possibility of underground escape routes as the German police were later in the cases of Erlemann and Oetker. The search for Lesley Whittle went cold. There were no more messages from the kidnapper and no sign of the victim. A full seven weeks later Staffordshire police found a ransom note from Neilson in the park. It had been found previously by children and thrown away, but it led the police to search the drainage system where they quickly found the remains of Lesley Whittle. They also picked up a mass of evidence left by Neilson, some of which had earlier been seen in his van. Booth's excuse for not searching the park more thoroughly was that he did not want the kidnapper to think that he was playing a double game: in public, via the Press and television, he kept reassuring the kidnapper that the ransom would be paid and pleaded with him, frequently in highly-charged and emotional tones, not to harm the victim.

The Whittle case left relationships between West Mercia and Staffordshire in tatters, while the Yard had nothing to boast about. In fairness, the Yard's small squad was obliged to obey orders from senior local officers and had no chance to use its skills fully. Each time the Metropolitan police leaves London to support forces elsewhere its officers face the same difficulties. The London police gain much experience with rarer crimes that is denied to other forces and often know more about a subject than their provincial brothers; they believe they are an elite, but after the incompetent search of Bathpool Park their reputation took a beating and did not recover till Lesley's body was found and a senior Murder Squad detective was sent from the Yard to head the investigation.

Lesley Whittle's kidnap and murder sadly underlined all the shortcomings that had seemingly been glossed over after the Muriel McKay case. The police could not respond effectively to a kidnap investigation. They could not provide sensitive surveillance—born of good training and technological sophistication. They had no idea about negotiating with kidnappers—they could not resolve the conflict of priorities between the policeman's traditional role of catching the villains and saving the victim's life. They could not organize the necessary and considerable resources of manpower and money—the McKay case cost over £200,000 and filled forty-five filing cabinets—and they had no coherent command structure with the necessary authority to co-ordinate all this. The autonomy of county forces made resolution of these problems all the more difficult, and, to some extent, this is still the case.

Surveillance is certainly a crucial part of an investigation to find the kidnap gang and to recover the victim alive. Both mobile and static surveillance: of the victim's house, of the intermediary on his way to make the payment, of places designated on the drop run, of houses and buildings where the victim may be held. Out of the Whittle case grew a conviction in the Metropolitan police that kidnap surveillance should be handled by Scotland Yard's specialist surveillance team, C11, a group of around fifty highly trained officers who concentrate full-time on this complex skill. This department is trained to watch and follow targets for long (generally boring) periods, irrespective of the time of day or of the weather, and using state-of-the-art technical equipment. Like most elite units, C11 does not court publicity, rarely coming to light, as it had to in January 1985 when one of its number, P.C. John Fordham, was stabbed to death by bullion dealer Kenneth Noyes whose movements he was trying to observe in a covert but out-on-a-limb, position, in the grounds of Noyes' Kent house. Noyes was acquitted of murder in December the same year. The verdict has immense and far reaching implications for C11 surveillance operations. The jury's 'not guilty' verdict said in effect that P.C. Fordham had been lawfully killed, thus depriving his widow of the right to claim compensation from the Criminal Injuries Compensation Board. This precedent means that, for the sake of officers' families, the Yard cannot allow its surveillance teams to be as exposed as tactical circumstances generally demand. This development could have serious implications of reduced police capability in future kidnap cases, when surveillance exposure often needs to be greater than for average police work.

Fortunately, more than mere increased awareness of the problems developed from the McKay and Whittle cases. Senior Scotland Yard officers started thinking urgently about how to improve their response to kidnap. They had their eyes on Italy (where in 1975 alone there were seventy-seven officially reported kidnaps) and on Central and South America. The Yard identified command and control as the key elements. In the Whittle case their men had been subordinate to the local chief investigating officer, Bob Booth of West Mercia, who, like every other police officer in the United Kingdom at the time, knew next to nothing about kidnap negotiations. However, even if the Yard developed a kidnap response blueprint—and it was the natural force to do this—there was no certainty of it being adopted outside the Metropolitan area. The autonomy of each constabulary meant that the Yard might be called in but they had no automatic right of command. The problem would be compounded if, as in the Whittle case, the ransom trailed across several force boundaries.

A senior Scotland Yard officer was detailed to draw up the blueprint. This officer took pains to research the subject carefully, even talking to jailed kidnappers. The results of his work formed the basis for the present British police response and are widely disseminated to other constabularies during seminars, for example at the Police Staff College at Bramshill, so that while the problems of county autonomy remain, police across the United Kingdom have available the necessary advice for a measured response. The details of this response remain secret but the bare bones of it are as follows.

The officer concluded that the typical British kidnap gang would be small, probably no more than five people: three to take turns guarding the victim, one to negotiate and one to handle the administration of supplying cars, leaving messages, buying provisions and so on.

Perhaps the most important aspect of any operation is to settle the objectives first. The officer quickly realized that these are somewhat different in kidnap cases to other run-of-the-mill criminal investigations. What were the priorities? Capture of the criminals? Recovery of the money? Releasing the victim alive? He decided that it had to be the last. If the choice was between letting the villains go and saving the victim's life, or capturing him and risking the victim's death, the police must let the kidnappers go. This would be a major stumbling block in persuading other officers to accept the blueprint because catching criminals is what policework is about. It is traditional. However, he decided that in any given case this order of priorities had to be established clearly from the outset. The victim's life was top priority. All other aims were subordinate. The next priority was the arrest and conviction of the kidnappers. Other objects such as recovering the money and controlling the risk to Lloyd's insurance market in an insured case came lower down the list of priorities.

Who was to run the show? Someone with the necessary authority at the right level. A Chief Investigating Officer (C.I.O.) had to be placed at the titular head of the whole operation—perhaps an assistant Chief Constable in a provincial force and in London a senior Metropolitan police commander. Next, the blueprint placed the C11 chief in actual practical command of the operations. His job would be to run the case in detail, reporting to and taking orders, generally of a strategic kind, from the C.I.O. He would also have to guide the C.I.O. in understanding the unusual order of priorities.

What sort of operation would they be directing? From this study of kidnapping cases, the officer recognized and established three areas of work. The first, coded Red, dealt with the victim's family, home and place of business. He understood that the gang would contact the victim's family, and realized that building up a relationship with the family called for great sensitivity, not least because of the inevitable threat not to contact the police. The Red team would be sent to the family as quickly as possible and, headed by a Detective Chief Inspector, would be responsible for the delicate interface between the police operation and the family. D.C.I. Red's job would include coping with the distraught family, explaining that the police understood the danger to the victim, and communicating the police priorities (which, with the new decision, now accorded with those of most families), and organizing his group of technicians to tape telephone calls and so on. This team would arrive covertly, suitably disguised, in case the kidnappers had thought to put someone watching the house. D.C.I. Red would stay with the family for the duration of the kidnap and it was crucial that he and his team arrived as soon as possible, before the family received any wrong and misleading advice from anyone else. Once installed, D.C.I. Red had to win the family's trust so he could advise them of how to negotiate and pass on the instructions handed to him by his boss, the head of C11, with whom he had to maintain constant liaison. This aspect of a kidnap adviser's job calls for exceptional powers of tact and resourcefulness. One stipulation the blueprint made was that he got plenty of sleep. The senior officer researching the new strategy found that the small numbers in the average gang were a disadvantage to the kidnappers that became greater and greater the longer the case wore on. The police could afford to get a decent rest, a gang of five could not. The resulting difference in operating efficiency could be critical when the key decisions had to be made at the climax of a case.

The second team, coded Blue, would be the surveillance unit plus a mobile operations room when necessary. They would start work soon after C11 was alerted, when there were suitable targets to observe, such as the victim's house, and then spread their net or concentrate on particular avenues of inquiry as the investigation and ransom negotiation progressed.

The third team, coded Green, would be the central operations unit, designed to link Red and Blue teams on the ground with the Chief Investigating Officer at the strategic level and with all the other agencies that might get involved. D.C.I. Green was to be in charge of this administration. The head of C11, the operational controller, would be based at this hub, with D.C.I. Green, until he thought it necessary to move out with a mobile operations room to be nearer the action of a surveillance task. This set-up, with an operations room (the Green team) at the centre, controlling the surveillance (the Blue team), the liaison with the family (the Red team) and every other agency, yet working to an overall commander (the C.I.O.), is similar to the system adopted with such success by the Dutch police during the Heineken case, though there has been no contact between the Amsterdam police and Scotland Yard over kidnapping.

The head of C11's first action would be to order D.C.I. Green to start a log of events, and the first thing to be noted would be the priority: to save the victim.

The next step would be an innovative and controversial one: to seek a total media blackout on the case, so that the public would be quite unaware that a kidnap was going on. For the police, one of the worst aspects of the McKay and Whittle cases had been the fact the news leaked out within a few hours of the victims' disappearances and thereafter reporters pestered the police and families throughout. Kidnap is a dramatic crime. It is ideally suited to sensational treatment: the horror of the abduction, the awful plight of the victim, the anguish of the family, the 'cloak and dagger' business of negotiating, and finally the excitement of the ransom payment. Human emotions, the chance of action, blood and death: such ingredients are hard to resist. There are also endless red herrings to pursue. In the kidnaps of McKay and Whittle, the police investigations had been bedevilled by hoaxers trying to get the families to pay them some easy money after they had heard of the kidnap through the media. Press reporting caused so much confusion to the police investigation that it jeopardized the victims' lives. Acting on advice from his head of Press relations, Malcolm Johnson, Sir Robert Mark who was Commissioner of the Metropolitan police, called a conference of newspaper editors to put forward the idea of a news blackout. There were naturally deep suspicions among the Press at the thought of agreeing to any infringement of their existing freedom to report. The Yard attempted to allay these by promising to keep the media informed of the progress of the investigation, even though they would be sworn to silence, and to cooperate as fully as possible with information as soon as the victim was released. This arrangement had the advantage of ensuring that in the end accurate and comprehensive reports would be filed.

Many police officers had grave misgivings about this idea too. They did not trust the Press to keep their side of the bargain. If one editor broke, they all would, that was certain, as each competed furiously with the other for the best story; and all would be lost. The police were also reluctant to say too much about the investigation, for fear that leaked details would compromise its success. These doubts, natural among police officers in any event, were fuelled by the bitter memories of the cases of McKay and Whittle. But the police doubters underestimated the Press's ability to keep a secret, and did not understand their delight at being taken into the confidence of the police in such dramatic circumstances.

The big tactical advantage of the blackout is that it leaves the kidnappers in the dark. The Yard officer asked to produce the blueprint had learned that British gangs were small and inexperienced by comparison with the *cognoscenti* in Italy. Starving them of news in papers and on the television would seriously weaken their knowledge of what was going on. To such men (and probably to experienced kidnappers too) the blackout meant cutting off a valuable source of intelligence about the family's reactions and the police effort. Furthermore, without news there would be a tremendous temptation for the gang to set a watch on the victim's family home to see if the police had actually been informed, or to check on their activities. This possibility would provide the police Blue team with an initial surveillance task: to watch for the watchers.

The blueprint specified one further detail of paramount importance. It was essential to ask, and if necessary insist on, proof that the victim was alive. This basic question was not demanded during the McKay case, nor in many other sad cases mentioned in this book. *It is always crucial.*

* * * *

The first test of the blueprint came in November 1975. Fortunately the case was in London so there was no problem of briefing a provincial force. On Thursday 6 November, Aloi Kologhiro, an eighteen-year-old Greek Cypriot girl studying in London, was kidnapped from the home of her brother and sister-in-law in Outram Road, Wood Green, North London. In a curious echo of the McKay and Whittle cases, the kidnappers had meant to seize somebody else: in this case, her sister Krini. But when they burst into the house, Aloi was the only person there. They dragged her off, leaving a note demanding £60,000, to be paid in one week in used £5 and £10 notes. The note added a dire, though typical, warning: if the police were contacted Aloi would be killed. This scrap of paper was found ninety minutes later when Krini returned home. She contacted her husband, Loucas Neocleous, a twenty-five-year-old accountant, and he raced to join her. They were shattered but, despite the kidnappers' note, they wisely decided to call the police.

The kidnap blueprint was put into operation for the first time after a senior officers' meeting at Scotland Yard. Here, the priority of saving the girl's life was established. Then, the operations centre was set up—under D.C.I. Green. D.C.I. Red moved his men secretly into the house with Krini and Loucas, a covert observation unit under D.C.I. Blue took up station to watch the house and surrounding area, and the following day confidential letters were delivered by hand to the editors of the major newspapers and news editors of the broadcasting organizations.

The text of this letter referred to 'an alleged kidnapping of a Greek Cypriot female in the London area', mentioned the ransom demand and said there appeared to be no political motive. It went on to ask the editors to refrain from publishing any information about the case—or from acting on any such information. By that the Yard meant that the last thing they wanted was a horde of journalists descending on the scene and alerting the kidnappers, even if nothing was actually published. The letter promised that newspapers and the other media would be kept informed of developments. The media agreed to the deal: nothing leaked out and the general public knew nothing of the drama.

Now that foundations had been laid, work started in earnest. Over the weekend, the police contacted Aloi's father, a semi-retired businessman who lived in Cyprus, and arranged for him and his wife to fly to London. Then, on Monday, case-day five, the negotiation for

Aloi's life began with two brief telephone calls from the kidnappers, received by Loucas Neocleous, who acted as the family's negotiator with the kidnap gang throughout the case. They repeated the ransom figure and threatened to kill the girl if the police were called in.

The next day, the Yard called a confidential Press conference to thank the media for their co-operation so far and to provide an account of the case, without naming the girl or her family. Mr Jock Wilson, assistant Commissioner (Crime), and the C.I.O., said that the fact that the gang had called twice in a day, from public phone boxes, indicated a certain anxiety on their part. He believed matters were getting to a critical stage and he asked for a twenty-four hour extension. It emerged that the police thought a group of Cypriots were responsible—Wood Green has a large and tightly-knit Greek Cypriot community. The family was not wealthy enough to pay the ransom of £60,000 demanded and though the police were advising closely they did not interfere with the family's decision to pay a ransom.

The secret Press briefings became daily events, with the blackout being extended day by day. The agreement was holding. The media co-operated fully with the police who were delighted. They realized how helpful it was to work without pressure from reporters and the public. Mr Wilson told the reporters: 'The big mistake that was made in the McKay and Whittle cases was the bloody publicity. If this one comes off, it will be down to you.'

Meanwhile, the gang were making regular calls, maintaining their hard-line threats to kill Aloi and insisting on their £60,000. Loucas, speaking for the family, argued that £60,000 was out of the question and demanded proof of life. The original deadline of a week expired without the gang providing it. Mr Wilson told the Friday conference that the kidnappers seemed to know what they were doing. But on that Friday, case-day eight, the gang turned their negotiating tactics volte-face and abandoned their brutal refusal to consider any reduction. They finally provided proof that Aloi was still alive and agreed to drop their demand to £17,000, which was all that Loucas had said the family could offer.

Next day, Saturday, they gave instructions how the ransom was to be paid: the money was to be wrapped in plastic and left in a rubbish skip near the tube station in Kentish Town, a suburb of North London. The police, keeping in close touch with the family through D.C.I. Red, agreed to allow the payment to be made.

Aloi Kologhiro was released soon after the payment, blindfolded, near Bounds Green tube station, not far from Wood Green. A drunk, staggering about by the station was not what he seemed. He was a policeman in D.C.I. Blue's team, disguised for covert surveillance duties and carrying a concealed radio. He alerted his back-up team, and the gang were quickly followed and arrested.

Aloi's uncle was charged with the kidnapping but acquitted by an Old Bailey jury. Four other men who pleaded guilty received sentences ranging from eight to twelve years. For the Yard, the case had been a success. The girl was saved, the criminals were caught, the money was recovered, and the news blackout had worked. In summary, the new blueprint worked.

* * * *

Since then, there have been eight kidnaps for ransom in the Metropolitan police area in which the media blackout policy has been repeated. On each occasion, the victim has been rescued, the ransom, if paid, has been recovered and arrests made. Of course, the media blackout is not the only reason for this run of success. It is merely one part of that original Scotland Yard blueprint, which has been refined and improved over the years in the light of lessons learned in each case.

In several instances, the behaviour of the kidnappers underlines the theory that the crime does not seem to attract the keenest criminal minds nor the professionals in Britain. Eighteen-year-old Robert Goldstein, son of a wealthy Essex property developer, was clearly seized by inexperienced men. He was kidnapped in March 1983, from outside the estate agent's office where he was a trainee, and a £200,000 ransom was demanded. It was left in a suitcase by the M11 motorway, but never picked up, and the young man was happily released unharmed after a short but frightening twenty-nine hours of captivity. Once the young man was freed, the police were able to continue their investigation unencumbered by the priorities of kidnapping, and C13, the anti-terrorist squad, arrested four men a week later. It is always the case that when the kidnap victim is recovered the police pursue the outstanding detection in the normal way.

In June 1981, Reem al Harithi, daughter of a retired Saudi Arabian General, was kidnapped as she was being driven to school from her parents' Knightsbridge home. It transpired that the family's chauffeur had cooked up the plot, and he held the girl hostage in a North London flat for two days. The chauffeur, Susantha Karunartne, who was born in Sri Lanka, pretended to her that he too was a victim of the 'gang' and meanwhile tried to extort a ransom of £150,000 from her father. Karunartne's choice of payment positively identifies him as an ignorant kidnapper—though fortunately the girl was not to suffer as a result of his inexperience, as Leslie Whittle had done. He settled on a direct swap of the ransom money for the girl at a pre-arranged rendezvous at the Odeon cinema in Swiss Cottage. This place was well covered by the men of D.C.I. Blue's surveillance team who arrested the kidnapper with two accomplices and freed the girl. Karunartne got fifteen years, his two assistants, twelve and three years. Reem survived her thirty-two-hour ordeal with remarkable sang-froid.

The police blueprint suffered its fullest test during the kidnap of Maria and Emmanuel Xuereb. This couple's nightmarish experience began in January 1983, only five months after they were married, when they returned to their Kent home from a shopping spree in the January sales, their arms laden with parcels. They were seized by masked men, shoved into a car and driven away. Emmanuel Xuereb, thirty-four years old and of Maltese origin, was a wine merchant and, perhaps more importantly from the gang's point of view, the son of a wealthy Hatton Garden jeweller, Anthony Xuereb.

The first contact from the kidnappers came that same evening, to the home of Anthony Xuereb who lived six miles away. The call was taken by Mrs Mary Xuereb, Emmanuel's stepmother, who was a solicitor. She called the police at once and D.C.I. Red and his team, who arrived quietly and unobtrusively, were present for the succession of calls that followed. One was from Emmanuel; the kidnappers made him call to prove that he had been kidnapped. Anthony went to his son's house and found it had been ransacked. Soon after midnight came a gruesome message, typical of kidnappers world-wide: 'We have your son. Don't delay or we will send you a finger a day . . . Fail to follow orders and you will receive your son's head in a box.'

Scotland Yard's anti-kidnap programme was activated without delay and a media blackout was asked for the following morning. The Press and other media agreed and the first briefing was held. That afternoon, Anthony Xuereb went to Emmanuel's office in Wapping to receive a telephone call from the kidnappers. He listened to his son's voice, on a tape playback, pleading for his father to pay the ransom.

The gang wanted £2 million. Then, another voice took over and showed a considerable knowledge of Anthony Xuereb's financial affairs. That same night the kidnapper called again twice, once to raise the ransom demand and then to drop it. This indicated a preparedness to negotiate and was an encouraging sign to the head of C11. He had deployed his resources in the three Red, Blue and Green teams and was now in the business of analysing the calls from the gang. After the reduction in ransom demand, the kidnapper threatened to cut off Emmanuel Xuereb's hand if the money was not paid within two days. There was comfort even in this grim threat: the gang had rather larded on the threats of chopping off pieces of their victim—it was still early days and they had no reason to issue more than the standard initial death threat to frighten the family.

The next afternoon Anthony Xuereb was told to go at once by taxi to St Katherine's dock, a Victorian dockyard beside Tower Bridge recently developed into an expensive marina, large hotel and conference hall, the World Trade Centre, where he was to look for a telephone box containing a package. C11's surveillance team, Blue, discreetly followed him. Anthony found the package. It contained four Polaroid pictures, and in two of them the father was shocked to see the hostage couple standing naked side by side. It was a particularly distasteful way of exerting pressure on the family. The other two showed Emmanuel alone. There was also a cassette of his voice pleading to be released: 'They will kill me if you don't pay,' and there was a crude drawing of a hand with a finger cut off with the message in red ink: 'One a day every day.' Doubtless this unpleasant package seriously upset the family and, had the police Red team not been helping, might have unbalanced the family's negotiating strategy. However, the threats were a repeat and variation of the earlier warnings and their very quantity began to dilute the impact of the kidnappers' tough line. Further calls to the Xuereb home and office led to some hectic bargaining. On Thursday night, case-day three, Anthony Xuereb said he could raise only £200,000 as a first instalment by the following Monday. The kidnappers' spokesman rejected the offer. Like all families after a rejection of their best offer, the Xuerebs were deeply depressed. The newly-wed pair had only been captives for forty-eight hours but it seemed a lifetime to their family.

Though the gang had appeared professional (relative at least to other British kidnappers), and certainly ruthless until then, they made an extraordinary mistake on the Saturday, the fifth day of the kidnap.

They agreed to release Maria Xuereb. At 4 p.m. Anthony Xuereb was amazed to receive a call from her. She was free and standing in a telephone box at Mitcham, on the South London–Surrey border. D.C.I. Red, in the house with the Xuereb family, alerted D.C.I. Green in the operations centre and a taxi, one of the Blue team's covert surveillance fleet, was dispatched immediately to pick her up.

She explained she had been blindfolded and driven to Mitcham by one of the kidnappers, and showed why they had decided to release her: she handed over a message about the ransom. They had reduced their demand to £525,000—£200,000 to be paid in notes, the same in gold and 500 krugerrands. Like other inexperienced gangs worried by the complications of what they had let themselves in for, the Xuerebs' captors had turned their hard line strategy on its head, released one of their bargaining counters and reduced their demand all at once. More than that, they had grossly underestimated Maria's astonishing ability to remember detail about them and their hide-out.

This sudden and welcome coup was not entirely unexpected. The head of C11 had remembered the research that had been done into kidnap gangs: on average they are small, of five men. He reasoned that with two hostages to guard they would find the negotiation very hard going unless they were exceptionally experienced in this crime. That was unlikely, in Britain, so he maintained the momentum of the negotiation, through Anthony, as much as he could, by arranging for frequent calls to discuss every aspect of the case over and over. This would keep the gang occupied and ultimately they would get tired, more tired than the police who had the numbers to take turns and the time and place to sleep undisturbed. Then, at what he thought was a critical moment, the officer suggested through Anthony, the family's negotiator, that if the gang were really serious about releasing the couple, they let Maria go unharmed as a gesture of good faith. Clearly the gang had no idea that the police were helping the family, or working on the case at all since there had been no reports of the kidnap. This, coupled with their growing tiredness, crucially tipped the balance of their judgement and they released Maria.

She was a godsend, a mine of information. She turned out to be a most impressively resourceful woman, who, from the moment she was kidnapped, had been doing everything she could to leave evidence that might help track down and convict the gang. In the house where she and Emmanuel had been held, she had bitten off some fingernails and pushed them under the carpet. She had pulled fibres off the same carpet and hidden them under other nails so, if her dead body had been found, forensic scientists would have been able to connect it with the site of their captivity. When the kidnappers took her from the house, blindfolded, she had determinedly counted the seconds of her journey to Mitcham. She had reached 179 when she was pushed out of the car. She also gauged the speed of the car as medium (probably driven carefully within the speed limits). Separated from her husband, taken out blindfolded to an unknown fate, such courage was exemplary.

The police analysed everything she gave them assiduously. It meant that the house where she had been held was no more than two-and-a-half miles from the spot where she had been left. There was more. Maria reported she had heard trains running in front of and behind the house: those in front sounded as if they had been at an angle to it, those behind higher up. The search was concentrated on the Croydon area and seven sites were picked out as possibilities.

A massive surveillance operation was started. All seven sites were covered by mobile and static teams looking for signs of the kidnappers. The head of C11 was elated by the upturn of events, but he was uncomfortably conscious that even if they were to find the house where Maria had been held, it did not follow that her husband Emmanuel was still there. His men could not afford to alert the kidnappers of their watching presence for fear of what they might do to Emmanuel. None the less, morale improved when several sites where eliminated after inquiries and observation. It was Maria Xuereb herself who provided the final clue: she remembered that the telephone in the house was of the warbling variety, not a standard model with straightforward ringing tones. A check with British Telecom revealed that only one of the houses left on the police shortlist had a Trimphone. That was number 56, Kemble Road, Croydon.

D.C.I. Blue re-grouped his surveillance forces. They were taken off the dead-end leads, some were stood down to get some rest, and he switched his main effort to organizing a rota of officers to observe activities at the target house. This work confirmed Maria's information. The kidnappers were using the house. But, were they using it only as their operations centre? Was it just the place where they had their 'councils of war' and decided on the flavour of their next threats? Or were they keeping Emmanuel Xuereb there too? If the police raided this house would they jeopardize Emmanuel's life somewhere else? These questions burned in the imagination of C11's operational chief. He was faced with the same dilemma as the Dutch head of operations, Kees Sietstma, before he gave the order to raid the woodyard where he thought Freddie Heineken was being held. A mistake at this juncture could ruin what had until then been good police work, and perhaps lead to the killing of Emmanuel Xuereb.

The decision was taken. On Sunday 9 January, at 5 a.m. when the gang were judged at their lowest, a massive police unit burst into the house in Kemble Road. They found three kidnappers—and Emmanuel Xuereb. The kidnappers were two Cypriot brothers, George and Anastasi Panae, and a West Indian assistant, Donald Gray. George Panae was a dangerous and resourceful burglar who had learned of Anthony Xuereb's wealth in his dealings with Hatton Garden jewellers. He was later sentenced to eighteen years imprisonment, his brother to ten years, and Gray, who turned Queen's evidence, to eight years.

This case showed the Yard's strategy to full advantage. The basic three-group, colour-coded system pre-organizing responsibilities, the media blackout working perfectly and a family prepared to follow police advice on negotiating strategy and accept tactical ploys, such as telephone scripts, combined to form the ideal response. As the case developed, the police advisers, working through Anthony Xuereb, had tightened the screws on the kidnappers, maintaining the momentum of the negotiation, making them tired, subtly taking the initiative from them until the gang unwittingly allowed the police to take Maria from them, with all her wealth of information which in turn led to the discovery of their hide-out within twelve hours.

The police were quite prepared to risk handing the money over to the gang, had they needed to. This tactic is an accepted part of the blueprint, because it acknowledges that all kidnappers only receive the 'reward' for their endeavours when they emerge from obscurity to grab the ransom. This does not mean that the Metropolitan police sanction kidnap payments, just that the police have now accepted that certain traditional approaches must be reappraised when dealing with kidnapping. During the payment kidnappers are especially vulnerable to quality surveillance such as that mustered by C11. The money can be bugged, as it was in America for Frank Sinatra's son, the serial numbers are recorded and the notes put on microfilm.

As technology advances, so the job of the surveillance teams becomes easier. There is never any replacement for the eyes and judgement of a trained surveillance officer, but certain equipment vastly improves the reach of the human eye and ear: electronic listening devices, infra-red cameras that 'see' at night, lasers that 'tell' when to begin recording and microscopic fibre-optics that 'spy' unseen through tiny holes at the unwitting target. Improvements are researched constantly, as they are in the area of forensic science where advances in voice analysis helped to trap one of the gang responsible for a kidnap in 1983. Voice analysis has been researched by criminologists, speech and language experts for years, notably by Germany's Bundeskriminalamt in Wiesbaden and the Federal Bureau of Investigation in America, separating and identifying the most minute characteristics of a recorded voice to match it with its owner. The goal has been to establish a vocal fingerprint.

Kidnappers regularly use the telephone to pass on their instructions and police forces have dutifully taped masses of evidence, but it has rarely been possible to match voices to men conclusively. Vocal fingerprints are an important new weapon against kidnapping, and in 1985 the judge in the Old Bailey trial of William Davies accepted such a piece of evidence which proved crucial to Davies's conviction for the kidnap of Mrs Shirley Goodwin.

This kidnap was unusual because, when Mrs Goodwin was snatched from her home in Hackney, East London, her husband, John, was in prison, serving ten years for alleged 'jury nobbling'. (He was later freed by the Appeal Court.) The police immediately activated their kidnap blueprint, including the media blackout, not least since the gang had left the unnerving message for the Goodwin children: 'If you go to the law, then Mum will think she's in Belsen. I can be a nice guy or a wicked bastard.' The tone echoed the phraseology of the underworld in which John Goodwin himself moved, and the police quickly realized that no blueprint covers every eventuality, for this family was not the sort readily to report their problems to them, even a kidnap. Their solicitor, however, had no such qualms; but, though he informed the police, relations between D.C.I. Red and the family were always strained. In particular, it grated with the police that communications with the family were non-existent until John Goodwin gave the go-ahead, from inside his cell in Wandsworth prison.

The police decided not to allow him out of the prison to help with the negotiations. Instead, they fixed up a direct telephone link to him in his cell and worked with him to free his wife. The combination of

Goodwin's understanding of criminal behaviour and the Yard's surveillance by C11 was to prove highly effective.

The ransom demanded was £50,000 and the gang clearly believed Goodwin owed them money. They issued a series of threats, including a tape recording of the distraught Mrs Goodwin pleading for her family to pay a ransom to the accompaniment of rattling chains in the background. Goodwin's eighteen-year-old son Spencer showed himself an effective negotiator at first, feeling strong enough to hold his own in a shouting match with a kidnapper on the telephone, saying that the gang would get nothing until they supplied proof of life. Goodwin's sister, Mrs Janice Pullen, took over the role of negotiator—the gang apparently did not suspect the police were helping, perhaps because of the media blackout—and she obtained proof on a tape left in a phone box at a pub nearby. As in the Xuereb case, the gang then made an incredible blunder (there are so many which can be made during a negotiation against sophisticated police teamwork) when they agreed to send a mini-cab to collect a letter from Goodwin which Mrs Pullen insisted was of vital importance. Of course the cab was followed by C11's Blue team which was staking out the Goodwins' apartment. They also followed another car that arrived the next evening to pick up the ransom, in a suitcase the kidnappers thought contained the £50,000. Certainly there was money inside, but it was a lot less than £50,000: some real notes had been skilfully arranged to appear to be the agreed amount. The police were prepared to risk a payment of some kind to get closer to the gang and their victim.

With these leads, it was a relatively simple affair for the Blue team to track down both the gang and the place where Mrs Goodwin had been held: a holiday chalet on the Isle of Sheppey, a secluded enough hideaway out of season. In fact she had been released when the payment was made, and dropped off in Mitcham, oddly enough the same area where Maria Xuereb was freed. The gang, who had actually driven to the Goodwins' apartment to collect the ransom, had clearly never realized that the police knew of the case and this underlined the importance and success of the media blackout. The other mainstay of these last two successes had been excellent surveillance to develop the leads that emerged. Some countries might find a media blackout hard to arrange (though the F.B.I. have used it successfully in the United States) but there is no doubt that skilled surveillance is critical.

Scotland Yard's one hundred per cent record from 1975 to 1985 in solving kidnap cases, recovering the victims safely and seeing the offenders convicted is impressive and a tribute to the blueprint thought up in the early 1970s. This very statistic probably measures the greatest deterrent to more thoughtful, organized criminals in Britain. It has been widely admired, and policemen from forces all over the world have come to absorb the lessons for their own benefit. But this sort of kidnap response does have its drawbacks, as Yard detectives admit. It is a great and costly drain on resources, in training, equipment and especially in manpower; and the Yard is probably the only force with the justification for an expert unit like C11, which has constant employment in the Metropolitan area. For example, C11 has to deal with three to four cases of blackmail in the London area every month. Blackmail has similar characteristics to kidnap, without the threat to human life, and the police response uses a system of three groups like the kidnap blueprint's Red, Green and Blue. The frequency of blackmail cases ensures that skilled sectors needed for the less frequent crime of kidnap, especially the surveillance teams, are kept to high standards.

Provincial forces must depend heavily on the Yard for support, but the autonomy of County Chief Constables means that they are not obliged to call for this help, though they are unlikely to match the experience and technique of the London team. Manning is also a problem for the Yard. The Commissioner of the Metropolitan police might be reluctant to commit so many valuable men out of his area for any length of time. So, senior Yard officers with experience of kidnap have given in-depth briefings to Regional Crime Squads, which cross provincial boundaries, on how to tackle kidnapping. Sadly, government spending cuts that Chief Constables were forced to meet in the mid-1980s have depleted the strengths of the Regional Crime Squads and may have weakened police capability against kidnap.

* * * *

What of political kidnappings? Britain has suffered several, all in Northern Ireland and all linked inevitably to the Irish Republican movement. The Provisional I.R.A., or at least elements within it, have frequently used kidnapping as a means of attempting to raise funds with which to continue their war against the security forces in Northern Ireland. In 1975, a Dutch industrialist resident in Ireland, Dr Tiede Herrema, was kidnapped but eventually released after a long police siege of a council house in County Kildare. The leader of the gang, Eddie Gallagher, lover of Rose Dugdale (an English doctor turned Republican activist) gave himself up and was sentenced to twenty years imprisonment. The Irish government set a pattern it was to follow consistently during subsequent kidnaps: it negotiated with the kidnappers but refused to pay money, arguing that to agree to a ransom payment would be tantamount to subsidizing a terrorist organization whose eventual aim was to overthrow the democratically elected government of Ireland by violent means. The British government adopted this policy too and made it public that, should any member of the Cabinet be kidnapped, there would be no question of acceding to any demands whatsoever. These policies turned Scotland Yard's blueprint priority on its head: no longer was safe release of the victim paramount. The authorities acknowledged their responsibility to the ordinary citizen in commercial kidnaps, but made it quite clear that in political cases, when terrorists threatened to increase their funds or force the freeing of prisoners, then the victim came second to the interests of the State.

Dramatic reinforcement of this principle came in 1981 when Ben Dunne, heir to the Dunne supermarket chain fortune, was kidnapped by a renegade band of I.R.A. men operating from the town of Dundalk, just south of the border between the Irish Republic and Northern Ireland. Several attempts were made by the Dunne family to pay the £400,000 ransom demanded; they even tried loading the money into the boot of a car and driving it from Dublin towards the border where Dunne was being held. The car ran into numerous Garda road blocks and was forced to turn back. The victim was eventually freed into the hands of Belfast journalist Eamonn Mallie, who was instructed to go to the churchyard at the tiny village of Cullyhanna, south of the border, where he encountered to his surprise the dishevelled figure of Dunne. The gang clearly found the Garda and Irish Army hunt too hot for comfort.

The big question remains: did a ransom eventually find its way to the I.R.A. after Dunne's release, in the manner of an extortion payment? Rumours persisted that this is what happened. The malign influence of the I.R.A. on many levels of Irish society, north and south of the border, is hard for a company with many employees and assets to ignore. The kidnap ransom becomes, in effect, protection money (which businesses in Belfast have been paying to the I.R.A. for more than ten years), or what the Basque terrorists call 'the revolutionary tax'.

This issue came more fully under the spotlight of publicity after another kidnapping in the Irish Republic—that of Don Tidey in November 1983.

This case is particularly interesting since Tidey was seized in Southern Ireland by the I.R.A. (who had ambitions to finance in Northern Ireland), his company head office was in London where Scotland Yard became involved, and he was insured on a policy which guaranteed a ransom on the Lloyd's market. This was an international case throwing the usual order of priorities up for grabs.

Tidey was the managing director of another supermarket chain, Quinnsworth, a subsidiary of the giant U.K. food combine, Associated British Foods (A.B.F.), which is controlled by the Weston family. He was driving his daughter to her Dublin school, intending to go on to the airport, when he was flagged down by a man who appeared to be a policeman. When he gave his name the 'policeman' produced a gun, held it to Tidey's head and bundled him into a car waiting at the side of the road. Hooded and blindfolded he was driven off, with another kidnapper sitting on top of him. After an hour he was transferred to a different car and taken on a long, twisting drive. At one point his kidnappers stopped to question him about contacts they could make for the ransom negotiation. Finally he was forced to walk across country until he reached a tent, where he was chained by the wrists, ankles and knees. He remained trussed and blindfolded for the next twenty-three days. His hood was removed only to allow him to wash. He never saw his captors' faces; they talked only in low voices or whispers.

The kidnap had been carried out so publicly that the Garda were swiftly alerted, and because Tidey was employed by a British company, Scotland Yard was immediately informed. So too were the Royal Ulster Constabulary because of the instant and well-justified suspicion that the I.R.A. were responsible. The Yard's response was to get a senior officer round to A.B.F.'s headquarters as fast as possible to get in first before private consultants could become involved. As it turned out the Yard's instincts were right. The London security consultants Control Risks were called in to advise the company on its tactics.

Since A.B.F. controlled the purse strings, the negotiations with the kidnappers would be from the Republic to London, which meant that the Yard's kidnap team, not the Garda, were at the hub of the case. The officer who went to A.B.F. arranged for several sets of tape recorders to be attached to the telephones, one sealed for evidential purposes (to prevent any potential claim that the tapes had been tampered with if the case ever got to court).

The involvement of three different police forces made it a unique case in the Yard's experience. Things looked good at first; the Garda seemed glad for the Yard to take charge, given their greater experience in kidnap cases, but politics soon intervened. The Irish government was determined that its police force should take over, for obvious reasons of nationalistic pride.

On the same day that Tidey was kidnapped, a telephone call to A.B.F. made it clear that their executive was in the hands of the Provisional I.R.A. and that they wanted a ransom of £5 million. Other calls made it plain that the money was to be handed over near the border, in the South. It was to be a confused negotiation—demands which had to be followed up came flooding in from a whole series of hoaxers. The kidnapping had been so public that there had been no chance for a media blackout to be imposed before the Press got hold of the story, even if the Irish authorities had wanted one—which was unlikely. The priority of the British and Irish governments was to emphasize their policy that no money was to be paid to political kidnappers whatever the circumstances. It was not enough to tell A.B.F. and their advisers, Control Risks, that this was so. The kidnappers had to be told too, or they would assume the firm was stalling and Tidey's life would be further endangered.

On 1 December, Lord Elton, a junior Home Office minister, publicly reaffirmed the British government's stance. The next day the Irish Justice minister, Mr Michael Noonan, announced in the Dáil (Irish Parliament) that his government would not acquiesce to ransom payments to paramilitary organizations. Mr Garry Weston, head of A.B.F., issued a statement admitting that a ransom had been demanded, that the Irish police believed the I.R.A. was responsible, but that the British government had asked the firm not to pay the money. Although he expressed his deep concern for Tidey, 'an admired and respected colleague', and emphasized that the company was prepared to consider whatever steps were necessary to free him, Mr Weston said he was bound to respect the government's wishes.

When that statement was blazoned across the front pages in both Britain and Ireland, the message to the I.R.A. was clear: there would be no ransom. The speeches and statements had been co-ordinated to make that absolutely plain.

Meanwhile a massive hunt for Tidey went on but it was not until 16

December that the searchers found him and then at a tragic cost. A joint Irish army and police patrol stumbled across the kidnappers' camp in a remote forest in County Leitrim. In the ensuing shoot-out a trainee policeman and a soldier were killed and the gang got away, but without their hostage who survived the raid.

With Tidey's release Scotland Yard bowed out of active involvement in the case. One of the gang was arrested and was later jailed for twelve years while two other men received lighter sentences for helping to imprison Tidey; but the principal kidnappers got clean away. It is thought they included some of those who had escaped from the Maze prison in the mass break-out of September 1983.

The case did not end with Tidey's freedom and the subsequent court cases. In February 1985 the Irish government announced that it had traced nearly £2 million to a Bank of Ireland account held at the Navan branch, thirty miles from Dublin. The government claimed the account had been opened by the I.R.A. to hold money 'raised through extortion, under the threat of kidnap and murder'. Irish government sources linked this money to the Tidey kidnap, implying that a form of ransom or protection money had been paid. The government passed emergency legislation to freeze the account.

In December 1985 the London *Sunday Times* alleged that the money in the Navan account had originally been paid into a Swiss bank account by A.B.F. after threats by the I.R.A. to attack company personnel and property after Tidey's release. The *Sunday Times* also confirmed that Control Risks had advised A.B.F. during the case and claimed there was 'heated argument' within Control Risks over whether the post-kidnap payment demand should be met. The money was paid after Control Risks said it would have to withdraw from its consultancy role if A.B.F. insisted on going ahead. The *Sunday Times* story was never denied by Control Risks or A.B.F. and the allegations were amplified by Labour M.P. Dale Campbell-Savours under the protection of parliamentary privilege.

This postscript to the Tidey affair demonstrates that ransom money can still reach kidnappers long after the danger of that happening appears to have passed, and this makes a mockery of government attempts to prevent money being paid to terrorists. However, the British blueprint response to kidnapping has an impressive record which should not be confused with the problems of investigations into subsequent extortions or 'revolutionary tax' demands.

* * * *

Organized criminals the world over are routinely 'laundering' their profits through a variety of convoluted offshore and overseas banking and business transactions, of which the I.R.A.'s Swiss bank account is an example. The latest experience of European police forces is that kidnapping, like other organized crime, is increasingly international.

This was amply demonstrated in January 1986 in the kidnapping in London of Muhammad Sadiq al-Tajir, brother of one of the world's richest men, Muhammad Mahdi al-Tajir, ambassador of the United Arab Emirates in London. Snatched outside his Knightsbridge home, he was held captive in a South London suburban house for eleven days while his brother negotiated his freedom. There was a Scotland Yard media blackout which again operated perfectly (although news of the kidnap did appear in a couple of Gulf newspapers while it was going on).

By monitoring the kidnappers' calls and being at the ambassador's side throughout, Scotland Yard and various European forces called in to help, were able to follow the gang's negotiator through Europe. But the negotiations were conducted by telephone from the U.S.A. and European capitals and the ransom figure finally agreed on (£2 million compared to a first demand of £50 million) was paid over through a bank account in Beirut, well outside European police forces' jurisdiction. Thus the police were rendered powerless by a sophisticated use of modern communications. Whatever happens to anybody ever brought to trial in the West for the crime, it is a fair bet that the money has disappeared into the wilderness of modern Lebanon for ever.

ELEVEN

A Summary: The Right to Protection

Kidnapping is rightly classified as a 'serious crime'. The spectacle of the police desperately casting about to find a gang which has seized a victim with apparent impunity, stripped him of human rights and made outrageous demands, undermines a society's attitude to law and order, even though the crime is infrequent compared to murders and armed robberies. In countries suffering a higher than usual incidence, kidnap is tacitly condoned—for example Colombia and Italy, where in 1983 a record ninety-two cases were officially registered (though an underwriter noted he paid out insured ransoms in several cases which did not appear on the official list). In those countries, in the words of the head of Dutch Special Branch, the kidnappers are truly 'mightier' than the police.

There has been too little publicly explained about kidnap and people have no yardstick by which to judge the crime. However, the German Bundeskriminalamt believe kidnap is their most newsworthy crime. Sensational coverage is the norm for every kidnapping, especially at the start and at the payment, yet little is known about the course of the negotiation between. The emotional dramatization of events, often concentrating on the wealth of the victims, the brutality of the abduction and even lending a certain glamour to the kidnappers, has too long concealed an honest look at the hard facts.

Cesare Pagani was right: kidnapping is a 'dirty' crime. Kidnappers prefer, unlike terrorists, to work in the dark and, as Pagani and victims in Germany (notably, Richard Oetker) found out, they wreak a secret, bitter revenge on their helpless captives. Worse, at the start, the authorities have not the slightest idea where to look for a kidnap gang. This is in direct contrast with terrorism (the great obsession of law enforcement agencies over the last three decades) when the authorities control the very destiny of terrorists who defy them with hostages in known locations: on aircraft or in buildings like the Iranian Embassy in London. Kidnappers are shadows that speak occasionally and emerge briefly from obscurity for the pay-off.

Unfortunately, the act of kidnap is easy. In the United States, John La Marca, who was suffering a minor cash-flow problem, seized his victim on the spur of the moment. When he realized getting the money was more complex than he thought, he abandoned the baby to die at the side of the road.

Neither the public, nor the criminals it spawns, realize how complex negotiations are. No matter how educated or organized — like the recent kidnap gangs in Holland—kidnappers continually underestimate the sheer problems of how to negotiate the payment, hold the victim and avoid the police. Clearly the kidnappers of Jennifer Guinness in Dublin in 1986 had no idea that they would cause such a furore of local and international interest; they hid in silence after seizing her until being found and arrested by the Garda a week later.

It is a fact that organized, experienced criminals get away scot-free from a surprisingly high percentage of crimes, eighty per cent or more in most countries, but the chances of a kidnap gang staying free to enjoy the ransom are quite the opposite, twenty per cent or worse. An offender's chances of getting away in Italy used to be better (57.7% in Sardinia in 1965 to 1970) but at last the Italians are getting a grip on their appalling kidnap problem and now claim to identify over seventy-one per cent. In South American countries, like Colombia where over 3,500 guerrillas roam freely about large areas of inhospitable jungle, the authorities have little or no control, but in Germany kidnappers are caught at the rate of eighty-six per cent.

Ad hoc attempts by individuals are usually doomed to failure: doubly-doomed because the victim is particularly at risk from this brand of kidnapper. The inexperienced criminal has little or no understanding of how to conduct a negotiation, or how to rate his victim's financial potential or the 'going rate' in his area. He is inflexible, often gratuitously brutal and dangerous. The deaths of Lesley Whittle in England and Gernot Egolf in Germany are examples. Understanding the character of the gang, from the kidnap itself and the facts that emerge during the negotiation, is one of the most important jobs for the family, police and negotiator.

The maximum commitment is required from the authorities to catch kidnappers. It is not good enough to put just a couple of dozen police officers on the anti-kidnap team and expect results, as was the case in Rome in 1979/80 (the Italians excused this by saying they were busy fighting terrorism instead). Several hundred men are needed, as the American and Dutch experience recently has shown. Kidnap investigations place the greatest strain on the most difficult of police skills: scene-of-crime work, forensic analysis, speech and handwriting analysis, surveillance and house assault. All these disciplines demand manpower, and plenty of time, training and constant updating of techniques that keep the police one step ahead of the criminals.

Control is a key factor in successful kidnap investigations. The Dutch cases, which crossed back and forth over international boundaries, were directed with expert central control. The early American experience showed how laws had to be changed to give the F.B.I. overall authority and the necessary powers to cross state boundaries. A senior officer at Interpol headquarters at Saint-Cloud, in Paris, believes that command of big operations is too often given to policemen without the necessary years or experience, and, in Italy, it must be galling for the Polizia and the Carabinieri to have to take orders from young magistrates in charge of their investigations.

Police forces need the support of their governments. Research (e.g. into speech analysis and the use of computers by the F.B.I. and the BKA) and training (particularly for surveillance and house assault) need generous budgets. But more than money, the police need public and administrative commitment from their governments.

All policemen agree that public co-operation is very important. Not all police forces get it. In kidnap investigations, where the offenders are hard to identify, this support makes all the difference. During the kidnap of Hans Martin Schleyer, the German police were inundated with information from the public and could not process it fast enough; while the locating of Heineken and Doderer—and their ransom—in Holland was the result of excellent public co-operation. It is unfortunate that in countries with a high incidence of kidnapping the public seem indifferent, perhaps inured, to kidnap, and the fault must ultimately lie with governments. If they were to support their police and simultaneously come to grips with the underlying socio-economic problems of their people (for example as a recent report on the phenomenology of kidnappings in Sardinia, the South of Italy, Spain and Central and South America has shown), they might reap the benefit of increased electoral support.

Beyond the police skills already mentioned, how many police forces can negotiate a long-term kidnap? Ironically, in countries with a great deal of kidnapping, the police are often excluded altogether from family negotiating conferences, while in other places, like the U.S.A., Great Britain, Holland and Germany, the police have had relatively little experience of long-term cases. Some officials believe in a policy of 'No deal!', but this is hardly reasonable except in cases where government itself is held to ransom. Negotiating certainly reduces the amount of money released on to the criminal 'market'; in Sardinia it has been found that in 66.7% of cases negotiating made savings in the ransom demanded of between forty per cent to over ninety per cent. More important than the money, the mere act of communicating with the gang lessens the danger to the victim.

Negotiations should be the job of the police. But, if the police cannot, will not, or are not trusted to negotiate, families—and companies—will turn to other intermediaries, like Juan Felix Eriz, for help through the crisis. Policemen may not approve, but they cannot realistically expect that families, left in the lurch, will not look about for another practical solution to their problems. Most policemen know it occurs and tacitly condone it, while doing their best. I have heard families say that the police are 'following clues'. It is the business of police to follow clues but families need more than that during a kidnap negotiation.

Kidnap negotiators should have few illusions about the less pleasant side of human behaviour. Wide experience of any sort is necessary, but a military or police background in operations dealing actively with crime and terrorism is particularly useful. The revelation of life's nastier realities leaves a certain objectivity when confronted by the threats and difficulties of kidnapping.

Objectivity is vital. Families use negotiators as a brick-bat for all their worries and cool reasoning is essential. In the words of Eriz: 'All the responsibility for a man's life rests on your shoulders.' Firstly, organization is needed: setting up a small crisis management committee, choosing a chairman (who can take decisions), allocating responsibilities (like Press, police and judicial liaison), and explaining how a negotiator leaves the family able to continue running the business (big multi-national companies ought to think of a system for these things before the disaster occurs). Then, one assesses the kidnappers, not being fooled by their threats (of death, sickness, deadlines, silence for weeks, doubling or demanding a second ransom), examines the facts (that mass of information left at every kidnap and all the contacts afterwards), and decides what the gang are likely to do. Against this analysis, the negotiator can choose, and select from, a family's options.

Negotiations have something of the theatre in them. The wife of one victim put down the telephone after a frenetic call to her husband's kidnapper which was agonizing to hear, and said calmly to me, 'Wasn't I good?' Extreme threats produce extreme reactions. Negotiations are a ritual where the rules are unwritten but it is important, for the credibility of each side, that family and kidnappers maintain their proper roles. It is the family's role to lead convincingly by example, showing itself willing to negotiate.

Demanding proof of life is essential: it is the most important first step for every family. This communication, perhaps more than any other, underlines the basis of negotiations: giving something—ransom—for something in return—the victim alive. After the gruesome example of Giovanni Palombini, Polaroid photographs of the victim holding a recent copy of a newspaper are not conclusive, though I thought the Stendals' idea of sending a T-shirt with a message printed on it, in which Russell could be photographed by the guerrillas, was cunning. The most heartening proof, for victim and family alike, is to pose a question which only the victim can answer.

'How much can we afford to pay?' It is hard for any family to put a price on the victim's head but that is what they must do as soon as possible. If they chop and change the total figure the negotiation will lose stability. The main themes in any negotiations are time, the amount of money on offer, and the momentum of the negotiation. If the family keep changing their minds about the final ransom they will seriously upset the momentum of the negotiations, since gangs respond suspiciously to any inconsistencies with threats, action or silence. One gang in Rome, annoyed that the family had actually reduced their offer, blew up the family's new Mercedes outside their home. Balance and momentum are most vital of all, for they have a direct influence on the gang's treatment of the victim.

Many families worry that the gang knows all about their finances. This is unlikely though political gangs—like ETA in Spain, the Red Brigade in Italy and the R.A.F. in Germany—do interrogate their prisoners. 'Commercial' gangs do little more than question their victims about the family's finances, and the victims do well if they deny all possibility of a large ransom—like Sergio Martinelli—and leave the negotiation to those 'outside'; the family, not the victim, must draw the money from the bank and pay it. In any case, kidnappers have their own idea of a family's wealth; they are unlikely to believe the full story is revealed in tax statements any more than an inspector from the Inland Revenue.

Politics certainly confuse the issue. Money demands are already complicated enough with their various threats, without talk of freeing prisoners (the R.A.F. in Germany), publishing political tracts (the *Grupo Revolucionario* which held William Frank Niehous of the Owens Illinois Corporation for three years and four months in Venezuela), or demolishing a power station (ETA and the Lémoniz power station in Spain). The negotiation is still one for the life of the victim, so the basic values do not change, but introducing politics brings governments into the action, and increasingly authorities world-wide are taking a hard line. In such cases, the chances of the victim's survival depend on the character of the kidnappers.

Negotiators should select a flexible strategy, one that credibly reflects the family's—or company's—actual circumstances. The family have the money, true, but the gang have the more important bargaining counter, the victim. A strategy of apparent co-operation with demands is better than an aggressive approach designed to break the kidnappers' will. Aggressive postures generate aggressive responses, increasing the possibility of grisly evidence like amputated ears (Giorgio Calissoni) or fingers (Baron Edouard Empain). Negotiators and intermediaries can always take the heat from a situation by having to 'refer back to the family' and choose a strategy that will gradually reduce the gang's expectations of reward.

No doubt kidnap is serious, but humour is not unknown. It is sometimes macabre, like the Guatemalan gang that sent one of its victim's amputated fingers to the parents in a hot-dog roll. It is sometimes straight comedy, like Matteo and I laughing at the idea of Martinelli's lawyer trying to conceal a vast bundle of notes about his already bulky person. It is sometimes farcical, like Count Antolini-Ossi's chauffeur who was ordered to find a message from the gang in a rubbish bin. Twice he went down the stairs from his top-floor flat, fruitlessly emptied out a long line of big dustbins on the pavement, enduring the abuse of other disgusted residents, and twice he swore at the kidnapper who rang to check he had found it. Finally, filthy and humiliated, he realized the message was in a small bin on a lamp-post beside the dustbins. Humour is a rare but wonderful safety-valve.

Contacts, like the message in the dustbin, vary. Letters, telephone calls and parcels are common, but most dangerous and daring are the face-to-face encounters like those of Eriz and the Stendals' contacts in the jungle. In Europe, it is likely that the use of intermediaries in this way speeds up the negotiation, but at a risk. These courageous people, often acting for no reward, are essential in some rural areas and with certain types of kidnappers, but they have been beaten up and always run the risk of being murdered by the kidnappers.

The Press is generally manipulated as a channel of communication. Kidnappers instruct that coded advertisements be placed in newspapers, and families place their own appeals and articles to influence the gang. Press silence has its uses during the negotiation, to protect the victim, especially with inexperienced gangs or individuals. The London Metropolitan police persuaded representatives of all branches of the media not to report the course of kidnaps and it is hoped to extend the policy to all British kidnaps. The American Press stayed silent in the Quinonez case at the request of the F.B.I. which was worried about increasing tensions in the gang holding Mrs Clelia Quinonez. The Stendal family were careful not to use the Press at all, mindful that the F.A.R.C. has killed victims before for bad Press coverage. Some families are influential enough to suppress Press interest—and get space for articles—while police depend on journalists' co-operation. This is usually freely given, but occasionally communications with the gang have been disrupted because a keen journalist has checked all the columns and eagerly reported his coup of finding the family's coded ad.

It is likely that publicity is the real reason why judges freeze a family's assets, to show the authorities are taking major, though not very subtle, steps to control the crime. This happens in many countries, like France, Italy and Spain, and magistrates explain that it is their task to see that such large amounts of money do not reach the criminal classes. The attitude is gaining popularity. During Jennifer Guinness's kidnap, Dr Garret FitzGerald spoke for the Irish government and the Garda when he stated there could be no ransom payment allowed, and the British government backed him to the hilt; this was an echo of the hard line both governments had taken during the kidnap of Don Tidey in 1983. There can be few more aggressive actions by the authorities against a family suffering a kidnap than this. The judiciary or the police ought to take a family into its confidence before taking this step: scant co-operation can be expected from a family, if not. Besides, the sequestration of assets can provide a good excuse for not having sufficient ransom. While governments have a duty to refuse payment when their employees, diplomatic or any other, are seized (since governments ought not to allow themselves to be held to ransom), banning payment because the money will be used to fund terrorism (Don Tidey) is a less easily supported argument when the family is unconnected with government. A distinction must be made between what the authorities are obliged to say publicly, in the fight against terrorism, and what they say to the families privately. Unfortunately, governments, however democratic, have their own priorities which clash badly with the raw emotions exposed during a kidnap, especially when the family is being told they must sacrifice their loved one for the common good (Jennifer Guinness). The need for sensitive understanding by the authorities cannot be stressed enough—a difficult task that settles on the negotiator or, if the family are lucky, a sympathetic policeman. Finally, governments should forget their laudable ideals for a moment and see the facts: no matter what the authorities say, mothers and fathers will find some way of paying to see their sons or daughters again. Freeze their assets, they will borrow on trust. Spy on them and they will slip the surveillance teams. I do not know of a case in which the hard line has prevented a family paying up.

It is true that justice must be seen to be done, but seen to be done quickly. Control of kidnapping requires strong laws and swift justice in the courts. The Americans changed their laws to cope in the 1930s and the Italians changed theirs in the late 1970s and 1980s (Articles 605, 648, but notably changes in Article 630 of the Penal Code), but the Italian judicial system is still subject to long delays, as cases take between two to three years for the inquiry, and then 1st degree trials last an average of 290 days. The process is swifter in Holland and Germany and one may suppose that the public have a greater regard for the shorter system.

Kidnap negotiation is probably illegal. There is a strong argument that negotiators are breaking the law: by assisting in the payment of ransom money to kidnappers they are 'aiding and abetting' criminals. Not for them the defence of acting under duress; consultants are paid. But so are lawyers, who often advise during kidnappings, and charge their fee. The F.B.I. do not object to families employing advisers of any sort—provided that they co-operate fully with the police. This proviso of co-operation is perhaps the crux of the problem and the worst example is seen in those countries that strongly object to kidnap negotiators—where kidnaps are more frequent than in the United States. Negotiators run the risk of upsetting the local magistracy. Several have been locked up in the past and security consultants infuriate the local police by supplanting them. They certainly fulfil a practical need in some countries, but the legality of their job remains to be settled.

Perhaps kidnap insurance is illegal too. Several European countries are certain of this, holding that it acts against the public interest. This form of insurance is banned in Italy and Germany where the authorities, with those of Eire, believe it actually encourages kidnapping, prevents co-operation with the police (since they say the family will agree to pay what is assured immediately without reference to the police), and hands money to the criminals. They further raise the accusation that potential kidnappers will be encouraged by finding out who is insured. Such lapses of security are unlikely in Lloyd's where great care is taken to preserve the names of those who pay these controversial premiums. The anti-kidnap lobby in the European Community has grown stronger, and after the kidnaps of Don Tidey and Jennifer Guinness, has found vibrant echoes in Britain where the Prime Minister, Mrs Margaret Thatcher, and other Members of Parliament led by Mr Dale Campbell-Saviours, have condemned kidnap insurance. Though Britain, with Holland, has refused in the past to ban the insurance when pressurized to do so by the other members of the E.E.C., it is likely that by the time this book is published Lloyd's underwriters will have had to move their lucrative business elsewhere, for example to Miami. However, a committee of representatives of E.E.C. Interior Ministers is trying to persuade the Americans to ban kidnap insurance as well. If it was banned in the E.E.C., in Britain and Commonwealth countries, in Japan, the United States and her satellites, the weight of opinion would be so heavily set against kidnap insurance as to seriously jeopardize its future altogether. Even now, underwriters are paying the fees of international lawyers specializing in insurance for advice on relocating their business in countries such as Liechtenstein and Switzerland where the head, not the heart, holds sway in business. If they succeed in their lobby, politicians may bask in the glow of moral self-satisfaction; and ignore the fact that kidnappers will continue to kidnap. Of all the kidnaps that take place every year, fewer than one per cent are insured, so the existence or not of insurance will not make the slightest difference to the kidnappers.

Whether kidnap insurance is right or wrong, companies with operations in risk areas ought to pay for this insurance. They owe a duty to their employees who work for the good of the company in dangerous areas, and they owe a duty to the shareholders to protect the company's profits which might otherwise go into the pockets of the kidnappers. However, private individuals, with none of the responsibilities of large multi-national companies, may find their money better spent in directly dissuading potential kidnappers with increased personal security. Ninety-five per cent of kidnap victims are attacked on the home-to-work route, sixty per cent within a few miles of home, and eighty per cent while they are in a vehicle. But there is hope for the determined, since, in Sardinia, one in five people escaped as the kidnappers attempted to seize them, generally using cars, carrying pistols and machine-guns, and in the evening. These and other readily available statistics point to areas of a person's life that would benefit from extra security measures. Some choose armoured cars, steel doors and fences, television cameras and bodyguards, while some hate the idea of being restricted at all. The purpose of all these measures, even if only taking the trouble to adopt an irregular daily routine, is to make the kidnapper think twice. Then they will look for another, easier victim, and there are plenty of those.

Another form of 'direct insurance' is paying protection money, or the 'revolutionary tax' as ETA call it in Spain. It is hard to estimate how much has been paid by individuals and companies to criminals in the world's riskier areas. One example only: Eriz has taken part in forty deals for the 'revolutionary tax' in Spain. For some, the choice between Lloyd's insurance, personal security or paying the gangs directly must be hard.

In the final analysis, the responsibility lies with State, through the police, to protect its citizens. In 1973, Lord Denning said the police should act so that 'honest citizens may go about their affairs in peace.' The police have a duty to enforce the law. They must choose their priorities of action with due regard to the victims suffering the consequences of the State's inability to control this serious crime. The safe return of the victim, catching the gang and doing the best to recover the money, in that order, are the priorities claimed by all police. Not all act in accordance. A hard line—catching the gang at the payment regardless—may solve the case but it does little to encourage families' co-operation in the future.

The Heineken-Doderer kidnap case provides a fine example of successful police work. The Dutch point the way to future success, though the cost is high in men and material. But what constitutes a police success, or, by contrast, the failure of the gang? It is not whether the victim escapes in the kidnap attempt, or whether the ransom is finally paid. It is whether, after the safe release of the victim, the kidnappers are caught and swiftly sentenced to a goodly term. That is deterrence.

The victims have the final word. They suffer, sometimes for months, fearsome treatment by men—and sometimes women—who are often described as 'insane' or 'beasts'. It is too easy to write them off as different from the rest of us. Kidnappers, except the occasional lunatic who generally acts in lonely ignorance, are as sane as anyone; it may be surprising for Britons to learn that eight per cent of women and thirty-one per cent of men will be convicted of a listed offence—not a motoring offence—in their lives. How many of us think of crime? Perhaps only a short step along that dangerous path, kidnappers recognize no moral law or precept whatsoever.

Most victims decide to survive. Cesare Pagani, Sergio Martinelli, Russell Stendal and Paola Brunelli were all determined to survive. Pagani was repulsed by his food but he decided to eat what he was given. Stendal, Martinelli, Edith Rosenkranz and Enrico Oetiker trusted in their religious faith to carry them through the extraordinary test. A few tried to negotiate their own release and suffered beatings. Nearly all managed to form some human contact with their guards which may be described as the kidnapping version of the Stockholm Syndrome. Though he shot one guerrilla at the start, Russell Stendal, when he was given a second opportunity to escape, found he did not have it in him to kill the guard he had known for three months. Perhaps these strange liaisons do more than help the victim keep his sanity. Surely the guards develop a relationship with their victim that makes it harder for them to carry out the final act of murder?

It is hard to believe that any good can come from kidnapping. If it does, then it is right that the victim benefits. Over half of kidnap victims suffer their experiences with an impressive degree of calm. I hope that they all learn the depth of understanding and humanity that Cesare Pagani alludes to when he said: 'Such a shattering experience changes you deeply. It is a point of reference. After it, your scale of values is very different. It is something that is past and closed, but it is also something that I will carry with me all my life.'

TWELVE

The Lebanon Hostages

Since 1985, more than 30 foreigners have been kidnapped in Lebanon. At the time of writing (December, 1987) two of those kidnapped at the start of this unprecedented wave of hostage-taking are still being held prisoner and so are many of those abducted since. Several were murdered; several were released in a variety of circumstances. The plight of the Lebanese hostages captured the attention and the sympathy of the world. It also placed firmly before the world the dilemma familiar to everybody involved in the more private business of kidnap for ransom, whether they were victim, family or firm: is it ever right to negotiate with kidnappers and pay a victim's release? As the kidnap victims of Beirut sat chained and blindfolded in the city's southern suburbs, the argument raged back and forth across the Western world. A succession of attempts by the Western nations to resolve it led to a succession of political and personal disasters and gave little hope to the hostages while strengthening the hand of their captors.

One attempt, masterminded by Lieutenant-Colonel Oliver North, dealt a huge body-blow to the Reagan Administration, until then the most popular US presidency of recent times, and led to the embarrassment of the Iran-Contra congressional investigation and report. Another saw the Archbishop of Canterbury's personal envoy, Terry Waite, who had until then been the most successful negotiator for the hostages' freedom, himself became a prisoner. And two others, by West Germany and

France, resulted in hostages being freed but also caused an open split in the European Community, with Mrs Thatcher's Government accusing its two partners of aiding and abetting terrorists by negotiating with them and acceding to their demands. While kidnap for ransom in the West was becoming an increasingly risky and ineffective criminal activity, the Beirut hostages repeatedly proved to be extraordinarily useful cards in an international poker game where one side appeared to have all the aces – and to play them at all the right moments.

Kidnap is always an unpleasant business for the victim, but the ordeal of most of the Beirut hostages surpassed that of any others in modern history. The Islamic fundamentalist groups that held them appeared to have no sense of compassion for their prisoners or their loved ones. (The label 'Islamic fundamentalist' should be qualified in two respects: first, the victims were frequently abducted by common criminals who then sold them on to political groups like Hizbollah or the shadowy umbrella known as Islamic Jihad. Second, as the personal account of one of the hostages, the American journalist Charles Glass, revealed, his captors evinced little devotion to any of the tenets of Islam but displayed a keen interest in such examples of Western decadence as whisky, discos, television, videos and pop music.)

The treatment of the hostages and their families back home was brutal in many different ways. The first hostage to be taken, William Buckley, abducted in March 1985, was the CIA's station chief in Beirut. He was hideously tortured to force him to divulge information about US intelligence work throughout the Middle East and is believed to have died under torture in October or November of that year. A French Arabist, Michel Seurat, was murdered in February 1986 after ten months in captivity. A British journalist working for the United Nations, Alec Collett, was kidnapped nine days after Buckley and is believed to have been hanged some 14 months later as a reprisal for the US bombing of Libya, and Britain's logistical help in it. A macabre video showing a man being hanged was sent to a Beirut television station at that time; Collett is feared to have been the victim. Two British teachers, Philip Padfield and Leigh Douglas, and an American librarian, Peter Kilburn, were killed for the same reason.

The kidnappers provided very little information about their victims and allowed next to no communication between them and their families. The second hostage to be taken, Terry Anderson, Beirut bureau chief of the Associated Press, was allowed one letter to his family in the US in the two and three quarter years he had been held captive at the time of writing. 'I didn't think it was possible to hurt this much,' he wrote. His kidnappers let him see his baby daughter, born after his kidnapping, on television but that was a rare moment of kindness. A video recording of him was also released to the media at Christmas 1987. At least his family knew he was alive. They were able to gather more information about his situation as other hostages, who had been with him in captivity, were released. Their accounts are extremely moving and bear fresh testimony to the capacity of human beings to stand up to the most appalling suffering without the least preparation.

David Jacobsen, administrator of the American University Hospital in Beirut, was kidnapped in May 1985. He was released 17 months later and his account of his captivity, published in Britain in *The Observer Magazine*, revealed that he shared a room with Anderson, the Reverend Benjamin Weir, Father Lawrence Jenco and Thomas Sutherland, an academic at the American University, for much of that time. He spent his first month in solitary confinement, and was then moved into a room with Andersen. In July 1985 all five American hostages were brought together in one room. This was clearly a big improvement on solitary: a group will always help to keep up one another's morale. As Jacobsen wrote: 'We lost all of our freedoms except two: the freedom to pray and the freedom to think.'

Charles Glass, the American journalist who was kidnapped in Beirut in June 1987 and escaped from his captors two months later, appears to have shared many of Jacobsen's reactions. He has written how he learned the value of prayer, particularly when he started to pray for others rather than for his own release. Like Jacobsen, he found solace in fantasising, particularly about his family. Glass would pretend to have a different member of his family with him every day. Jacobsen pretended to be at a son's wedding or another's birthday.

Both Glass and Jacobsen were forced to obey the traditional kidnapper's demand that they write (or in Glass's case record on video) a message written for them by their captors. They played it differently: Jacobsen wrote a letter contrasting his apparent abandonment by the Reagan Administration with the efforts being made on behalf of the journalist Nicholas Daniloff, briefly imprisoned in the USSR. He did his best to correct all the mistakes in his captors' grammar, but, suspecting a trick, they insisted he write it exactly as they dictated. When all their mistakes were picked up by the outside world, his kidnappers accused him of sending coded messages and beat him. Glass, on the other hand, left in most of his kidnappers' grammatical mistakes and read out a statement 'admitting' he was a CIA agent. He used a Southern American accent to try to indicate he was being held in Beirut's southern suburbs. (Nobody in the outside world seems to have realised this but Glass's wife knew instantly she saw the video that her husband was acting). Long after they became free men again, the fate of the other hostages weighed heavily on both men's minds.

The French photojournalist Roger Auque, who was kidnapped soon after Terry Waite early in 1987, also provided a graphic account of his captivity when he was freed after ten months, together with TV technician Jean-Louis Normandin, who spent 21 months as a prisoner. From their knowledge of his movements, Auque realised his kidnappers had been following him for months. For the first few hours, after he had been manhandled into a car and taken to a garage, he was assured he would be freed that same day. Only later did the kidnappers tell him they told all the hostages that to allay their initial panic.

He was held in three different places: the first was a room in the basement of an apartment block so tiny he could barely stand up straight and could not stretch out fully when he lay down. For two weeks he shared it with a South Korean diplomat who was later freed for a large ransom. He told Auque there were seven other hostages in the same building, Americans, French and British. Auque's second prison was a room in an apartment where other hostages were held. He believed one of them was Terry Waite. Auque would always put on his blindfold when his guards were about to come in. They told him they did not belong to Hizbollah; he believed they were Palestinians from the Organisation of Revolutionary Justice. They admitted to being supported by Iran, which was confirmed when Auque's release was swiftly followed by a deal between Paris and Tehran. They claimed to like the French while hating America and Britain (but for all that deceived Auque into thinking they had sent six letters he had written to his family). Auque's final prison was another flat, like the first two near the airport. He was the only hostage there. He thought he might be able to escape but desisted from trying as he was told he would soon be released. He thought he might get out before Christmas and he did. During his captivity, he said, he came to believe in God and prayed every day. This appears to be an experience common to almost all kidnap victims, whatever their beliefs before they were abducted and imprisoned.

The ordeal of Jacobsen and Auque eventually ended – but there was a total silence from the kidnappers of many of the other hostages, such as John McCarthy, a British television journalist kidnapped on his way to Beirut airport soon after the Libya raid, and Brian Keenan, an Irish teacher taken at the same time. Twenty-one months after their abduction, their family and friends had heard nothing, not even whether they were alive or dead. Such an ordeal must be almost unbearable for both victims and family. The British Government's consistent refusal to countenance any negotiation with the kidnappers gave the families little hope their nightmare would soon be over.

As Charles Glass has pointed out in one of a series of articles written since he escaped, kidnapping has been endemic in Lebanon since the start of the civil war in 1975, with Christians abducting Muslims or Palestinians and vice versa. A spiral would develop, kidnappers' relatives being themselves snatched as bargaining counters. It was a natural development to extend the practice to foreigners to use as bargaining chips against the West, for ransom (to help finance further terrorist activity), arms (for Iran, the Lebanese fundamentalists' virtual controller, locked in its seemingly endless war with Iraq), or in exchange for Arab terrorists imprisoned in the West.

The Lebanese kidnappers used their hostages ruthlessly and effectively in their dealings with the Western nations whose negotiators were often naive and who frequently emerged from a negotiation with the worst of all worlds: they achieved only part or none of their objectives while giving the kidnappers most or all of what they wanted – which included the retention of enough hostages to continue using as negotiating pawns in future. Some of the negotiators, like North and Waite, were also in a weak position from the start in that they represented a Government whose public posture was dead against any form of negotiating with terrorists, or because they could not deliver what they promised. While President Reagan publicly proclaimed at every available opportunity that the US would never deal with terrorists, North and his colleagues were busily negotiating with Iran, one of the chief sponsors of terrorism against the West.

North offered missiles, which Iran needed against Iraq, in exchange for US hostages held in Lebanon. But the missiles were delivered before any hostages were released. Over a period of 14 months, three American hostages, Weir, Jenco and Jacobsen, were freed with the help of Terry Waite (and Oliver North, though the public did not know that at the time). But two of the Americans kidnapped at the start of the hostage-taking – Anderson and Sutherland – were still held captive, and several more were to follow them, leaving the kidnappers with as many cards as before. When the US's secret negotiations, inevitably to be dubbed 'Irangate', were revealed by a Beirut magazine, *Al-Shiraa*, the resulting outcry meant that there could be no return to negotiations, at least during Ronald Reagan's presidency.

The leaking of the story to the magazine is thought to have been done by hardliners in Tehran who wanted no truck with negotiations with the US. At that time, November 1986, Terry Waite was deep in negotiations aimed at securing the release of Jacobsen, Anderson and Sutherland. In the event, only Jacobsen was freed: the Iranians had reneged on the deal and the most important factor was probably that Waite had not been able to deliver a previous understanding, as the kidnappers saw it at least, that Kuwait would release 17 people imprisoned there for bomb outrages. This undermined Waite's future hopes of deals and he cannot have been helped by the revelation that he had met North several times in the previous year, clearly as part of their efforts to free hostages. Waite was probably kept in the dark about the deals North was offering to the Iranians but in the kidnappers' eyes he was somehow mixed up in the US package and that must have contributed to his own eventual disappearance. His fate illustrates the danger to which intermediaries can expose themselves. In the delicate three- or four-way negotiations in which he was engaged, he appears to have had no option but to meet the kidnappers face to face, a risky enterprise at the best of times and possibly suicidal given the context in which Waite was operating by January 1987 when he failed to return from a negotiating mission in West Beirut. It might be suggested that he failed to appreciate the very different perspectives of the kidnappers. In all kidnap negotiations the negotiator has to try to understand the objectives of the other side. It is questionable whether the hard-line Muslims with whom Waite was dealing were ever really impressed by his status as a special envoy of a foreign religious leader, as was commonly supposed in the West.

Given France's historic ties with Lebanon and its continuing presence there via the United Nations peacekeeping force, it was inevitable that its nationals would be as much of a target for the kidnappers as Americans. Ten were kidnapped between March 1985 and February 1987. The French Government took its customary pragmatic view and negotiated with the Iranians to secure the successful release of five of them by the end of 1986. But it made the cardinal mistake of failing to deliver on a promise, in this case to free Georges Abdallah, a convicted murderer and terrorist, in exchange for a Frenchman who was released in Lebanon. After that, the kidnappers could not trust the French and no more hostages were released. Indeed, the wave of bombings that hit Paris in late 1986 was attributed to Abdallah's relatives avenging themselves for his continued detention.

France took a tough line on terrorism in public, subscribing to the European Community's apparently united stance against it. But after two of the five remaining French hostages, Jean-Louis Normandin and Roger Auque, were unexpectedly freed in November 1987, a series of developments followed which had all the appearances of a ransom deal. The sieges of the Iranian embassy in Paris and the French embassy in Tehran were lifted and an Iranian interpreter allegedly wanted for terrorist bombings in Paris was allowed to go home in exchange for a French diplomat accused in retaliation in Tehran; France agreed to repay some of a debt outstanding since the days of the Shah and since frozen; and, it is believed, a ransom of $5 million was also paid. But the Lebanese still held three hostages kidnapped way back in early 1985 at the outset of the whole hostage-taking drama. Add to that West Germany's apparent payment of a ransom for one of its citizens kidnapped in Beirut after the Libya raid and the whole edifice of a united European stand against negotiating with terrorists lay in tatters. Only the British Government reiterated its determination never even to talk to the Lebanese kidnappers – and left little or no hope for an early release for John McCarthy and Terry Waite.

It could be argued that Waite had been warned, before his last mission, that he should not go to Beirut again, as his safety could not be guaranteed (and he himself acknowledged he could easily end up as a hostage). It could also be argued that John McCarthy was an experienced journalist who knew the risks of being in Beirut at all at that period. As 1987 neared its end with nothing being done for Waite or McCarthy beyond private initiatives and appeals by their families and friends, the crucial dilemma was no nearer resolution for them and the other 20-odd foreign hostages still held in the most appalling isolation and misery in Lebanon: was it ever right for governments to negotiate with terrorists or countries that sponsored them to enable kidnap victims to regain the precious freedom the rest of us take for granted? Or did such negotiations merely encourage more terrorist actions such as kidnappings – and endanger the future freedom of others?

Bibliography

ALIX, Ernest K: *Ransom Kidnapping in America, 1874–1974: the Creation of a Capital Crime* (Carbondale, Southern Illinois University Press, 1978)

ANCIPINK, Patricia: *Business as usual—at gunpoint* (*Best's Review*: Property Casualty Insurance edition, vol 81, June 1980)

BECKER, Jillian: *Hitler's Children* (London, Panther, 1978)

British Perspectives on Terrorism (*Terrorism*, vol 5, Nos 1 & 2, 1981 whole issue, including articles by M. Tugwell, E. Moxon-Browne, E. O'Balance, M. Rees, F. Gregory, R. Clutterbuck, C. Aston, and P. Wilkinson)

CLUTTERBUCK, Richard: *Living with Terrorism* (London, Faber and Faber, 1975)

CLUTTERBUCK, Richard: *Guerrillas and Terrorists* (London, Faber and Faber, 1977)

CLUTTERBUCK, Richard: *Kidnap and Ransom* (London, Faber and Faber, 1978)

COLE, Richard B: *Executive Security: a corporate guide to effective response to abduction and terrorism* (New York, Wiley, 1980)

CONNOLLY, Colm: *Herrema: Siege at Monasterevin* (Dublin, Olympic Press, 1977)

CORSI, Jerome R: *Terrorism as a Desperate Game* (*Journal of Conflict Resolutions*, vol 25, March 1981)

DEELEY, Peter and WALKER, Christopher: *Murder and the Fourth*

Estate: an Investigation into the Role of Press and Police in the McKay case (London, Gollancz, 1971)

DILSHAD, Najmuddin: *The Kidnappings of Diplomatic Personnel* (a paper presented to the International Police Academy, Washington D.C., 1971)

Dokumentation zu den Ereignissen und Enscheidungen im Zusammenhang mit der Entführung von Hanns Martin Schleyer und her Lufthansa-Maschine Landshut (Bonn, Presse und Informationsamt der Bundesregierung, 1977)

FAIRBAIRN, Geoffrey: *Revolutionary Guerrilla Warfare, Countryside Version* (London, Penguin, 1974)

FREIFELD, Sidney A: *Diplomatic Hostage-taking: a retrospective look at Bogota* (*International Perspectives*, Sept–Oct 1980)

GERAGHTY, Tony: *Who Dares Wins* (London, Arms and Armour Press)

GOTT, Richard: *Rural Guerrillas in Latin America* (revised edition. London, Penguin, 1973)

HALPERIN, Ernst: *Terrorism in Latin America* (Washington D.C., Washington Papers No. 33, 1976)

HERMANN, Kai and KOCK, Peter: *Assault at Mogadishu* (London, Corgi, 1977)

International Terrorism (Milwaukee, Institute of World Affairs, University of Wisconsin-Milwaukee, 1974)

JACKSON, Sir Geoffrey: *People's Prison* (London, Faber and Faber, 1973)

JENKINS, Brian: *Terrorism and Kidnapping* (Santa Monica, California, Rand Corporation, 1974)

JENKINS, Brian: *Numbered Lives: some statistical observations from 77 international hostage episodes* (Santa Monica, California, Rand Corporation, 1977)

KENNEDY, Ludovic: *The Airman and the Carpenter* (London, Collins, 1985)

LAQUEUR, Walter: *Terrorism* (London, Wiedenfeld and Nicholson, 1977)

LANZ RODRIGUEZ, Carlos: *El Caso Niehous y la Corrupcion Administriva* (Caracas, Editorial Fuentes: Ediciones Tres Continentes, 1979)

MESSICK, HANK & GOLDBLATT: *Kidnapping, the Illustrated History* (New York, Dial Press, 1974)

MILLER, Abraham H: *Negotiations for Hostages: Implications from the*

Police Experience (*Terrorism*, vol 1, No 2, 1978 pp 125–46)

MOOREHEAD, Caroline: *Fortune's Hostages* (London, Hamish Hamilton, 1980)

PERICARD, Michel: Director of *Radio France Presente* (Les Dossiers de France-Inter, Presses de la Cite, 1977)

PISANO, Vittorfranco S: *Terrorism in Italy: the Dozier affair* (*Police Chief,* vol 49, April 1982)

PROYER, Ronald: *Stories of Famous Kidnappings* (London, Barker, 1972)

RADWANSKI, George, and WINDEYER, Kendal: *No Mandate but Terror* (Richmond Hill, Ontario, Simon and Schuster of Canada, 1971)

ROYAL UNITED SERVICES INSTITUTE, *Ten Years of Terrorism* collected views (New York, Crane Russak and Company, 1979)

SHAFFER, Daniel E: *Crisis Management: the Challenge of Executive Kidnapping and Extortion against Corporations* (F.B.I. Law Enforcement Bulletin, vol 48, May 1979)

STENDAL, Russell: *Rescue the Captors* (Burnsville, Minnesota, Ransom Press International, 1984)

UNITED NATIONS SOCIAL RESEARCH INSTITUTE: *Phenomenology of Kidnappings in Sardinia* (Rome, Fratelli Palombi Editori, 1984)

WALLER, George: *Kidnap; Story of the Lindbergh Case* (New York, Dial Press, 1961)

WILKINSON, Paul: *Political Terrorism* (London, Macmillan, 1974)

WILKINSON, Paul: *Terrorism and the Liberal State* (London, Macmillan, 1977)

WILLIAMS, Dr Geoffrey: *The Corporate Sector* (University of Perth, Western Australia, 1982)

STAR BOOKS BESTSELLERS

	JACK GERSON	
0352316187	**The Back of the Tiger**	£1.95
0352314672	**The Whitehall Sanction**	£1.95*
	ADAM HALL	
0352316071	**Northlight: A Quiller Mission**	£2.95*
	NOEL HYND	
0352319410	**Flowers from Berlin**	£3.25*
	ADAM KENNEDY	
0352313145	**The Domino Vendetta**	£1.80*
	MICHAEL KILIAN	
0352317574	**Blood of the Czars**	£2.25*
	HAROLD KING	
0352316314	**The Hahnemann Sequela**	£2.75*
	PETER LESLIE	
0352316683	**Death Mail**	£1.95

STAR Books are obtainable from many booksellers and newsagents. If you have any difficulty tick the titles you want and fill in the form below.

Name _____

Address _____

_____

Send to: Star Books Cash Sales, P.O. Box 11, Falmouth, Cornwall, TR10 9EN.

Please send a cheque or postal order to the value of the cover price plus:
UK: 55p for the first book, 22p for the second book and 14p for each additional book ordered to the maximum charge of £1.75.

BFPO and EIRE: 55p for the first book, 22p for the second book, 14p per copy for the next 7 books, thereafter 8p per book.

OVERSEAS: £1.00 for the first book and 25p per copy for each additional book.

While every effort is made to keep prices low, it is sometimes necessary to increase prices at short notice. Star Books reserve the right to show new retail prices on covers which may differ from those advertised in the text or elsewhere.

**NOT FOR SALE IN CANADA*